Gentlemanly Capitalism, Imperialism and Global History

By the same author

INTERNATIONAL ORDER OF ASIA IN THE 1930s (*in Japanese, co-editor with N. Kagokani*)

THE BRITISH EMPIRE AND THE INTERNATIONAL ORDER OF ASIA *(in Japanese)*

Gentlemanly Capitalism, Imperialism and Global History

Shigeru Akita

First published 2002 by
PALGRAVE MACMILLAN
Houndmills, Basingstoke, Hampshire RG21 6XS and
175 Fifth Avenue, New York, N.Y. 10010
Companies and representatives throughout the world

PALGRAVE MACMILLAN is the global academic imprint of the Palgrave
Macmillan division of St. Martin's Press, LLC and of Palgrave Macmillan Ltd.
Macmillan® is a registered trademark in the United States, United Kingdom
and other countries. Palgrave is a registered trademark in the European
Union and other countries.

ISBN 0–333–99306–3

This book is printed on paper suitable for recycling and made from fully
managed and sustained forest sources.

A catalogue record for this book is available from the British Library.

Library of Congress Cataloging-in-Publication Data

Gentlemanly capitalism, imperialism, and global history / edited by Shigeru Akita.
    p.   cm.
    Revised versions of papers originally presented at the workshop "Gentlemanly
    Capitalism and its Impact on Global History", held in Osaka, Japan, Oct. 7–8, 2000.
    Includes bibliographical references and index.
    ISBN 0–333–99306–3
    1. Capitalism—Great Britain—Colonies—History.   2. Imperialism—
    Economic aspects—Great Britain—Colonies.   3. Great Britain—Colonies—
    History.   4. Great Britain—Colonies—Asia—History.   5. Great Britain—
    Colonies—Economic conditions.   I. Akita, Shigeru.

DA16 .G46 2002
325'.341—dc21   2002025147

10   9   8   7   6   5   4   3   2   1
11   10   09   08   07   06   05   04   03   02

Printed and bound in Great Britain by
Antony Rowe Ltd, Chippenham and Eastbourne

Contents

Part I: British Imperialism and the Global Order

Part II: Gentlemanly Capitalism and Informal Empire in East Asia

List of Maps and Figure

Notes on the Contributors

Shigeru Akita is Associate Professor in the Department of Area Studies at Osaka University of Foreign Studies, Japan, where he specializes in the history of the British Empire and Commonwealth. His publications include 'British Informal Empire in East Asia, 1880–1939: a Japanese perspective', in Raymond E. Dumett (ed.), *Gentlemanly Capitalism and British Imperialism* (1999), *1930-nendai Ajia Kokusai-Chitujyo* [*International Order of Asia in the 1930s*] (2001) (coed. with N. Kagotani) and *Igirisu-Teikoku to Ajia Kokusai-Chitujyo* [*The British Empire and International Order of Asia*] (2002). He is also involved in research on global history.

H.V. Bowen is Senior Lecturer at the Department of Economic and Social History, University of Leicester, UK. He is the author of *Revenue and Reform: the Indian Problem in British Politics, 1757–1773* (1991), *Elites, Enterprise, and the Making of the British Overseas Empire, 1688–1775* (1996) and *War and British Society, 1688–1815* (1998). He is currently engaged in an economic and administrative history of the East India Company in Britain between 1750 and 1850.

P.J. Cain is Research Professor in History at the Department of History, Sheffield Hallam University, UK. He has published numerous articles on British imperial expansion and theories of imperialism in learned journals. He is the author of *Economic Foundations of British Expansion Overseas, 1815–1914* (1980) and *British Imperialism, 1688–2000* (with A.G. Hopkins) (2001). He has just completed a study of J.A. Hobson and the development of the theory of economic imperialism which will be published in 2002.

John Darwin is Fellow of Nuffield College and Beit Lecturer in the History of the British Commonwealth, Oxford University, UK. He is the author of *Britain, Egypt and the Middle East: Imperial Policy in the Aftermath of War 1918–1922* (1981), *Britain and Decolonization: the Retreat from Empire in the Post-War World* (1988) and *The End of the British Empire: the Historical Debate* (1991). He is currently working on a history of the British Empire as an international system c. 1840–1970.

A.G. Hopkins, formerly the Smuts Professor of Commonwealth History at Cambridge University, is now the Walter Prescott Webb Professor of History at the University of Texas in Austin, USA. He has published widely in the field of African and imperial history, beginning with a pioneering synthesis, *An Economic History of West Africa* (1973), and continuing with the work that is the subject of the present volume of essays, *British Imperialism, 1688–2000*. This study, written with P.J. Cain and first published in two volumes in 1993, is currently available in a 2nd edition in one volume (2001). His most recent book is an edited collection entitled *Globalization in World History* (2002).

Naoto Kagotani is Associate Professor at the Institute for Research in Humanities, Kyoto University, Japan, where he specializes in Asian and Japanese economic history. He is the author of *Ajia Kokusai Tsusho Chitujyo to Kindai Nihon* [*International Trade Order of Asia and Modern Japan*] (2000) and *1930-nendai Ajia Kokusai-Chitujyo* [*International Order of Asia in the 1930s*] (2001) (coed. with S. Akita). He is currently working on merchants' networks in Asia and Japan 1931–55.

Yoichi Kibata is Professor at the Graduate School of Advanced Social and International Studies, the University of Tokyo, Japan. He is the author of *Shihai no Daisho: Eiteikoku no Houkai to 'Teikokuishiki'* [*Price of Imperial Rule: Imperial Mentality and the Break-up of the British Empire*] (1987) and *Teikoku no Tasogare: Reisen ka no Igirisu to Ajia* [*The Twilight of the Empire: British Policy towards Japan and Malaya 1947–1955*] (1996), and the editor of *The History of Anglo–Japanese Relations, 1600–2000: the Political and Diplomatic Dimension*, 2 vols. (2000). He is currently working on decolonization, Anglo-American relations and international relations in Asia in the 1950s and 1960s.

Gerold Krozewski is currently research fellow in the Department of History, Sheffield Hallam University, UK. He is the author of *Money and the End of Empire: British International Economic Policy and the Colonies, 1947–1958* (2001). His principal research interests relate to British, and more generally European relations with the non-Western world.

Niels P. Petersson is Lecturer in Modern and Contemporary History at the Department of History and Sociology, University of Konstanz, Germany. His publications include *Imperialismus und Modernisierung: Siam, China und die europäischen Mächte* (2000), 'Ostasiens Jahrhundertwende. Unterwerfung und Erneuerung in west-östlichen

Sichtweisen', in Ute Frevert (ed.), *Das Neue Jahrhundert. Europäische Zeitdiagnosen und Zukunftsentwürfe um 1900* (with Jürgen Osterhammel) (2000) and 'König Chulalongkorns Europareise 1897: Europäischer Imperialismus, symbolische Politik und monarchisch-bürokratische Modernisierung', *Saeculum*, 52–2 (2001). He is currently working on globalization, crime and international financial transactions.

Ian Phimister is Professor of International History at University of Sheffield, UK. He has published no less than 50 articles and chapters in books on African economic and social history. He is the author of *Zimbabwe: an Economic and Social History* (1988) and *Keep on Knocking: a History of the Labour Movement in Zimbabwe* (1997) (with Brian Raftopoulos). He is currently engaged in research on British overseas investment.

Kaoru Sugihara is Professor at the Graduate School of Economics, Osaka University, Japan, where he specializes in modern Asian international economic history. He is the author of *Ajia-kan Boeki no Keisei to Kozo* [*Patterns and Development of Intra-Asian Trade*] (1996), *The East Asian Path of Economic Development: a Long-term Perspective* (2000) and 'Oceanic Trade and Global Development, 1500–1995', in Solvi Songer (ed.), *Making Sense of Global History: the 19th International Congress of the Historical Sciences Oslo 2000 Commemorative Volume* (2001). He is currently working on the rise of the Asia-Pacific economy 1945–2000, and its significance for global history.

Shunhong Zhang is Professor and Chairman of the Section of Modern History of Western Europe and North America, at the Institute of World History, Chinese Academy of Social Sciences, Beijing. He is the editor and author of *Da Ying De Wajie* [*The Collapse of the British Empire*] (1997) and *Ying Mei Xin Zhiminzhuyi* [*Anglo-American Neocolonialism*] (with Meng Qinglong and Bi Jiankang) (1999). He is currently doing research on the British colonial system in the twentieth century.

Acknowledgements

This volume is the result of a 2-day Workshop on 'Gentlemanly Capitalism and Its Impact on Global History', held in Osaka, Japan, on 7 and 8 October 2000. The aim of the Workshop was to consider the new perspective of global history, focusing on gentlemanly capitalism as a bridge from imperial history to global history. We had organized a 3-year joint-venture project on global history with Prof. Patrick O'Brien, the Convenor of the Programme in Global History, the Institute of Historical Research, University of London. The Workshop was part of the International Conference on 'The Formation of Global History and the Role of Hegemonic States, 2000', and was financially supported by the Japanese Ministry of Education and Sciences and the Osaka University of Foreign Studies. I would like to express my appreciation for their generous financial support, especially to Prof. Osamu Akagi, the President of Osaka University of Foreign Studies, and the head of the Project, Prof. Yujiro Aga.

Nine papers were submitted to the Workshop and intensive discussions took place during this 2-day period. Each paper has been revised in the light of further exchanges that have occurred since then. I would also very much like to express my appreciation to our discussants, Prof. Raymond E. Dumett (Purdue University), Dr Harumi Goto-Shibata (Chiba University), and Professors Minoru Kawakita (Osaka University), Katsuhiko Kitagawa (Kansai University), Man-houng Lin (Academia Sinica, Taipei) and Yukio Takeuchi (Nihon University) for their helpful comments and suggestions to broaden our perspectives on global history. I am also grateful to the audiences who came from all over Japan, for their useful comments.

The Fellowship of the Japan Foundation 2001 has enabled me to be attached to the Economic History Department, LSE, University of London and to edit this volume. The discussions on global history with my colleagues at LSE, especially with Prof. Patrick O'Brien, have been very helpful for my editorial work.

Finally, I would like to thank Professors P.J. Cain and A.G. Hopkins for their contribution, which has made this volume more fruitful.

Shigeru Akita
January 2002

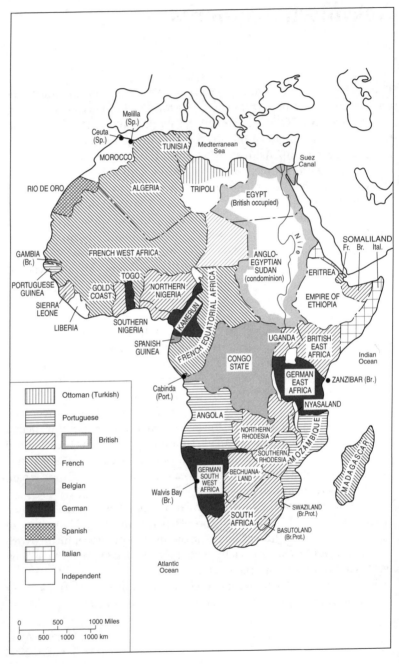

Map 1. The Partition of Africa by 1902

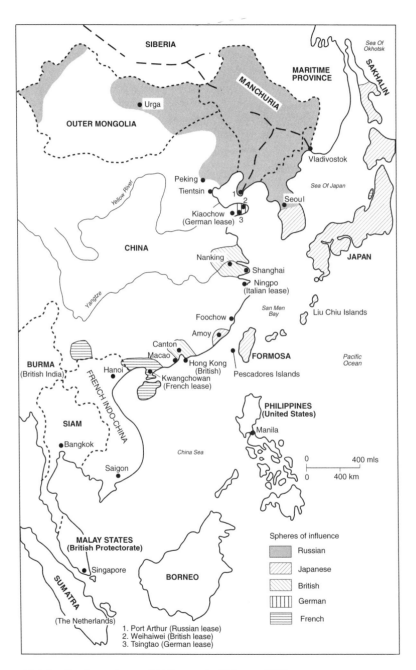

Map 2. Foreign spheres of influence in China, c. 1900

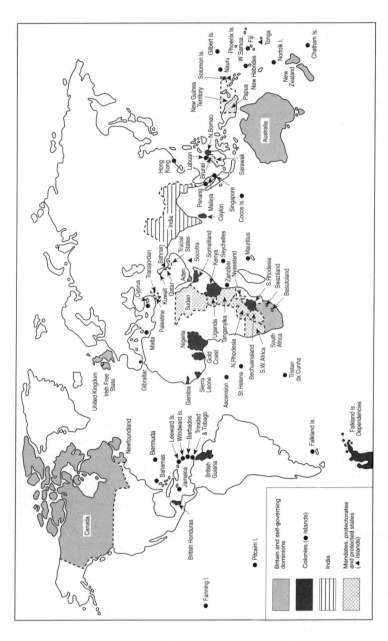

Map 3. The British Empire c. 1931

1
Introduction: from Imperial History to Global History

Shigeru Akita

I

The main aim of this book is to update the debate on British imperialism by relating it to new developments in the history of globalization, as well as by looking at Western historiography from a comparative, Eastern perspective. The focus of this study is therefore less on British imperial history *per se* than on that segment of global history that was powerfully driven by British imperialism. We hope to bring together two separate branches of historiography: imperial history, with its predominantly Eurocentric or broadly Western orientation, and East Asian studies, which are typically confined by the needs of regional specialization and are rarely connected to broader, global issues.

Within this overarching theme, the central concern of the essays in this volume is the study of power in international relations, and one of the key concepts of the book is 'informal' or 'invisible empire'. Informal empire attracted attention after the publication of Gallagher and Robinson's famous article 'The Imperialism of Free Trade' in 1953.[1] British imperial historians continue to debate the strengths and weaknesses of the concept[2] as the recent *Oxford History of the British Empire* bears witness.[3] Informal empire is essential for the analysis of British influence in areas such as Latin America, the Middle East and China. Recently, in an attempt to take the debate on British imperialism beyond the confines of formal/informal debate, Tony Hopkins has distinguished between two forms of power in the international system and made use of the concepts of 'structural power' and 'relational power', as a means of interpreting the British presence in Latin America, especially in Argentina in the nineteenth century. 'Structural power' allows its possessors to determine, or at least exert, a predominant influence, and to lay down the general rules of the game governing international relations and it was fundamentally a manifestation of the core values and policy priorities of the British liberal state, with its preference for free trade, low taxation and sound money. On the other hand, 'relational power' deals with the negotiations, pressures and conflicts that determine the outcome of particular contests within this broad framework.[4] These concepts of 'structural power' and 'relational power' originate with Susan Strange, an eminent specialist in international political economy. She identified four aspects of structural power: control over credit, control over production, control over security, and control of knowledge, beliefs and ideas.[5] We will try to apply these concepts to the broader context of global history, and extend our study of power in international relations from imperial history to global history.

In this book, we use the term 'global history' in the context of the formation and development of a capitalist world-economy. As Patrick O'Brien has pointed out, 'comparisons and connections are the dominant styles of global history'.[6] In other words, an important aspect of global history is the history of the formation of mutual interdependence or interconnectedness between the various regions or areas in the world under the framework of a capitalist world-economy. The progress of globalization has promoted the formation of interconnected economic linkages beyond national borders at various levels of transnational movements including exchanges of goods, peoples, money, technology and information. In this historical context, British imperial history can now be seen as a bridge to global history. Cain and Hopkins suggest, in the last chapter of their second edition of *British Imperialism 1688–2000*, that imperialism and empires can be viewed as globalizing forces.[7] Through the study of the process and progress of globalization, we can better interpret modern world history not only from comparative perspectives, but also from the perspective of the formation of relational history within a capitalist world-economy.[8] The chapters in Part I of this study take a predominantly metropolitan view of the globalizing forces unleashed by British imperialism; those in Part II focus on the international order of East Asia that was partly shaped by Britain's influence but which kept a relatively unique 'autonomous' status in a capitalist world-economy. In Part II especially, we are exploring a new interpretation of the relational history within a capitalist world-economy through the evolution of globalization.

The progress of globalization has been promoted and accelerated by the presence of hegemonic states in a capitalist world-economy, especially by the primacy of Great Britain in the nineteenth century, the 'Pax Britannica', and the predominance of the United States in the twentieth century, the 'Pax Americana'.[9] A hegemonic state provides 'public goods' for the international system as a whole. These international public goods include 'peace, safe access to international waterways, international laws for the protection of property rights, an open regime for foreign trade, and an international monetary system'.[10] As O'Brien has observed over the nineteenth century, 'trade promoted and was in turn sustained by movements of capital, migrations of labour and transfers of technology and information around the world on an unprecedented scale and at ever increasing speeds. Political impediments to international flows of exports, imports, money, credit capital, labour, technology and information diminished sharply during the liberal international order that prevailed between 1846 and 1914'.[11] In this book, we evaluate the role played by Great Britain in a capitalist world-economy and its implications for international relations.

II

The starting point for any discussion of the British Empire and British imperialism is now *British Imperialism, 1688–2000*, by Cain and Hopkins. This study attracted very considerable attention both in the press when first published in 1993, and subsequently, in a wide-ranging and now long-running scholarly debate. Cain and Hopkins's concept of 'gentlemanly capitalism' became a key term in Will Hutton's best-selling book, *The State We're In*.[12] It featured prominently in Philip Augar's well-publicized study, *The Death of Gentlemanly Capitalism*,[13] and it has been adopted and criticized by specialists of British history and Area Studies alike. The concept and the general interpretation of the cause and course of British imperialism derived from it has also been the subject of a book edited by Raymond E. Dumett, *Gentlemanly Capitalism and British Imperialism: The New Debate on Empire*.[14] As Cain and Hopkins have themselves recently reviewed the main criticisms generated by their interpretation, it is unnecessary to deal with them in detail here.[15] However, although the debate has been extensive, large gaps still remain and important angles have yet to be explored. Furthermore, the subject has moved on, partly under its own momentum and partly in response to changes in the world at large.

Essentially, the current debate concerns the process of modern economic development in Britain and the causes of British imperial expansion. Cain and Hopkins offered a metropolitan perspective on British imperialism that raised three large and still unresolved questions. First, is their assessment of the predominantly gentlemanly forces within Britain driving imperial expansion persuasive? Secondly, have they attached sufficient weight to influences outside Britain that were, to varying degrees, beyond British control? Thirdly, are they correct in arguing, against conventional wisdom, that 1914 was not a turning point that marked the decline of Britain's power and influence? This book covers these three questions about the Cain–Hopkins interpretation from the perspective of external relations.

The first question prompts us to investigate the definition of 'the gentlemanly elite', the character of the British state and the role of financial and service sectors in the British economy. These topics have already been addressed in Dumett's volume, but this did not deal with the formative period of gentlemanly capitalism in the late eighteenth century or in the last stage of decolonization in the 1950s and 1960s. Cain and Hopkins referred to both periods only briefly[16] and some questions still remain. For example, although the transformation of British society was reflected in the composition and changing nature of gentlemanly capitalists, there remains a need for studies of the mutual interactions between the British 'gentlemanly capitalists' and the colonial elite of immigrants or indigenous people. We need to know more about the formation of the 'gentlemanly capitalists' at home and their 'export' overseas. We deal with these subjects in Chapters 2 and 5.

Our second question raised by Cain and Hopkins is concerned with the linkages between British imperial expansion and globalization. All chapters deal with this second question to some degree. For example, Chapter 2 treats an early phase of globalization and its limits, and Chapter 3 is particularly concerned to weigh up the relation between domestic imperial impulses and international constraints on British overseas expansion. Chapters 4 and 6 present local examples of these international constraints in the cases of the Partition of Africa and the scramble for spheres of influence in China at the turn of the 19th–20th centuries. These two chapters are concerned with the height of 'modern' or 'imperial globalization', as defined by Cain and Hopkins.[17]

The second question is also closely related to another key concept used by Cain and Hopkins, that is, 'informal' or 'invisible empire'. As mentioned in Chapter 3, there are common grounds and differences between Gallagher and Robinson and Cain and Hopkins on this issue. Gallagher and Robinson have directed their attention to the manufacturing interests and trade policies as a driving force behind the expansion of British interests overseas, whereas Cain and Hopkins have concentrated their analysis on the roles of the financial and service sectors, or the City of London. But both pairs of scholars agreed that the growing influence of Great Britain was based on powerful economic sectors at home, whether manufacturing or finance. Chapter 4 offers an exploration of the concept of informal empire in the South African context.

The term 'informal empire' was mainly applied to areas and regions of the non-European developing countries, as the original definition of the term assumed the unequal political and economic status of these countries. However, the overseas influence of Great Britain ranged far beyond the confines of formal and informal empires, due to the global network of the City of London and the financial and service sectors in a capitalist world-economy. In the context of British imperial history as shown in Chapter 6, China used to be regarded as a typical example of informal empire in the nineteenth and the early twentieth centuries. On the other hand, after the conclusion of the Anglo-Japanese Alliance in 1902, Japan was treated as an ally of Great Britain rather than as part of the British informal empire.[18] Nevertheless even in the 1930s, the United Kingdom continued to exert financial influence upon Japan and the colonies of other Great Powers through the establishment of the sterling area, by setting 'the rules of the game' for international finance in East Asia. At that time, as we will see in Chapters 8 and 10, the Chinese Nationalist Government strengthened its political authority, and partly manipulated the balance of power in East Asia as a newly emerging nation-state. Thus debates continue about the validity of applying the concept of informal empire to China. Jürgen Osterhammel favours analyzing the dynamic interactions between the British government, the Nationalist Government of China and her 'bureaucratic capitalism', as well as the evolution of a Japanese informal empire in East Asia, by using a more sophisticated version of informality.[19] But perhaps the best way to consider these interactions is to use the new concepts of 'structural power' and 'relational power', which incorporate these kinds of autonomous activities by the non-European countries, and allows us to understand the extent to which the United Kingdom exerted her influence upon international relations.

The third question has been relatively neglected by Cain and Hopkins's critics, most of whom concentrate on nineteenth-century imperialism. However, a large part of *British Imperialism 1688–2000* is concerned with post-1914 and the authors insist that, in relative terms, Britain's power and influence did not undergo severe decline until just before the Second World War. The British Empire also had something of a renaissance, though under American auspices, for a while after 1945.

Chapters 3 and 5 deal with important aspects of Britain's twentieth-century imperial history and test some of the claims made in *British Imperialism 1688–2000*. Moreover, Cain and Hopkins's description of Britain's continued economic influence in the interwar years, including their emphasis on the importance of the sterling bloc in the 1930s, suggests important linkages between imperial history and the process of globalization in the twentieth century. Most of the chapters of Part II in this book, especially Chapter 9, present separate answers to this question from Asian perspectives. We will later refer to some more specific points of the arguments of each chapter in section IV.

Next we look briefly at the new historiography in Asian economic history in order to understand the connection between British metropolitan and Asian and Japanese perspectives.

III

Until recently, 'most of the literature on Asian economic history has been written within the intellectual framework of the Western impact versus each region's response to it, and the element of intra-regional economic intercourse in Asia has not been properly assessed in a wider comparative perspective'.[20] Recent scholarship, led by Japanese economic historians, has offered a new perspective on Asian economic history. It enables us to look at individual Asian countries in the context of an integrated Asian regional economy, and to construct the framework of an evolving relation between the British Empire and the Asian regional economy, within a capitalist world-economy. It is worth mentioning here the works of three distinguished Japanese scholars, Takeshi Hamashita, Heita Kawakatsu and Kaoru Sugihara, who share a common critical viewpoint towards Eurocentric or Western-oriented historiography. Hamashita has insisted on the importance of the development of a Chinese-centred world-system and its resilience based upon the tributary trade system. He also has emphasized the importance of silver-currency circulation and the active roles of Asian merchants' networks for the promotion of intra-Asian trade.[21] Kawakatsu has pointed to two different paths of development followed by the Western European and Japanese cotton textile industries, and revealed the coexistence of coarse Asian cotton goods with fine cottons from Manchester.[22] Nevertheless, the arguments of Hamashita and Kawakatsu are oriented towards the identification of indigenous roots of Asian regional economies, and have not been able to incorporate the global linkages or the development of a capitalist world-economy.

In contrast with these two scholars, Sugihara has revealed the formation and development of intra-Asian trade from the late nineteenth century to the early 1940s, by using multinational archives of trade statistics. The uniqueness of his research is to offer two key insights into the pattern of modern Asian economic development, that is, the emergence of 'cotton-centred economic linkages' on the supply side, and the effects of 'final demand linkage' on the demand side. At the turn of the 19th–20th centuries, a unique chain of linkages was formed between Indian raw cotton, cotton yarn exports to China from British India and Japan, the production of cotton piece-goods in China based on imported yarns, and a peculiar pattern of consumption of Asian cotton goods. These linkages depended on the development of cotton industries in Japan and British India, and Japanese imports of Indian raw cotton. Meanwhile, Southeast Asian countries, such as Burma, the Straits Settlements, and the Dutch East Indies, specialized in the production and export of primary products to European countries. In return, they earned hard currency, sterling, and imported cheap consumer goods from Japan or British India. Sugihara sees that industrialization in Japan and British India was not only generated through the 'cotton-centred' linkage, but was promoted by the rise in income as a result of the growth of exports of primary products to the West, and calls this the 'final demand linkage effect'.[23] Both sets of connections contributed greatly to the promotion of industrialization-based trade under the umbrella of the 'Pax Britannica'. In this context, Sugihara's work links with imperial and international history and he stresses the vital importance of the 'Western Impact' for the development of intra-Asian trade.

In order to connect the Asian or Japanese historiography with that in the West, one can here point to a mutual connection or interdependence of economic interests between the 'structural power' of Great Britain and the peripheral East Asian countries. We can detect several kinds of 'complementarity' from the turn of the 19th–20th centuries. For example, complementarity evolved between rapid Japanese industrialization and increased British exports of capital goods.[24] The decline of British cotton goods export to Japan was traded off against the growth of Japanese demand for capital goods, especially for British-made cotton textile machinery. Also, in 1904–05 the Japanese government issued five Russo-Japanese war loans on the London and New York money markets, by using the international networks of merchant banks. Some British banks, such as the Hong Kong and Shanghai Bank and Parr's Bank, brought loan issues on the London capital market and floated them in conjunction with Baring Brothers and Ernest Cassel.

Total foreign war loan issues amounted to £107,000,000, out of which London absorbed £42,500,000. Similarly, during the period 1900–13, Japan's large capital imports accounted for over 20 per cent of total foreign government loan issues in London.[25] This close Anglo-Japanese financial relationship and Japanese dependence upon the City of London is another aspect of Anglo-Japanese complementarity in economic relations.

This complementarity between British financial power and East Asian economic development is an important theme of Part II of this book. It remained an important element in Anglo-Japanese economic interaction until the late 1930s. Similar relationships can be recognized in the l930s, after the restoration of China's tariff autonomy, between Chinese industrialization and British financial interests. In regard to the economic interaction between the UK and East Asia, Chapters 8, 9 and 10 present a new interpretation of the international order of Asia up to the 1930s.[26] In that decade, the Chinese currency reform of 1935 was the central focus of economic interaction. After the success of the currency reform, the new Chinese dollar was stabilized against sterling and the US dollar, and was *de facto* linked with sterling. Stabilization of currency promoted the development of Chinese industrial production and the export of consumer goods which accrued under the protectionist policies pursued by the Nationalist Government.[27] Thus the rise of economic nationalism in China was achieved by taking advantage of the international order of Asia and the financial influence or the 'structural power' of Great Britain. In British India, economic development, also centred on cotton goods, was helped by the rise of tariff protection after the acquisition of 'fiscal autonomy' in 1919. As long as British financial interests were protected by the high fixed exchange rate of the Indian rupee at 1s 6d, the Government of India allowed Indian industries to grow and export their products to Asian countries.[28]

We can clearly understand these unique developments by reference to the Cain–Hopkins thesis that the core of British economic interests had shifted from manufacturing to finance and services, the main economic base of gentlemanly capitalism. This kind of complementarity, which in effect encouraged industrialization in East Asia, represents a special relationship, especially in the non-European worlds. It implies not rivalry or competition but co-operation or alignment as long as individual national interests are in concert with each other. The co-existence between British economic interests and East Asian industrialization added to the 'structural power' of Great Britain, and strengthened the status of the City of London as an international centre of high-finance.[29] The future task is to compare this nexus of connection with other networks of trade and finance, for example, the African networks in order to reveal the successes and failures in early industrialization.

IV

The book is divided into two parts. Part I deals with the metropolitan basis of British imperialism and the issues raised in section II above. In Chapter 2, Huw Bowen discusses the making of a global British Empire in the eighteenth century which is vital for an understanding of the British-centred globalization or the 'Pax Britannica' of the nineteenth century. Bowen illuminates two important factors for the formation of a global empire in Asia as well as in North America.[30] He refers to recent studies of cultural and material aspects of imperialism in the United States. These factors have been concerned with the links between gentlemanly capitalists at home and overseas actors, such as the North American elite and the East India Company. Bowen's important contribution to the Cain–Hopkins debate is to identify the emergence of an 'international British elite or transoceanic imperial elite' in North America and Bengal through the 'anglicization' of overseas high society. In the case of Bengal, powerful private interests, supported by a strong state, played an important role in spreading British influence in Asia, and their activities were closely connected with 'country' or intra-Asian trade. In this context, Bowen's arguments are connected with Part II of this book, which exposes the impulses from the periphery behind the formation of a global British Empire and its relationship to the metropolis.

In Chapter 2, John Darwin reconsiders British power in the nineteenth and twentieth centuries in a global context, and explores the mutual relationship between globalism and British imperialism, or the link between imperial history and global history. First, he recognizes the common ground between the Cain–Hopkins and Gallagher–Robinson theses, especially the notion of informal influence. In considering British power in the global context, he assumes that there were two basic constraints on British power from the world economy and geopolitics. The first is that 'as an open global system, the British empire was acutely sensitive to the pressures and prospects of the international economy'. The second is that 'the world-wide span of British imperialism made it vulnerable to political change' in East Asia and the Euro-Atlantic world as well as in the empire. He proposes the three 'long swings' of the world economy as the chronological matrix for the rise and fall of the British Empire: the approach (1830s–70s), formation (1880s–1920s), and crisis (1930s–40s). From his viewpoint of constraints under global circumstances, 'there was no mid-Victorian "global hegemony"'; and 'globalism set in after 1870', when 'the economic inter-dependence of regions and markets reached a critical stage creating for the first time a "world economy"'. He reveals the limits of British power projection in international relations through the coexistence between an empire of trade and an empire of rule. In this sense, as he stresses, 'the full implications of that protean concept, the "imperialism of free trade" have yet to be worked out',[31] even after the publication of the Cain–Hopkins thesis.[32]

In Chapter 4, Ian Phimister offers a revisionist account of that classic case study of late nineteenth-century imperialism: the Partition of Africa. He examines Cain and Hopkins's interpretation of the scramble for Africa, and criticizes two aspects of their arguments. First, Phimister points to a global dimension of the partition of Africa in the context of the transformation of international relations which witnessed the rise of Germany and the United States. He stresses the importance of international rivalries among European Powers for the acceleration of the partition in tropical Africa. Phimister's second argument concerns the relationship between economic imperialism, informal empire and territorial empire. Focusing on British expansion in Southern Africa, he presents a new interpretation of the Selborne Memorandum of 1896, and insists that the success of financial imperialism and informal empire in the South African Republic threatened British governmental plans for uniting South Africa. His conclusion is that the South African crisis revealed a conflict between two arms of gentlemanly capitalism, one led by the City of London and the other in government.

In Chapter 5, Gerold Krozewski is concerned with later stages of British imperialism between 1945 and the early 1960s, giving particular prominence to international finance. Krozewski provides a critical assessment of the applicability of gentlemanly capitalism to the post-1945 period, and criticizes the 'continuity theory' of Cain and Hopkins. He suggests that the transformation of British society and the British state before and after the Second World War, especially the changing role of the state and the coming of welfarism, reduced the influence of the gentlemanly elite. He then argues that the changing structure and constraints of international relations after 1945, especially the emergence of liberal multilateralism in a new international economic order dominated by the United States, exerted a strong influence on Britain's international position and policies. Briefly stated, his argument is that the social and economic conditions, both within Britain and in the wider world, that nurtured gentlemanly capitalism no longer existed after 1945. Krozewski also refers to 'complementarity' as a systemic component of international relations and outlines how regional economies interconnected with each other. This point is closely related to the arguments in Part II and is explored in more detail in Chapters 8 and 10. His analysis, which draws on his recently published book on British international economic policy and the colonies,[33] emphasizes the importance of the 'structural domestic and international context' of the post-1945 period, and he prefers to analyze 'Empire' as a 'system' rather than as a set of bilateral relationships between the metropole and colonies.

Part II links international and general themes to East Asia – a huge area that felt the British presence and influence but largely escaped formal imperial control. This section of the book not only explores the extent of, and limits to, British influence, but also demonstrates the unique status of East Asia in global history and underlines the autonomy of its own dynamics in creating a globalized order. Furthermore, Part II reconsiders the meaning of 'informal empire' in East Asia from an Asian perspective.

In Chapter 6, Niels Petersson looks at European imperial rivalry and the concept of informal empire in China before the First World War. He reveals the specific circumstances under which gentlemanly capitalism exerted an influence on China, and offers 'an international or transnational history of empire' by using archival evidence from Britain, France and Germany. Petersson illuminates the favourable international and peripheral context of 1905–11 in which Britain pursued foreign-financed railway construction in China. This specific but only brief period is regarded as the height of gentlemanly imperialism in China, and he represents its peculiar character as 'co-operative financial imperialism', a phrase he takes from Jürgen Osterhammel.[34] Petersson also identifies a three-level structure for the analysis of co-operative financial imperialism: at metropolitan, international and peripheral levels. In the shaping of global history, the interconnectedness between the second and the third levels is seen as essential, and 'British policy within the framework of co-operative financial imperialism was distinguished from that of other powers by the conscious pursuit of "structural power"'.[35]

In Chapter 7, Shunhong Zhang presents a Chinese view of British imperialism and decolonization from the perspective of scholarship that is beginning to engage with Western historiography while still emerging from its Marxist inheritance. Zhang, a scholar from the Chinese Academy of Social Sciences in Beijing, appraises the Cain–Hopkins thesis as an explanation of British expansion overseas from a metropolitan perspective. However, he primarily offers three criticisms of their interpretation. The first is that they underestimate the role of British industrial capitalism in China. The second, like Petersson, again points to the changing balance between all three factors which determined the power of 'imperialism'; the core, the periphery and the international power structure. His third criticism addresses the treatment and interpretation of decolonization, where he emphasizes the role of the Soviet Union. Based on his own research on the disintegration of colonial empires,[36] Zhang presents us with a more rigid definition of decolonization. He emphasizes the roles of national liberation movements and indigenous nationalism in accelerating decolonization, and plays down financial causes.

In Chapter 8, Naoto Kagotani and Shigeru Akita use recent research by Japanese historians to reconsider the nature and formation of the 'International Order of Asia' in the 1930s, and emphasize the importance of indigenous forces in creating it. First, we present a framework and viewpoint for analyzing the Asian international order in the 1930s. We explore the formation of economic interdependence and complementary relationships in Asia at the metropolitan-peripheral as well as inter-regional levels, the historical significance of Asian industrialization in the 1930s, and the 'openness' of the sterling area and the imperialistic international order of Asia. We then analyze British perceptions of Japanese economic development in the 1930s, as an ideal case of economic 'complementarity', by referring to the *British Commercial Reports on Japan* written by the Commercial Counsellor, Sir George Sansom. Finally we consider Japanese 'cotton-textile diplomacy' with British India and the Dutch East Indies in the first half of the 1930s. We conclude that Japan's ability to import huge quantities of primary products from the British Empire was indispensable for colonial debt servicing, and that there was a clear complementarity between European financial interests and Japanese exports to the Asian markets which stimulated the networks of Asian merchants.

In Chapter 9, Yoichi Kibata reconsiders the influence of Great Britain in East Asia in the 1930s to test the proposition that Britain remained an assertive, global power in the inter-war years. Kibata, who is one of the editors of the Anglo-Japanese History Project,[37] combines an analysis of British policy in China and Japan, and relocates the Cain–Hopkins thesis in the context of the changing nature of the British Empire, especially in East Asia. He examines British attitudes to Japan from the Japanese invasion of Manchuria in 1931 to the Sino-Japanese War in

1937, and reveals the continuity of Britain's accommodating attitude to Japanese diplomacy and the formation of Britain's appeasement policy towards Japan in the mid-1930s. He argues that the British Government pursued coexistence with Japan in China for the purpose of containing rising Chinese nationalism and prolonging the imperialist world order in East Asia. British appeasement policy reflected the contemporary sense of weakness in the 'official mind' and the changing nature of Britain's status in international relations. Kibata's article is also concerned with the political significance and the validity of the concept of British 'informal empire' in China.

In Chapter 10, Kaoru Sugihara reveals the interconnectedness between the City of London as the chief source of international capital and Asian industrialization in the twentieth century, and develops an argument that relates the trajectory of British imperialism with the global diffusion of industrialization in the development of a capitalist world-economy. First, Sugihara points to the formation of 'complementarity' or a particular kind of 'division of labour' between the City of London and East Asia's industrialization over the first half of the twentieth century. The City benefited from the growth of 'intra-Asian trade'[38] and the industrialization of Asian countries. He also analyzes the 'link' of Japan in 1932 and China in 1935 with the sterling area and the extension of sterling's influence outside the British Empire in the 1930s. Sugihara then broadens his arguments to cover their implications for global history. He explores the new international division of labour between the United States and other Asian countries under the Cold War regime, and its similarity to the former relationship between the City of London and East Asian countries. He observes that 'the peculiar relationship, identified as the Cain and Hopkins perspective, has arguably survived the hegemonic shift, and has remained a central device for the development of the capitalist world economy to this day'.[39] The role of the financial and service sectors is generalized as a vital facilitator of technological transfer and the global diffusion of industrialization in the context of global history.

V

At the end of the book, Peter Cain and Tony Hopkins respond fully to every chapter and show that they are looking ahead as well as reflecting on their earlier work. They make it clear, as do the other chapters in this volume, that imperial history is a lively subject and one that is taking new directions. It is also a subject for the twenty-first century and not, as many commentators have supposed, one that is or should be confined to the age of great empires alone. Empires did much to shape the form of globalization that characterized the world order before our own, post-colonial age.

As noted at the outset, the main aim of this book is to renew the debate on British imperialism and the British Empire by combining Western and Asian historiography, and to construct a new 'global history' for the understanding of globalization. Globalization is now becoming a new and important field in historical studies. 'Global history' attracts attention not only from historians but also from social scientists. Tony Hopkins has shown a keen interest in the history of globalization,[40] and Cain and Hopkins have added a new chapter, 'Afterword: Empires and Globalization' to their second edition of *British Imperialism, 1688–2000*. For their part, Japanese historians have also taken a strong interest in world history since the 1960s, and they have written several series of world history from a global perspective.[41] Thus academic discussions on globalization have begun on both sides of the globe. By learning more about the imperial element in the history of globalization, we can come to a better understanding of what is truly novel about the process of globalization in the late twentieth and twenty-first centuries.

Notes

1   John Gallagher and Ronald Robinson, 'The Imperialism of Free Trade', *Economic History Review*, 2nd series, Vol. VI (1953).
2   W.R. Louis, *Imperialism: the Robinson and Gallagher Controversy* (London and New York, 1976).
3   Editor-in-Chief, W. Roger Louis, *The Oxford History of the British Empire*, 5 vols (Oxford, 1998–99), especially Vol. IV: *The Twentieth Century* and Vol. V: *Historiography*.
4   A.G. Hopkins, 'Informal Empire in Argentina: an Alternative View', *Journal of Latin American Studies*, 26 (1994), pp. 469–84; P.J. Cain and A.G. Hopkins, 'Afterword: the theory and practice of British imperialism', in Raymond E. Dumett (ed.), *Gentlemanly Capitalism and British Imperialism: the New Debate on Empire* (London and New York, 1999), pp. 204–6.
5   Susan Strange, *States and Markets* (London, 1988), ch. 2.
6   Patrick K. O'Brien, 'The State Status and Future of Universal History', an Essay submitted for Major Theme 1A, 'Perspective on Global History, Concepts and Methodology' for the 19th International Congress of Historical Sciences, Oslo, 6–13 August 2000, p. 16.
    Patrick O'Brien is the Convenor of the Programme in Global History, the Institute of Historical Research, University of London.
7   P.J. Cain and A.G. Hopkins, *British Imperialism, 1688–2000* (2nd Edition, Harlow and New York, 2001).

8 Minoru Kawakita, 'Kindai-Sekai Sisutemu-ron wo megutte' [On the 'Modern World-System'], *Senshu-Daigaku Shakai-Kagaku Kenkyusho Geppou* [*Monthly Report of the Institute of Social Sciences, Senshu University*, Tokyo], No. 287 (1987).

9 Giovanni Arrighi, *The Long Twentieth Century: Money, Power, and the Origins of Our Times* (London and New York, 1994); Takeshi Matsuda and Shigeru Akita (eds), *Hegemoni-Kokka to Sekai Sisutemu* [*The Hegemonic States and the World System*] (Tokyo: Yamakawa-Shuppan, 2002).

10 Patrick K. O'Brien, 'The Pax Britannica and the International Order 1688–1914', Shigeru Akita and Takeshi Matsuda (eds), *Looking Back at the 20th Century: the Role of Hegemonic State and the Transformation of the Modern World-System* (Proceedings of the Global History Workshop Osaka, 1999, Osaka University of Foreign Studies, 2000), pp. 44–5.

11 O'Brien, 'The State Status and Future of Universal History', p. 8.

12 Will Hutton, *The State We're In* (London, 1994).

13 Philip Augar, *The Death of Gentlemanly Capitalism* (London, 2000).

14 Raymond E. Dumett (ed.), *Gentlemanly Capitalism and British Imperialism: the New Debate on Empire* (London and New York, 1999).

15 Cain and Hopkins, op. cit., 'Forward: the Continuing Debate on Empire'.

16 Ibid., chs 2 and 26.

17 Cain and Hopkins, op. cit., 'Afterword: Empires and Globalization', pp. 668–77.

18 Ian H. Nish, *The Anglo-Japanese Alliance: the Diplomacy of Two Island Empires 1894–1907* (London, 1966).

19 See C.M. Turnbull, 'Formal and Informal Empire in East Asia', in Robin W. Winks (ed.), *The Oxford History of the British Empire*, Vol. V, *Historiography* (Oxford, 1999) and Jürgen Osterhammel, 'China', in Judith M. Brown and Wm. Roger Louis (eds), *The Oxford History of the British Empire*, Vol. IV, *The Twentieth Century* (Oxford, 1999).

20 Kaoru Sugihara, *Ajia-kan Boeki no Keisei to Kozo* [*Patterns and Development of Intra-Asian Trade*] (Kyoto: Mineruva-Shobo, 1996), Introduction, pp. 1–2.

21 Takeshi Hamashita, *Kindai Chugoku no Kokusaiteki Keiki: Choko Boeki Shisutemu to Kindai Ajia* [*International Factors Affecting Modern China: Tributary Trade System and Modern Asia*] (Tokyo: Tokyo University Press, 1990); Takeshi Hamashita, *Choko Shisutemu to Kindai Ajia* [*Tributary Trade System and Modern Asia*] (Tokyo: Iwanami-shoten, 1997).

22 Heita Kawakatsu, 'International Competition in Cotton Goods in the Late Nineteenth Century: Britain versus East Asia', in W. Fisher, R.M. McInnis and J. Schneider (eds), *The Emergence of a World Economy, 1500–1914, Beiträge zur Wirtschafts und Sozialgeschichte*, Band 33–2 (Wiesbaden, 1986); A.J.H. Latham and Heita Kawakatsu (eds), *Japanese Industrialization and Asian Economy* (London and New York, 1994).

23 Sugihara, op. cit., ch. 1; Kaoru Sugihara, 'Japan as an Engine of the Asian International Economy, c. 1880–1936', *Japan Forum*, 2(1) (1990).

24 Shigeru Akita, '"Gentlemanly Capitalism", intra-Asian Trade and Japanese Industrialization at the Turn of the Last Century', *Japan Forum*, 8(1) (1996), pp. 51–65.

25 Toshio Suzuki, *Japanese Government Loan Issues on the London Capital Market 1870–1913* (London, 1994), pp. 1–3, 83–4.

26   See also, Shigeru Akita and Naoto Kagotani (eds), *1930 nendai no Ajia Kokusai Chitujo* [*International Order of Asia in the 1930s*] (Hiroshima: Keisui-sha, 2001).

27   Toru Kubo, *Senkan-ki Chugoku Jiritsu eno Mosaku: Kanzei-Tsuka Seisaku to Keizai Hatten* [*China's Quest for Sovereignty in the Inter-war Period: Tariff Policy and Economic Development*] (Tokyo: Tokyo University Press, 1999).

28   B.R. Tomlinson, *The Political Economy of the Raj 1914–1947: the Economics of Decolonization in India* (London, 1979); B.R. Tomlinson, *The New Cambridge History of India*, III-3, *The Economy of Modern India, 1860–1970* (Cambridge, 1993), chs. 3 and 4.

29   Shigeru Akita, *Igirisu-Teikoku to Ajia Kokusai Chitujo* [*The British Empire and International Order of Asia*] (Nagoya: Nagoya University Press, 2002).

30   H.V. Bowen, 'British Conceptions of Global Empire, 1756–1783', *Journal of Imperial and Commonwealth History*, 26 (1998), pp. 1–27.

31   Ch. 3, p. 60.

32   See also, John Darwin, 'Imperialism and the Victorians: the Dynamics of Territorial Expansion', *English Historical Review*, Vol. CXII, No. 447 (1997), pp. 614–42.

33   Gerold Krozewski, *Money and the End of Empire: British International Economic Policy and the Colonies, 1947–58* (Basingstoke and New York: Palgrave, 2001 (now Palgrave Macmillan)).

34   J. Osterhammel, *China und die Weltgesellschaft. Vom 18. Jahrhundert bis in unsere Zeit* (Munich, 1989), p. 223; J. Osterhammel, 'Britain and China, 1842–1914', in A. Porter (ed.), *The Oxford History of the British Empire*, Vol. III: *The Nineteenth Century* (Oxford, 1999).

35   Ch. 6, p. 116.

36   Shunhong Zhang, *et al.*, *Da Ying Diguo De Wajie* [*The Collapse of the British Empire*] (Beijing: China Social Science Documentation Publishing House, 1997).

37   Ian Nish and Yoichi Kibata (eds), *The History of Anglo-Japanese Relations, 1600–2000*, Vol. 2, *The Political-Diplomatic Dimension, 1930–2000* (Basingstoke and London, 2000).

38   Kaoru Sugihara, *Ajia-kan Boeki no Keisei to Kozo* [*Patterns and Development of Intra-Asian Trade*].

39   Ch. 10, p. 197.

40   A.G. Hopkins, 'Back to the Future: from National History to Imperial History', *Past and Present*, No. 164 (1999); A.G. Hopkins (ed.), *Globalization in World History* (London, 2002).

41   Rekishigaku Kenkyukai [The Historical Science Society of Japan] (ed.), *Kouza Sekaishi* [*Lectures in Modern World History*], 12 vols, (Tokyo: University of Tokyo Press, 1996–97); *Sekai no Rekishi* [*A History of the World*], 30 vols (Tokyo: Chuokoron-Shinsha, 1998–99); *Iwanami-Kouza Sekairekishi* [*Iwanami Series in World History*], 29 vols (Tokyo: Iwanami-shoten, 1998–2000).

Part I

British Imperialism and the Global Order

2
Gentlemanly Capitalism and the Making of a Global British Empire: Some Connections and Contexts, 1688–1815

H.V. Bowen

During the eighteenth century, trade, discovery, warfare and settlement took Britons to all parts of the world. From the very beginning of the expansionist process, those extending British maritime and commercial enterprise beyond European waters and into the wider world had directed their energies and resources towards the east as well as the west, and towards the south as well as the north. As a result, although the overseas footholds established by the British were often uncertain and sometimes short-lived, they gradually began to constitute an empire whose chief characteristics were its diversity and widely scattered distribution. For all the obvious importance of trade and settlement in the Atlantic world, activity in Africa, India and the Pacific region was increasingly recognized as defining the full extent of British overseas ambition. Britain proved to be rather more successful than France, Holland and Spain in maintaining at least a token presence in all of the main spheres of European overseas interest, and it gradually became evident to Britons that their empire was taking a form that was unlike any other, past or present. Always seeking out comparisons and contrasts with the empires of ancient Greece, Rome and Persia, commentators duly noted that Britain was the first to exert influence in all parts of the globe. Slowly, but ever more surely after the end of the Seven Years' War in 1763, the British began to view their empire as a global one, and this found expression in their outlook, strategy, and resource calculations. Imperial attitudes had already begun to be embedded in popular political consciousness, and they now began to consolidate the identity of the British as a people who commanded a multiracial, multifaith empire of millions.[1]

The emergence of a global British Empire: causes, connections and consequences

There was of course no grand strategy or master plan involved in the creation of Britain's overseas empire, and such were the different spheres of activity that, on the face of it, there seems to be little if anything to link expansion in, say, North America and India. Indeed, an overview of British expansion might well suggest that it was an entirely haphazard, uncertain and discontinuous process, played out in far-distant and unconnected parts of the world. But although the acquisition of individual territories or possessions can often be explained by the fortunes of war, quirks of fate, or the rogue actions of a 'man on the spot', the steady establishment of a global empire implies the existence of deeper, strong-running causal currents. Two particularly strong currents were to be found in the long-term and reasonably consistent application of metropolitan resources to overseas activity, and in the creation of a set of common attitudes and assumptions among Britons everywhere. These helped to bring a peculiar strength, coherence and resilience to overseas activity, and enabled Britain, undeterred by the loss of America in 1783, to survive and then eventually to thrive as an imperial power.

If an overseas empire is, at least in part, an outward manifestation of the metropolitan power that first created it, then the establishment of Britain's global empire cannot be understood without consideration being given to developments that occurred in Britain itself during the eighteenth century. Indeed when Cain and Hopkins sought to re-examine the reasons that lay behind the growth of Britain's overseas empire, they were motivated by a strong belief that explanations of expansion should always begin at home. Accordingly, they challenged many of the existing orthodoxies by advancing a powerful case based upon the emergence in Britain of a form of 'gentlemanly capitalism' created by an alliance of mutual benefit forged between the representatives of land, trade and finance during the course of the eighteenth century.[2] Gentlemanly capitalists were located at the very heart of the expansionist process, notably in the City of London's burgeoning financial service sector, from where they were able to deploy resources, shape opinion and influence decision-making. Generally committed to innovation, 'improvement', and diversification, their gentlemanly ideals and entrepreneurial attitudes permeated the wider British elite, and helped to define patterns of economic, social and cultural behaviour. Above all, many were deeply committed to overseas enterprise and sought enthusiastically to exploit the opportunities offered by the nascent empire. For them, all the world was a stage, and as risk-taking merchant princes, investors, shipowners, insurers, lenders, bankers, land speculators, projectors and adventurers they focused their profit-seeking attention on distant horizons and thus helped to underwrite and sustain expansionist activity at far-flung peripheries. Indeed, the commercial sophisticates who led the way operated freely and comfortably across different sectors and regions in such an effective fashion that they were themselves able to establish miniature global business empires of their own. They became, as David Hancock has so ably demonstrated, 'citizens of the world',[3] and the scope and range of their activities was such that during the late eighteenth century one Dutch-based British entrepreneur, Robert Charnock, was able to anticipate such a description by pronouncing that he had become a 'burgher of the whole world'.[4]

Defining and tracing the emergence of metropolitan gentlemanly capitalists with a keen interest in overseas activity is, of course, as relevant to the study of imperialism as it is to our understanding of elite formation within British society, but this does not by itself explain how and why Britain was able to establish a *global* empire by 1815. After all, many of the eighteenth-century gentlemanly capitalists described by Cain and Hopkins never left Britain and were thus not in any real sense active agents driving forward the expansionist process in the wider world. They can be represented as the back-seat drivers of the imperial vehicle who paid for the fuel and supplied a route map but were unable to exercise tight control on the steering wheel. The real drivers were those operating at or beyond different frontiers who acted in their own interest, or who managed resources, made decisions, and undertook actions on behalf of those who remained at home. Of course, Cain and Hopkins acknowledge the critical role played by overseas actors within the expansionist process, and they do so within an explanatory framework that embraces both the imperial core and the periphery. As they put it:

> The chief aim of our interpretation is to establish the context within which actions took place; that is, to understand why actors of a certain

kind were where they were when they were, and why their views of the world inclined them to act in the way they did.[5]

Unfortunately for students of the eighteenth century, however, their necessarily compressed treatment of that important period meant that they were perhaps not able to explore as fully as they would have liked the interplay and associations that existed between those in Britain and those who moved in the wider world. As a result, although they eventually concluded in the first edition of *British Imperialism* that 'The configuration of wealth, status and power that materialised in gentlemanly forms of enterprise' made its mark on the overseas empire, both on the Atlantic colonies and on India,[6] they did not provide case studies of eighteenth-century expansion similar to those offered for the years after 1815.[7] This remains so in the recently published second edition of *British Imperialism* and thus there is still a need to examine further any relationship that might have existed between the post-1688 emergence of gentlemanly capitalism and the increasingly global exertion of British power and influence during the eighteenth century. In particular, it is necessary to establish the extent to which gentlemanly capitalist forces were felt in the wider world, and how, if at all, they served to influence the development of British activity in different regions. This is attempted here through the amplification of some of the points raised directly or indirectly in the work of Cain and Hopkins, and also by drawing on some of the many studies of the eighteenth-century empire that have appeared since the publication of the first edition of *British Imperialism* in 1993. The issues raised and discussed here (which are not intended by any means to be comprehensive in scope or detail) relate primarily to gentlemanly capitalism in its overseas context.[8] Emphasis is placed upon the nature and form taken by the British presence overseas, and the factors that served to underpin Britain's emergence as an imperial power whose influence was increasingly felt in all parts of the known world. It should be borne in mind, therefore, that in what follows metropolitan and overseas forms of gentlemanly capitalism are not regarded as being separated by geographical location, but rather as belonging to one increasingly interconnected transoceanic developmental process that bore heavily upon the establishment and expansion of a global British empire.

During the eighteenth century, Britons at home and abroad did not invest the word 'empire' with an exact meaning. This was a reflection of the fact that, as David Armitage has recently remarked, 'The unifying [political] concept of the British Empire left generous room for different conceptions of the Empire.'[9] Armitage's study of the emergence of conceptions of an empire that by the 1740s was characterized as being Protestant, commercial, maritime, and free adds much to our understanding of why the word 'empire' was not, as later, used narrowly or exclusively in relation to the conquest of territory and the rule of alien people. Rather, as historians have long recognized, it was a word with multiple meanings applied across a range of overseas contexts, and as British activity changed and expanded during the eighteenth century so too a variety of different connotations and associations came into being.[10] In the early part of the century, for example, contemporaries often wrote or spoke of the 'empire of the seas', a reflection of the importance of the North Atlantic fisheries and the 'nursery of seamen' that provided manpower for the Royal Navy. At the same time, while the term 'colonies and plantations' was often preferred in discussion of the settlements peopled by migrants and slaves in North America and the West Indies, commentators also began to describe the existence of an English or British 'empire' in America. Only later, with conquest in India did the word 'empire' become commonly associated with the annexation of territory and the exertion of direct political and administrative control over large numbers of indigenous peoples. As a result, attitudes towards an increasingly polyglot empire tended to be conditioned by the branch being discussed, and language was adjusted accordingly. Metropolitan responses to white settlers or 'brethren overseas' were thus quite different from those offered to subordinated Hindus or Muslims, with the former invariably being located within an Atlantic 'empire of liberty'; the latter within an Asiatic 'empire of conquest'. These distinctions were reinforced by the geographical separation that existed between the empires of the west and east, and also by the variety of institutional arrangements that underpinned British activity in different parts of the world. Only slowly did ideas begin to coalesce around the notion that Britain possessed one empire, *the* Empire, and this ensured that the British never exhibited dogged adherence to an ideological template designed to impose a rigid framework upon imperial endeavour or overseas activity. Rather, they made a series of accommodations with different types of imperial enterprise. This undoubtedly helped Britain to survive the loss of the American Colonies in 1783 and it paved the way for the dual pursuit of both formal and informal empire during the early nineteenth century.

Although Britain's widely scattered overseas empire took many forms during the eighteenth century, expansionist tendencies were often at work simultaneously at different points of the compass. The growth of trade and commerce went hand in hand with the application of military and naval power to ensure that new possessions were acquired, frontiers were extended, and markets were established. But the extension of British influence occurred at an uneven pace and rhythm. In times of peace, expansion was usually creeping and steady, often passing unnoticed by those in the metropolis, but wartime victories against old rivals France and Spain could bring spectacular advances that were consolidated by peace treaties and widely celebrated by the British public. No more was this the case than during the Seven Years' War (1756–63) when victories in Europe, North America, India, Africa, and the West Indies, together with the establishment of naval supremacy, led many Britons to suggest that their nation was now able to exert power on the global stage.[11] Earlier triumphs, such as Anson's highly acclaimed heroic voyage round the world between 1740–44, had often been represented as evidence of such a capacity, but it was not until 1763 that, with France and Spain humiliated, the way seemed clear for Britain to embark upon a process of sustained world-wide expansion.

Of course, not all were convinced about the advantages to be gained from empire and those who feared the consequences of over-expansion were to be heard loudly proclaiming the virtues of caution and retrenchment. Yet although the gathering American crisis and signs of a French recovery ensured that any general mood of imperial optimism was short-lived, Britons acknowledged and reflected upon their global interests and possessions. The horizons of the gentlemanly classes were greatly furthered after 1763 as the editors of journals and the writers of pamphlets encouraged a 'swing to the east' in outlook by placing before their readers copious amounts of information relating to diverse British activities in India, China, the East Indies, the South Pacific and Australasia.[12] As this happened, the more practically minded politicians and commentators endeavoured to identify the connections that existed between different forms of overseas endeavour. The potential economic interdependence of different overseas possessions was explicitly stated and rudimentary attempts at imperial integration were made in an attempt to draw together and better exploit in far-distant peripheries.[13] Commercial and cultural integration had long been a feature of the Atlantic world, and it has received much attention from historians, but efforts were also made to establish sustainable economic connections between British Asia and the American colonies. That this failed in the short term when disaffected American colonists threw East India Company tea into Boston Harbour to trigger the events leading to the American Revolution should not obscure the fact that as early as the 1760s some thought was being given to the question of how relationships between peripheries might be more sharply defined. Those in the metropolis who thought about such things usually did so with their own interests in mind, but they were beginning to consider the empire as the sum of its many parts rather than as simply a collection of unrelated and randomly distributed overseas possessions. Underpinning this theoretical consolidation of the empire as a single entity or greater whole can be discerned demands for the more organized and rational ordering of possessions, the emergence of the metropolis as a more proactive agent for the reallocation of imperial resources, and the growing realization that losses in one sector or area might be offset by gains elsewhere. Not only did these lines of thought represent the beginning of a new approach to empire, but they also played their part in helping to ensure that, despite fears to the contrary, Britain was able to absorb the considerable economic and commercial impact caused by the loss of America.

The establishment of connections between the different branches of Britain's expanding empire was not only made by those who looked out at the world from the metropolis. As in the wheel of a contemporary wagon, Britain's eighteenth-century empire was given shape and definition by its rim as well as by the spokes that centred upon the axle. To a lesser or greater degree, and indeed sometimes only tenuously, provinces became linked with other provinces as well as to the imperial core, a process that was facilitated by increasingly long-distance flows of people, goods and information around the empire, and this enabled some of those at the outer edges to place themselves within a much greater whole. Those in the Atlantic colonies benefited from the material benefits of expansion in other parts of the world; they gloried in the success of British arms in far-distant theatres of war; and they believed themselves to be sharing the same rights and privileges as all other Britons, whether at home or abroad. Moreover, some within the overseas empire played a full part in the 'emergence of a pan-Atlantic conception of the British Empire',[14] and during the 1760s they, like their metropolitan counterparts, began tentatively to locate themselves within a broader, global empire.[15]

Informing the preliminary and often very hesitant attempts to come to terms with the practical realities of global imperialism was a growing awareness that financial and military resources derived from the overseas empire were becoming deeply embedded in the processes that sustained the strength of the metropolitan state and economy. The increased levels of trade and investment directed towards the empire were an obvious manifestation of this, but many in the metropolis were now expecting to draw some benefit from some of the more explicitly 'imperial' forms of endeavour that were being pursued by Britons overseas. This became abundantly clear as Britain began to accumulate possessions acquired by military conquest rather than settlement, notably in India where the East India Company's greatly expanded private army established control over Bengal and the surrounding provinces during the 1760s. Not only did the Company's Indian army represent a considerable cost-free addition of strength to the metropolitan state that could be deployed in the global struggle against the French, but the Company's deep involvement in the collection of territorial revenues after 1765 offered the prospect of a substantial surplus being remitted to Britain as a form of 'tribute'. The government fully expected to receive a share of this surplus, with the fruits of empire being distributed among the members of a mutually beneficial public–private partnership established between the state and the Company. Although the Company's financial and political difficulties ensured that such a relationship never properly developed, the matter greatly exercised the minds of some who began to regard the overseas empire as a fiscal cash cow that could be milked to the great benefit of a nation struggling with mounting financial problems. Revenue income derived from the periphery could be applied to the spiralling national debt, thereby easing the domestic tax burden and notionally offsetting some of the costs that had been incurred by the state in support of overseas activity.

With the empire being written into calculations of national wealth, strength, and prosperity, developments in the wider world could no longer be thought to have only a marginal effect upon the domestic economy. Historians have hotly debated the extent to which trade and imperialism influenced the growth of the eighteenth-century economy, but after the 1760s contemporaries were inclined to consider the empire as capable of exerting a major influence upon the economic well-being of the metropolis. Yet although the economic benefits of expansion were plain for some to see, others raised awkward questions about the ultimate value of trade in exotic goods and luxury items. Anxieties were also expressed about crisis at the periphery of the empire having a devastating financial impact upon the metropolis. It was thought, for example, that with considerable amounts of investment capital committed to the East India Company a serious setback in India could destroy confidence and badly damage the City of London. Some well-informed thinkers went as far as to suggest that imperial crisis could well serve as a prelude to national bankruptcy, and although events following the loss of America proved otherwise, such fears were usually sufficient to convince ministers that the state had some degree of responsibility for underwriting and sustaining those overseas activities deemed to be of importance to the national interest. As a result, although the establishment of Britain's fledgling global empire was never in any sense a state-sponsored or state-directed enterprise, the influence of the metropolitan state could always be felt in a number of different ways.

The eighteenth-century British state was, by instinct, non-interventionist and it exercised only a light touch on the development of overseas enterprise. At times, of course, the force of British arms and ships was felt in North America, the West Indies, India and elsewhere but for the most part Crown troops and administrators were conspicuous by their absence from the outer reaches of empire. Governments had inherited from their seventeenth-century predecessors a legacy that had established the outline features of overseas enterprise through legislation granting monopolies and privileges to a variety of trading companies, 'projectors', and territorial proprietors. Little direct control was exercised by the state over overseas possessions, and few efforts were made to direct or control the course of expansion. Instead, considerable autonomy had been devolved to local authorities such as the assemblies in North America and the West Indies or the East India Company in Asia. Indeed, there were no Crown or state representatives at all in Asia during the early part of the eighteenth century, and there was little by way of regulation or routine supervision of the Company in Britain. Yet this should not be construed as long-term indifference by the state towards overseas activity. Monopolies and the Navigation system had been established to enhance national financial and maritime power, and governments were usually prepared to commit manpower resources, at least on a temporary basis, to various peripheries in support of hard-pressed outposts routinely policed and defended by locally raised troops or militias. Although it can be argued that as a result of the harsh strategic reasons learned during the War of American Independence the navy remained reluctant to disperse its main forces to distant waters,[16] expeditions and squadron continued to be dispatched to the wider world and Britain retained the capacity to bring pressure to bear upon colonial theatres of war. There was no clearer indication of this than during the global warfare of 1793–1815, when not only were French threats to the empire decisively thwarted but Britain also emerged victorious as Europe's predominant imperial and maritime power.[17]

When pressed, the state also offered financial support to enterprises considered to be vital to national interests. This was most notably the case with the East India Company. The Company had been present at the birth of the eighteenth-century state during the 1690s when it loaned considerable sums of money to a hard-pressed wartime government. As such, it was embedded at the very heart of the system of public credit, and came together with the Bank of England to form the powerful 'monied interest', which represented the institutional meeting point between the worlds of private and national endeavour. Because of this, and because of the economic potential thought to be offered by the Company's expansion in India, the state was prepared to grant considerable financial support to the Company when it ran into trouble during the late eighteenth century. In return, the state began to exercise closer supervision of the territory being brought under Company control, but it did so at arm's length and the Company long continued to act as Britain's official agency in Asia. Governments were wary of the political problems associated with any challenge to the sanctity of chartered rights, but they were also all too aware of military and administrative realities. They did not have the resources, expertise, or capacity to govern vast tracts of overseas territory, and their attempts to assert authority over the 13 American colonies during the 1760s had only drawn them into crisis and a costly war. It was thought far better to continue to devolve power to others, such as the East India Company, who could act as representatives of British interests. This policy ran obvious risks when the Company pursued aims that were not in the wider national interest or was unable to control its own employees, and thus after 1773 Parliament began to establish the metropolitan bureaucracy necessary to supervise East Indian affairs. In the aftermath of American war, fears for the future of the empire combined with the anxieties of the revolutionary era led to similar developments becoming evident in other spheres of overseas activity. This is held to have heralded the beginning of a new authoritarian era in which more robust metropolitan attitudes towards the empire were translated into the establishment of the institutional apparatus of control and audit.[18] This was undoubtedly the case, but much tighter imperial regulation at the centre was not yet matched by effective control at far-distant peripheries, and the influence of the British state often remained very limited at times other than when troops and ships were deployed in support of local British representatives or communities. The limited overseas reach of the state was no better illustrated than in the case of India where the East India Company, despite its gradual loss of commercial privileges after 1793, remained firmly in place as a semi-autonomous governing agency.

Although the existence of a global empire began slowly to impress itself upon the minds of Britons everywhere, Britain's overseas possessions remained diverse in form, were scattered around the world, and could only be loosely controlled from the metropolis. Such characteristics militated against the development of closer imperial ties, but over time, and in spite of many differences borne out of a variety of local conditions, Britain's imperial possessions began increasingly to adopt patterns of sociocultural configuration that were similar to those evident in the metropolis itself. This served to impose some basic coherence and order upon an otherwise fragmented empire, and also helped to bind overseas territories to the imperial core and metropolitan society. Indeed, the unsuccessful attempts to redefine Britain's relationship with her American colonies during the 1760s and 1770s underscored the point that the Atlantic empire could be better sustained and exploited through the development of informal ties and associations than it ever could be by heavy-handed assertions of metropolitan authority that could not be backed by force.

In recent years, historians have begun to approach the study of eighteenth-century British imperialism from a range of new perspectives, and this is reflected in the number of terms they have employed to describe the defining features of the empire. Generally speaking, attention has shifted away from the imperialism that manifested itself in the administrative, constitutional and military studies of earlier generations of scholars. Much more emphasis is now placed upon the cultural and material aspects of imperialism, and Britain's Atlantic possessions are now thought to have belonged to an 'empire of goods' or an 'empire of paper'.[19] In different ways, these terms suggest the emergence of 'anglicized' overseas societies whose path to maturity was determined by powerful impulses emanating from the metropolis as well as by local conditions. Indeed, historians of colonial America have been ever more willing to draw comparisons rather than contrasts between economic and social development at the core and peripheries of the Atlantic empire.[20]

Gentlemanly capitalism and Britain's Colonial American Empire

Colonial America does not loom very large in the work of Cain and Hopkins, which is perhaps rather surprising in view of the extent to which historians have been inclined to portray members of the North American elite as archetypal gentlemanly capitalists. This might be held to represent something of a lost opportunity to locate gentlemanly capitalist influences at the outer edge of the eighteenth-century empire. Certainly, North American elites, like their provincial British counterparts, were active agents of anglicization and played the leading role in the establishment of the core–periphery links that secured for the colonies increasingly extensive levels of participation in the changing world of metropolitan etiquette, fashion, goods, news, ideas and learning. The gathering strength of metropolitan influence at the periphery was facilitated by better communications and improved levels of economic integration within the Atlantic trading world, and it found expression in the way that many of the material benefits associated with the consumer revolution were brought to bear upon North American society. As a result, an increasing sense of civility, improvement and order characterized many parts of the colonies by the middle of the eighteenth century, and this had an important bearing upon the lines of development followed by local elites. Different elites were able to confirm and reinforce their status in society through the purchase of a wide range of fashionable and luxury goods, and, in the absence of formal titles, ranks and privileges of the type found in contemporary Britain and Europe, 'conspicuous consumption' assisted with the demarcation of boundary lines within the social hierarchy. At the same time, elites were also able more sharply to define their sense of group identity and belonging by developing genteel, polite and well-mannered lifestyles similar to those that had emerged within metropolitan elite circles. Indeed, from a broader perspective, the all-pervasive influence of the metropolis can be seen to have contributed to a process, recently described as 'international gentrification',[21] which helped to establish a common pattern of social and cultural behaviour within the upper echelons of all Britain's imperial possessions. If the view that the 'spread of gentility created in America a conscious class of gentlemen united by common standards across colony lines' is broadly acceptable,[22] the extension of such an argument suggests that all elites across the entire British overseas empire were drawn together, united, and given a sense of identity by the same standards and codes of behaviour. They formed a transoceanic imperial elite and, although the members of this elite were, to varying degrees, rooted in quite different British colonial contexts, they nevertheless followed similar lifestyles, displayed many of the same characteristics, and developed a range of interests and associations that transcended local and regional frontiers. Drawing them together, and helping to establish a set of common social and cultural benchmarks, was their adherence to the English gentlemanly ideal, or at least to an adapted form of that ideal.

By the beginning of the eighteenth century, the North American colonies had moved beyond the initial uncertain stages of settlement and living standards had begun to improve. As this happened, members of the elite became enthusiastic participants in the various cultural, economic and social processes that helped to establish and sustain Britain's wider gentlemanly empire, and it is possible to identify many reasons why they became dedicated to what has been called the 'pursuit of fashion'.[23] However, although a strong case can be made for placing colonial elites within a general behavioural and cultural framework defined by metropolitan terms of reference – similar lifestyles, social activities, patterns of consumption and so on – it is nevertheless important that close attention is paid to the precise form taken by what Cain and Hopkins call the 'imprint' of the English gentleman in the overseas setting. There are a number of reasons for this. First, as Richard Bushman and others have argued, American elite lifestyles were founded upon rather more than the simple imitation or replication of British types of behaviour. Instead, cultural trends on both sides of the Atlantic belonged to what Bushman describes as the 'single integrated process' affecting all Britain's provinces. This enabled colonists to respond almost as quickly as those in the outer regions of the metropolis to behavioural and material influences emanating from London.[24] Second, the overseas elite never became unthinking clones of the metropolitan elite. Some were capable of displaying an independence of mind and action, and some were prepared to condemn those aspects of English culture they considered inappropriate or unsuited to their own particular environment.[25] Ian Steele has remarked that elites were capable of displaying a 'fascinating ambivalence' towards Britain.[26]Although they needed and indeed welcomed the many advantages that London bestowed upon them, they could at the same time demonstrate a deep suspicion and hostility towards key aspects of British economic and imperial policy, as of course was amply demonstrated during the events leading up to the American Revolution. Thirdly, whatever the strength of the influences exerted by the metropolis, other factors always played a very large part in shaping elite lives, experiences, and outlooks, with the result that local customs could find a place within adapted forms of genteel culture.[27] Kevin Sweeney stresses this in his recent exploration of these issues, and he makes the important point that 'the lifestyles of the colonies' social and economic elite were shaped by local conditions and vernacular traditions as well as by English goods and the pursuit of gentility'. Members of some elites did not possess the financial resources that were necessary to secure full-scale participation in the world of fashionable goods while others remained, through inclination and disposition, committed to the pursuit of a modest and simple lifestyle. As a result, the colonial pursuit of gentility could be both limited and, in certain contexts, 'selective'.[28]

It has, of course, long been acknowledged that the English gentlemanly ideal played a central role in the definition of elite status within the American colonies, and historians have often extended and, indeed to a degree, formalized this connection by making use of the terms 'aristocracy' and 'gentry' when describing quite different groups of individuals within colonial society. By doing this, and by using an English model of aristocratic or gentry behaviour, they have drawn comparisons, either explicitly or implicitly, between the lifestyles of their subjects and those of the landed and titled elements within contemporary British society. This is quite understandable because, with the exception of the important part played by slave ownership in helping to define gentlemanly status in the Chesapeake and the South,[29] the standard criteria that contemporaries had long applied to the definition of a gentleman in the North American colonies were much the same as those used in Britain. In particular, the possession of landed wealth and the accompanying personal qualities associated with civility, gentility, social responsibility and a sense of honour were all taken to represent the hallmarks of the colonial gentleman.[30] Yet, by the middle of the eighteenth century, it was increasingly possible to define a gentleman without narrow reference to land and birthright. Lifestyle, behaviour and manners could all help to secure entry into the world of the gentleman. In Britain, the exclusive associations between the landed gentry and the descriptive title of 'gentleman' had been broken before the beginning of the eighteenth century and the non-landed gentleman had come into being. Whereas all the gentry called themselves gentlemen, not all who called themselves gentlemen were members of the landed gentry. As a result, merchants, traders, financiers, and professionals of different types joined the gentlemanly ranks.[31] Similarly, changing perceptions and applications ensured that in the American colonies the term 'gentleman' could be used in a loose and flexible way to describe an increasing number of individuals who held little in terms of landed wealth but who were able to purchase the goods and possessions that had traditionally been associated with elite status.[32] In these cases, as in metropolitan society, consumerism advanced hand in hand with gentility, causing a redefinition of gentlemanly images and characteristics,[33] and it helped to ensure that the term 'gentleman' became associated with a wider range of occupations, qualities and characteristics than had hitherto been the case.[34] The effect of this was, in practice, to extend the boundaries of the gentlemanly order beyond those whose economic and social position was based entirely upon landownership. The colonial non-landed gentleman came into being and this ensured that the upper echelons of colonial society acquired some degree of the differentiation and diversity evident within the contemporary British elite.

On the face of it, therefore, it would seem that there are strong grounds to support the emergence of a colonial American form of gentlemanly capitalism, not least because the form taken by elite culture helped to establish and then cement a strong relationship between the advance of gentility and the development of capitalist or entrepreneurial activity. This is an issue recently addressed by Richard Bushman who suggests that material acquisition and the quest for refinement exerted powerful influences in the world of production and distribution, and thus ensured that 'capitalism and gentility came to reinforce one another'.[35] Engaging this issue from a slightly different perspective, it can be argued that, in part, such 'reinforcement' also resulted from the way in which gentlemanly values and codes of behaviour infused many forms of economic activity in North America,[36] while, as in the metropolis, innovation and enterprise established a place for themselves at the heart of the colonial gentleman's world. This bilateral exchange occurred against a general background in which entrepreneurial business methods and characteristics were becoming evident in all sectors of the colonial economy,[37] and it was assisted by the intermingling of different forms of economic activity. In the cultural and social sphere, the effects of this were such that they helped to remove, or perhaps prevent the establishment of, much of the hostility and antipathy that still occasionally characterized relations in Britain between the traditional landowning elite and those who operated in the world of business, commerce and trade.

In the Chesapeake, where the planter elite exhibited many of the behavioural, cultural and social characteristics of their metropolitan landowning counterparts,[38] choice or necessity dictated that fortunes were often established and then developed through a combination of tobacco planting, mixed farming, and a wide range of business enterprises including money-lending, land speculation, industrial activity, shipbuilding, and commercial operations. This not only enabled individuals to move away from a dangerous dependency on the success of their tobacco crop, but it also played an important part in the accumulation of wealth.[39] Detailed case studies reveal the extent to which local elites dedicated themselves to economic 'improvement' and to the diversification and development of their activities.[40] These individuals were neither crude caricatures of provincial British squires nor leisured *rentiers*. Rather, they were broadly similar to those British landowners who were genteel and civilized but who were also to be found in the vanguard of those promoting innovation, improvement and diversification within the British economy.

Other North American elites began to move along paths of socioeconomic development that were strikingly similar to those followed by elites in Britain. Boston, New York and Philadelphia all saw the emergence of powerful commercial groups that bore a close resemblance to metropolitan merchant elites both in terms of lifestyle and the range of their economic activities.[41] Although levels of personal wealth within North American commercial elites never reached the heights enjoyed by other colonial and metropolitan elites,[42] these men sought, in the selective manner mentioned earlier, to secure the trappings and social status of the gentleman. Accordingly, they kept one foot in the world of work and trade, but they were also often to be found purchasing land for speculative purposes and the development of the estates and country house that provided them with some of the material trappings of gentlemanly status. But land did not capture the attention of such entrepreneurs to the exclusion of everything else and there was no 'flight from trade'. Depending on local circumstances, it is possible to find plenty of examples of them diversifying their economic activities and moving into manufacturing, shipping, insurance, the iron industry, money-lending and privateering. Some long-established landed families beyond the Chesapeake also developed a close interest in trade and commerce, and their connections and involvement in such activity were often strengthened through marriage and family association. In New York many of the great landed dynasties had important branches of the family heavily engaged in trade, commerce, and industry by the 1750s.[43] Examples such as these illustrate that, broadly speaking, no firm line was drawn between land and trade, and this helped to bring elites drawn from a range of economic backgrounds into relatively close-knit alliances. These elites often displayed many of the character-istics of the most innovative and enterprising groups in metropolitan society, and, as was the case in South Carolina and Georgia for example,[44] this helped to shape the outlook and actions of those who acted as agents of economic growth and territorial expansion in colo-nial America. Lest the comparisons between colonial and metropolitan elites are too closely drawn, however, it is necessary to stress that those in colonies were unable to gain easy access to the centres of political and financial power in Westminster and the City of London, and thus the colonial gentleman lacked direct representation and, with only a few exceptions, he was unable to assume the role of public creditor and thereby become a stakeholder in the state and empire. Even so, although the colonial elite could never fully enter the world of the British gentleman, enough evidence has emerged in recent years to suggest that a variant form of gentlemanly capitalism exerted a consid-erable influence upon the economic and social development of the American colonies.

Gentlemanly capitalism and British expansion in Asia

It is also possible to discern gentlemanly capitalist influences at work within Britain's expanding empire in Asia. All too often Asia is regarded as a 'special case' in examinations of overseas expansion, and, Cain and Hopkins apart, few attempts have been made to integrate British India into general explanations of eighteenth-century imperialism. And yet, for all the obvious outward differences resulting from the formal struc-ture and form taken by the empire of the East, there are important simi-larities that allow British India to be tied into the wider empire, and incorporated within wider patterns of development evident in the imperial state. Three such general similarities are noted briefly here.

First, as elsewhere, the elite of British India endeavoured as far as possible to replicate the lifestyle, behaviour and patterns of sociocul-tural activity that were evident in the metropolis. The wider effects of this were of course diluted by the fact that the British community in India only ever represented a tiny minority of the population as a whole, but, as elsewhere, the elite strove hard to display all the up-to-date trappings of genteel style and fashion. In a harsh climate this brought them a degree of European-style comfort and luxury, but it also enabled them sharply to define their presence in alien and unfamiliar surroundings. Exchanges between the majority of Britons and the local Indian communities did not extend much beyond business and commerce, and the elite sought refuge, both literally and metaphorically, in what was familiar to them. This was most apparent, perhaps, in the 'White Town' of Calcutta, where, as P.J. Marshall has recently written, members of the elite 'lavished money and effort on creating for themselves the amenities of what they regarded as civilized British urban life', a process that formed a central element within their 'cultural self-sufficiency and insistence on maintaining British norms to the fullest extent'.[45] In this environment, the elite engaged in a full range of gentlemanly pursuits, and they exhibited all the social cultural characteristics of their metropolitan counterparts. Such actions served many purposes, but one of the most important was that they allowed the British in India to affirm their associate membership of the international order of gentlemen.

Second, recent work suggests that during the second half of the eighteenth century the British in India also succeeded in creating an adapted form of the 'fiscal-military' state that had been established in Britain after 1688. The East India Company's transition from trader to sovereign during the 1760s and 1770s obliged the British to move far beyond the management of commerce as they were taken into the realms of government and defence, and they became heavily dependent upon the regular collection of territorial revenues and customs duties. As a result, the Company's regime, driven by the need to support a vast army, increasingly resembled the centralized, highly bureaucratic fiscal system that supported the metropolitan state. The administrative settlement imposed upon British India by the Company required active support from an increasing number of civil officers of all types, and these men, confident of their legal authority, began to apply uniform methods and procedures in a variety of different contexts.[46] Although local circumstances dictated that the Company state could never fully replicate its metropolitan progenitor, the organizational characteristics that it exhibited indicate the extent to which core assumptions about military and fiscal power had been embraced by British elites everywhere.

Third, since the pioneering work of Holden Furber it has been acknowledged that one of the most important dynamics of eighteenth-century British expansion in Asia was provided by private enterprise.[47] While vigorous coercive action was always taken by the East India Company against rogue traders and interlopers attempting to establish illegal commercial links between Britain and the East, the Company's monopoly on British trading within Asia itself was never regarded as being absolute in all areas of commercial activity. Indeed, during the second half of the seventeenth century, the Company had granted 'indulgences' which permitted its servants to trade on their own account. It also issued licences to a small number of 'free merchants' and, unlike other European companies, it had effectively ceded intra-Asian trade or the 'country trade' to private individuals. There had long been an informal commercial presence operating within and often well beyond the formal boundaries demarcated by the Company's trade and territory, and thus the British presence in Asia was defined by both private enterprise and 'official' Company activity, with the two often operating in harness.

The private sector in India was remarkably vigorous, its innovative and diversified activities often being based upon partnerships between Britons and local traders and bankers. Naturally, the Company protected its own position as a trader in bulk commodities, but it allowed individuals plenty of scope for initiative. Such a policy ran obvious risks, such as when private traders became involved in disputes with local rulers, or Company servants became heavily indebted to Indian merchants, but there were plenty of advantages for the Company. By trading on their own account, Company servants could accumulate the large fortunes that would, they hoped, secure them a comfortable retirement in British landed society, and not only did this make the East India service attractive to adventurers, but it also gave the Company access to a large pool of private British funds that acted as an important local source of credit and working capital. Over time, the flourishing private sector took on an institutional form as partnerships established a large number of banks, industrial concerns, shipping companies and agency houses. Most notably, this sector came to dominate the 'country' trade, the expansion of which was of great importance to the Company because it allowed funds to be transferred from India to Canton in China where investment could be made in the all-important tea trade. Growing involvement in the China trade helped private traders to reassert themselves in eastern seas and this enabled a new sphere of British influence to be established. Since the middle of the eighteenth century, private traders from India had broken out of a traditional Asian maritime commercial system, and they moved far and wide, with their reach eventually extending from Australia to Britain. Thus, to take one late-eighteenth-century example, British private traders in Bengal were able to exploit important transoceanic commercial linkages that touched three continents as they endeavoured to transfer goods and funds to Europe via the United States of America.[48] In the words of P.J. Marshall, the operations of India-based British merchants 'now spanned the world',[49] and their activities well illustrate how, in certain instances, the process of global expansion and integration could be driven by powerful commercial impulses emanating from the periphery as well as the metropolis. This underscores the important yet often overlooked point that Britain's emerging global empire was given shape and definition not only by those looking out at the world from Britain, but also by those at the outer reaches who were capable of independently establishing links of their own with other parts of the world, as well as with the metropolis itself.

Conclusion

The examples offered by North America and India suggest that the different overseas spheres in which Britons moved during the eighteenth century perhaps had more in common than might have been first thought. In part, this was because these separate spheres were connected by the international order of British elites whose attitudes and assumptions were informed by a shared commitment to the gentlemanly ideal and the pursuit of enterprise. As the American Revolution demonstrated, this was not enough to override the tensions and divisions between core and periphery that could be caused by constitutional and political crisis, and more generally, one of the greatest perceived threats to the well-being of the metropolis always lay in the unfettered expansionist actions of gentlemanly capitalists in the wider world. Nevertheless, those located at the outer reaches of the eighteenth-century empire established social, economic and administrative systems that possessed many of the characteristics embodied in the metropolitan gentlemanly capitalism defined by Cain and Hopkins, and this helped to integrate Britain's diverse territories and possessions into a greater whole. The British had always adopted a flexible and broad-based approach to overseas activity, and when this legacy was harnessed to an increasingly strong belief in the value and importance of a global empire the potentially devastating loss of America became only a momentary setback to the processes of worldwide expansion and growth.

Notes

1   For recent discussions of the increasingly central place of empire in eighteenth-century political consciousness, see Kathleen Wilson, *The Sense of the People: Politics, Culture and Imperialism in England 1715–1785* (Cambridge, 1995) and Eliga H. Gould, *The Persistence of Empire. British Political Culture in the Age of the American Revolution* (Chapel Hill, 2000). For the part played by

the empire in the creation of a British identity, see the hotly debated study by Linda Colley, *Britons: Forging the Nation, 1707–1837* (New Haven, 1992).

2   P.J. Cain and A.G. Hopkins, *British Imperialism 1688–2000* (London, second edition, 2001), esp. pp. 23–103.

3   David Hancock, *Citizens of the World: London Merchants and the Integration of the British Atlantic Community* (Cambridge, 1995).

4   Holden Furber, *John Company at Work: a Study of European Expansion in India in the Late Eighteenth Century* (Cambridge, MA, 1951), p. 159.

5   Cain and Hopkins, *British Imperialism*, p. 59.

6   P.J. Cain and A.G. Hopkins, *British Imperialism: Innovation and Expansion 1688–1914* (London, 1993), pp. 467–8.

7   The overseas empire of the eighteenth century itself is discussed primarily in ibid., pp. 84–6, 320–3.

8   For a critical discussion of gentlemanly capitalism in an eighteenth-century metropolitan context, see H.V. Bowen, *Elites, Enterprise and the Making of the British Overseas Empire, 1688–1775* (Basingstoke, 1996), passim.

9   David Armitage, *The Ideological Origins of the British Empire* (Cambridge, 2000), p. 8.

10 See, for example, P.J. Marshall, 'Introduction' in idem (ed.), *The Oxford History of the British Empire. Vol. II: The Eighteenth Century* (Oxford, 1998), 4–9.

11 H.V. Bowen, 'British Conceptions of Global Empire, 1756–1783', *Journal of Imperial and Commonwealth History*, 26 (1998), pp. 1–27.

12 This emerges from a recent study of the late-eighteenth-century press, Jeremy R. Osborn, 'India, Parliament and Press under George III: a study of English attitudes towards the East India Company and empire in the late eighteenth and early nineteenth centuries' (University of Oxford D. Phil. thesis, 1999). For a detailed study of this theme, see P.J. Marshall and Glyndwr William, *The Great Map of Mankind: British Perceptions of the World in the Age of Enlightenment* (London, 1982).

13 Bowen, 'British Conceptions of Global Empire', pp. 13–19.

14 Armitage, *Ideological Origins*, pp. 170–1, 176–80.

15 See H.V. Bowen, 'Perceptions from the Periphery: Colonial American views of Britain's Asiatic empire, 1756–1783' in Christine Daniels and Michael V. Kennedy (eds), *Negotiated Empires: Centers and Peripheries in the New World, 1500–1820* (New York, 2001).

16 N.A.M. Rodger, 'Sea-power and Empire, 1688–1793' in Marshall (ed.), *History of the British Empire*, pp. 169–83.

17 Michael Duffy, 'World-wide War and Imperial Expansion, 1793–1815' in ibid., pp. 184–207.

18 C.A. Bayly, *Imperial Meridian. The British Empire and the World, 1780–1830* (London, 1989), 100–32.

19 T.H. Breen, 'An Empire of Goods. The Anglicization of Colonial America, 1690–1776', *Journal of British Studies*, XXV (1986); Ian K. Steele, *The English Atlantic, 1675–1740. An exploration of communication and community* (New York, 1986).

20 There is a vast and growing literature on this subject, but for a detailed and influential elaboration on these themes, see Jack P. Greene, *Pursuits of Happiness. The Social Development of Early Modern British Colonies and the Formation of American Culture* (Chapel Hill, 1988).

21   Cary Carson, 'The Consumer Revolution in Colonial British America: why demand?' in Cary Carson, Ronald Hoffman and Peter J. Albert (eds), *Of Consuming Interests. The Style of Life in the Eighteenth Century* (Charlottesville, 1994), p. 690.

22   Richard L. Bushman, 'American High-style and Vernacular Cultures', in Jack P. Greene and J.R. Pole (eds), *Colonial British America. Essays in the New History of the Early Modern Era* (Baltimore, 1984), p. 359. Bushman's views are discussed further in his *The Refinement of America. Persons, Houses, Cities* (New York, 1992).

23   These are examined and documented in detail in Carson, 'The Consumer Revolution' (quotation on p. 495).

24   Bushman, 'American High-style and Vernacular Cultures', pp. 366–7. A similar point is made with reference to the Chesapeake in Lois Green Carr and Lorena S. Walsh, 'Changing Lifestyles and Consumer Behavior in the Colonial Chesapeake' in Carson *et al.* (eds), *Of Consuming Interests*, pp. 59–60.

25   Steele, *English Atlantic*, p. 268. Carson, 'The Consumer Revolution', pp. 149–52. Of course, colonial condemnation of English cultural and social forms, and the boycott of goods, was to gather pace during the political crisis of the 1760s.

26   Ian K. Steele, 'The Empire and Provincial Elites. An Interpretation of Some Recent Writings on the English Atlantic, 1675–1740', *Journal of Imperial and Commonwealth History*, VIII (1980), 18.

27   For discussion of this, see Carson, 'The Consumer Revolution', pp. 508–9; Bushman, 'American High-style and Vernacular Cultures', pp. 370–6.

28   Kevin M. Sweeney, 'High-style Vernacular: Lifestyles of the Colonial Elite' in Carson *et al.* (eds), *Of Consuming Interests*, pp. 2, 32–6, 13. Thus, for example, a relatively small and dispersed colonial population could not support a commercialized leisure industry of the type that attracted widespread participation from the metropolitan elite (Carson, 'The Consumer Revolution', pp. 507–8).

29   Rhys Isaac, *The Transformation of Virginia, 1740–1790* (Chapel Hill, 1982), pp. 118, 132; Allan Kulikoff, *Tobacco and Slaves. The Development of Southern Cultures in the Chesapeake 1680–1800* (Chapel Hill, 1986), pp. 276–7.

30   For the 'ideal of cultivation' in a colonial context, see Bushman, 'American High-style and Vernacular Cultures', pp. 352–60.

31   For discussions of this process in Britain, see Peter Earle, *The Making of the English Middle Class. Business, Society and Family Life in London, 1660–1730* (London, 1989), pp. 5–9; Lawrence Stone and Jeanne C. Fawtier Stone, *An Open Elite? England 1540–1880* (Oxford, 1984), pp. 23–5.

32   For the ways in which 'competitive consumption' helped to redraw social lines, see Sweeney, 'High-style Vernacular', pp. 28–31.

33   Karin Calvert, 'The Function of Fashion in Eighteenth-century America' in Carson *et al.* (eds), *Of Consuming Interests*, pp. 252–83 (esp. 260–74).

34   See, for example, the cases cited in Robert E. Brown and B. Katherine Brown, *Virginia, 1705–1786. Democracy or Aristocracy?* (East Lansing, 1956), pp. 34–42.

35   Bushman, *The Refinement of America*, pp. xvii–xix.

36   This was most obviously reflected in some of the practices associated with debt, creditworthiness and business agreements. In some contexts, the form

taken by such arrangements was entirely based upon a gentleman's social standing and his word of honour. For a discussion of this with reference to the Chesapeake planter elite, see T.H. Breen, *Tobacco Culture. The Mentality of the Great Tidewater Planters on the Eve of the Revolution* (Princeton, 1986).

37 Edwin J. Perkins, 'The Entrepreneurial Spirit in Colonial America: the foundations of modern business history', *Business History Review*, LXIII (1989), 160–86.

38 See, in general, Isaac, *The Transformation of Virginia*, pp. 11–138; Greene, *Pursuits of Happiness*, pp. 92–100; Kulikoff, *Tobacco and Slaves*, pp. 261–313; Paul G.E. Clemens, *The Atlantic Economy and Colonial Maryland's Eastern Shore. From tobacco to grain* (Ithaca, 1980), pp. 120–67. For the relationships within families and the lifestyles of the Virginia and Maryland gentry, see Daniel Blake Smith, *Inside the Great House. Planter Life in Eighteenth-Century Chesapeake Society* (Ithaca, 1980). For details of the general improvement in living standards in the Chesapeake after the 1680s, see Lois Green Carr and Lorena S. Walsh, 'The Standard of Living in the Colonial Chesapeake', *William and Mary Quarterly*, 3rd series, XLX (1988), 135–59 and idem, 'Changing Lifestyles and Consumer Behavior'.

39 Aubrey C. Land, 'Economic Base and Social Structure. The Northern Chesapeake in the Eighteenth Century', *Journal of Economic History*, XXV (1965), 639–54; idem, 'Economic Behavior in a Planting Society. The Eighteenth-century Chesapeake', *Journal of Southern History*, XXXIII (1967), 469–85; John Bezis Selfa, 'Planter Industrialists and Iron Oligarchs. A comparative prosopography of early Anglo-America ironmasters', *Business and Economic History*, XXIII, 66–7.

40 Clemens, *Atlantic Economy*, pp. 134–5. For the development of varying patterns of diversification evident among the elite of Maryland, see Gloria L. Main, *Tobacco Colony. Life in Early Maryland, 1650–1720* (Princeton, 1982), pp. 79–91.

41 See, for example, Bernard Bailyn, *The New England Merchants in the Seventeenth Century* (Cambridge, MA, 1955), pp. 101–2, 134–42, 192–7; Virginia B. Harrington, *The New York Merchant on the Eve of the Revolution* (1935, reprinted Gloucester, MA, 1964), pp. 11–37, 126–63; Thomas M. Doerflinger, *A Vigorous Spirit of Enterprise. Merchants and Economic Development in Revolutionary Philadelphia* (Chapel Hill, 1986), pp. 11–164. For a recent discussion of the material world of these individuals and their influence on those around them, see Carson, 'The Consumer Revolution', pp. 607–10.

42 For some comparisons that underscore this point, see Doerflinger, *A Vigorous Spirit of Enterprise*, pp. 139, 158–61.

43 Sung Bok Kim, 'A New Look at the Great Landlords of Eighteenth-century New York', *William and Mary Quarterly*, 3rd. series, XXVII (1970), 579–614 (esp. 595–600).

44 Alan Gallay, *The Formation of a Planter Elite. Jonathan Bryan and the Southern Colonial Frontier* (Athens, GA, 1989). For the development of elite culture and the adaptation of the gentlemanly ideal to conditions in this region, see Richard Waterhouse, *A New World Gentry. The Making of a Merchant and Planter Class in South Carolina, 1670–1770* (New York, 1989).

45 P.J. Marshall, 'The White Town of Calcutta under the Rule of the East India Company', *Modern Asian Studies*, 34, 2 (2000), 308–9. For studies of British

social life in India during this period see, for example, Percival Spear, *The Nabobs. The Social Life of the English in Eighteenth-century India* (Oxford, 1932; new impression, 1980) and S.C. Ghosh, *The Social Condition of the British Community in Bengal 1757–1800* (Leiden, 1970), republished as *The British in Bengal. A study of the British society and life in the late eighteenth century* (New Delhi, 1998).

46   For the long-term evolution of the Company state and comparisons with the British domestic state, see C.A. Bayly, 'The British Military–Fiscal State and Indigenous Resistance. India 1750–1820' in Lawrence Stone (ed.), *An Imperial State at War. Britain from 1689 to 1815* (London, 1994), 325–30.

47   Furber, *John Company at Work*; idem, *Rival Empires of Trade in the Orient 1600–1800* (Minneapolis, 1976). For the importance of private trade, see also P.J. Marshall, *East Indian Fortunes: the British in Bengal in the Eighteenth Century* (Oxford, 1976) and I.B. Watson, *Foundations for Empire: English Private Trade in India 1659–1760* (New Delhi, 1980).

48   Amales Tripathi, *Trade and Finance in the Bengal Presidency 1793–1833* (2nd revised edition, Calcutta, 1979), pp. 79–80.

49   P.J. Marshall, 'Private British Trade in the Indian Ocean before 1800', in Ashin Das Gupta and M.N. Pearson (eds), *India and the Indian Ocean 1500–1800* (paperback edition, New Delhi, 1999), 299.

3
Globalism and Imperialism: the Global Context of British Power, 1830–1960

John Darwin

I

How do we account for the course of British expansion in Asia, Africa and the Middle East in the 'imperial century' between 1815 and 1923 and for the long contraction that followed? For nearly fifty years the high ground in this debate has been occupied by two great schools and the stage army of their critics and camp followers. The 'imperialism of free trade'[1] and 'gentlemanly capitalism' each provide a grand synthesis into which may be fitted the economic, strategic, international, domestic and colonial components of imperial growth and decline. Each has attracted a barrage of criticism: the 'imperialism of free trade' from those who resisted 'informal empire' as an implausible fiction;[2] 'gentlemanly capitalism' from those who rejected it as an inadequate description of the British economy[3] or who doubted the 'Schumpeterian rationality' of the City.[4] And each contained arguments and emphases at odds with the other. Robinson and Gallagher had stressed the importance of the colonial factor in the imperial equation, and seen strategic rather than economic motives as the force behind late-Victorian imperialism, Cain and Hopkins had insisted upon metropolitan dynamism as the engine of expansion and commercial gain as its target.[5] It was the Late-, not the Mid-Victorians, they argued, who won Britain a worldwide commercial *imperium*. For Robinson and Gallagher, the makers of British policy were a 'closed' elite of self-confident officialdom, whose 'special historiography' seduced or intimidated their political masters. For Cain and Hopkins, they were a more 'open' elite whose membership was commercial as well as political, reflecting the close alliance of Westminster, Whitehall and the City. These differences are important but they should not obscure the wide agreement on fundamentals: that the British Empire was a global system comprising both 'formal' and informal' elements; that it depended upon the collaboration of local interests constrained by the inequalities of 'structural power';[6] that it was governed by the prevailing assumptions of its policymaking elite; and that its ultimate fate depended upon the success with which it 'integrated new regions into the expanding economy'.[7]

In this chapter, it is this agreement on fundamentals that is the starting point for speculation. It is possible to take an unflattering view of the policymaking elite and its confident opinions: to doubt their coherence, suspect their provenance and question their authority.[8] But more interesting questions arise if we take seriously the link between imperial history and global history on whose importance Tony Hopkins has recently insisted.[9] To what extent was British imperialism, for all its subtlety and panache, an epiphenomenon of much larger forces at work in the world after 1830? Were the British surfing a global wave, or were they the hapless victims of a sea-change they could barely register? What combination of global circumstances allowed them to cut such a figure in the world for so long but then brusquely despatched them to the second rank? What interplay between the economic and political forces of 'globalism' – the drawing together of the world's regions into a single 'system' – lay behind the attrition of their imperialism in the 1930s but its paradoxical survival into the 1940s and 1950s? What conditions once favoured a loose-knit empire scattered broadcast across the globe, but then turned so many bridgeheads of influence into mere symptoms of 'overstretch'?

Such an inquiry risks undignified collapse into the mere recital of endless variables or the *reductio ad absurdum* of a monocausal theory. Global history is not easily rendered into usable fragments. In this paper it is argued that we can best approach the problem by invoking two 'terrible simplifications'. The first proposes that as an open global system, the British empire was acutely sensitive to the pressures and prospects of the international economy. Three 'long swings' – the approach (1830s–70s), formation (1880s–1920s), and crisis (1930s–40s) of the world economy – form the chronological matrix for its rise and fall. The second that the world-wide span of British imperialism, its loose, decentralized organization, its frequent reliance on 'informal' methods, and the limited means of coercion available to it, made it especially vulnerable to political change wherever strong states contested its claims. The logic of this assumption is that the flimsy maritime web that the British spun between the two poles of the Old World depended as much, if not more, on the state of politics in East

Asia and the Euro-Atlantic world as upon the variable scope for state-making in the vast region that stretched between them. The British were not the passive victims of circumstance. But perhaps it was these larger conditions that prescribed the limits of their initiative and fixed the domestic cost of empire.

II

After 1830 the British steadily transformed a straggling mercantile empire into a world-system. While their success owed much to a particular set of endowments and aptitudes, these in turn could hardly have come into play without favourable global conditions and the growth of new patterns of intercontinental trade and contact. It was once assumed that the 'spontaneous combustion' of home-grown industrial change had driven Britain's rise to global power. It is now plausibly suggested that it was the rapid intensification of commercial and cultural contact between European and Asian economies in the eighteenth century – expressed in the European demand for Indian textiles and Chinese tea, silks and porcelain – that was a crucial stimulus to British industrialization.[10] Britain was particularly receptive to Asian imports: its growing 'consumer culture' reflected the strong attraction to 'exotic' products. Early industrialisation in textiles and ceramics mimicked the artisan manufactures of India and China. The profits to be made from tea were the hidden spring of treasure in the East India Company and served indirectly to drive forward its frontier of rule in South Asia. But it was access to the North American market that was the pacemaker of British foreign trade.[11]

Thus well before the great age of Victorian expansion the British had been able to turn the Atlantic expansion of Europe and the commercial dynamism of Asian producers to their advantage. They had become the entrepot between the Eastern and the Western world. In the Napoleonic wars, they beat off French efforts to supplant them and tightened their grip on the financial as well as commercial branches of the entrepot trade. But it was the 1830s that saw the spectacular expansion of this entrepot empire into a world-system in the making.

The 1830s opened a new phase in the Euro-Atlantic economy and in Europe's relations with East Asia. European penetration of other large regions in the extra-European world reached a critical stage. The 'Eurasian revolution' that had begun with the European conquest of Bengal in the 1750s was reaching a climax. By 1830, the 'neo-Europe' in North America was undergoing a 'commercial revolution'.[12] With the land rush in Mississippi the 'cotton kingdom' had been staked out.[13] The era of railway-building was under way.[14] The inflow of European (mainly British) migration accelerated dramatically.[15] The American economy was being integrated much more fully than before into the economy of Greater Europe: as market, supplier and demographic over-flow.[16] With East Asia the volume of trade was much smaller. But there, too, the outcome of the political and commercial crisis of the 1830s was the (limited) integration of maritime China into the European trading system.[17] In the Middle East, the political and strategic catastrophe that threatened the overthrow of the Ottoman Empire had as its by-product the wedging open of Egypt and the Ottoman provinces to European trade. Even further afield, the 1830s were the crucial decade in the for-ward movement of the European pastoral frontier in Australia[18] and, perhaps, in the fraught relations between aborigines and white men.[19] In New Zealand, the dangers of unregulated contact between European sailors, traders and escapees and Maori communities had been recog-nized in the appointment of a British consul in 1833 and led by a wind-ing path to annexation and the treaty of Waitangi seven years later.[20] In Southern Africa a double revolution was in progress. There the consoli-dation of the Zulu state had unleashed a cycle of indigenous conflict – the *mfecane* – that opened the way for a huge extension of European control in the interior – the Great Trek.[21]

These events among others were symptomatic of a vast disturbance in the relations between Europe and almost every region of the extra-European world: perhaps the climacteric to a long period of ever-closer cultural, commercial and physical contact – the product of mutual attraction.[22] As the leading commercial state in the eighteenth century, Britain had promoted these contacts and, in turn, been shaped by them. But by 1830, she was, of all the European countries, much the best placed to take advantage of them and much the most exposed to their unpredictable consequences. This had less to do with the visions of policymakers than with the sociocultural formation of early Victorian Britain. Here the most obvious feature was an exceptionally dynamic commercial culture: the availability and cheapness of credit; the dense network of commercial intelligence; the sophistication of mercantile expertise; the appetite for exotic produce; and the supercharging of Britain's entrepot function by industrialized production. This commercial dynamism was closely linked to demographic instability. British and Irish labour was the most geographically mobile of any large European society and among the first to feel the effects of agricultural modernization.[23] With ready access to commercial shipping (and, perhaps, credit) it was no surprise that settlers from the British Isles formed the vanguard of European migrants in search of free land overseas.[24] Britain also boasted a markedly secular intellectual culture, sympathetic to scientific and geographical enquiry and to their commercial applications.[25] The creation of the Royal Geographical Society in 1830 marked a new purposefulness in 'intellectual colonization'.[26] Finally, and not perhaps coincidentally, early Victorian Britain also experienced intense religious anxiety, much of it channelled into missionary and humanitarian enterprise overseas: anti-slavery may have been the strongest public emotion of the Victorian age. In the new conjuncture of the 1830s, new trades, new lands, new peoples, new fields of spiritual endeavour and new sources of guilt and shame exerted a compulsive attraction for a society already attuned to pursuing commercial, demographic, cultural and spiritual opportunities overseas.

This cocktail of social energies was the fuel for the diversified, pluralistic expansion signified by the 'imperialism of free trade'. As Gallagher and Robinson indicated, Victorian governments intervened periodically at the behest of private interests[27] eager to exploit the main chance for trade, settlement or conversion. But we should not assume that the mid-Victorians possessed the means for universal dominion, formal or informal. The 'new order' of the 1830s was a pattern of constraints as well as opportunities. Britain might have gained more than other European states from the growing intimacy of intercontinental relations. But she had not been freed from the perpetual insecurity of European politics and the need to guard against domination or invasion by a continental league or a 'Napoleonic' superstate. Strategic vulnerability in Europe magnified the dangers of European competition elsewhere in the world. Fortunately for the British, neither France nor Russia, their principal rivals in an age of triangular imperialism, had the means or the will to shadow them everywhere. Even so, the conflict of interests was real enough. The British did not often enjoy a free hand: not in the Middle East;[28] not in East Asia;[29] not even in the South Atlantic.[30] Nor could they ignore the awkward corollary of American expansion: the impulses of 'manifest destiny' in Oregon, Maine and Central America. These had to be managed with extreme prudence, partly for fear of a transatlantic combination at Britain's expense.[31]

Nor was this the whole story. After 1830, many non-European societies had bent, but not broken. Eurasian states from China to Egypt retained significant autonomy and the ability to limit European intrusion, sometimes by playing off the interlopers against each other. It was not yet clear that they had lost the race to modernize and 'self-strengthen'. In many places, European intervention was necessarily circumspect. Even where Europeans appeared as conquerors, occupiers or settlers, for much of the period between 1830 and 1870 their predominance was contested or equivocal. This was true in New Zealand, where Maori resistance persisted into the 1870s and perhaps beyond;[32] in Southern Africa, the scene of innumerable 'frontier wars' lasting into the 1890s; and even in India, where the Mutiny left a durable legacy of unease. To one influential traveller in the 1870s, Turkish primacy in Western Africa seemed more likely than European.[33] There was no mid-Victorian 'global hegemony'. In reality, Britain's main spheres of influence skirted those of numerous strong or resilient states in Europe, Asia, the Americas and sub-Saharan Africa. The resort to 'informal empire' was in deference to local muscle as well as to imperial convenience. The achievement of a real international economy of integrated regions and open markets was in prospect but not in hand. The export of capital was modest. In the meantime, Britain's place in the new ensemble of global interests was bound to be uncertain as long as Europe's future in Afro-Asia was unsettled. Not even Palmerston favoured ubiquitous self-assertion.[34] His critics, including both Peelites and Cobdenites, railed against the dangers of aggression, isolation and over-commitment, in the Near East as well as in China.[35] Perhaps they hankered after a British *Sonderweg*: a new kind of world power based on the Concert in Europe and a pacific dominion of trade, settlement and religion beyond. If so, the new shape of world politics after 1870 was as disappointing to them as to any disciple of Palmerstonian braggadocio.

III

It is still a commonplace in histories of British imperialism (despite the efforts of Cain and Hopkins) that the late nineteenth century was a time of trial. The competitors closed in. The stakes were raised. The costs went up. Much useless property had to be bought. Good money was thrown after bad. But for all the effort to prop it up, Britain's world position grew inexorably weaker and the outposts of empire more vulnerable. The grand extensions to the old imperial fabric in tropical Africa, Southeast Asia and the Pacific were a dangerous illusion. The high noon of empire was really an age of hubris.

It is easy to reach this conclusion if we draw our evidence from the usual witnesses: the dispatches of diplomats, the speeches of politicians or the warnings of pundits. But if we take a more panoptic view of the global conditions under which British imperialism was bound to operate, the picture seems much less clear-cut. It was certainly true that the shape of 'geo-economics'[36] and geopolitics had been sharply modified. The economic interdependence of regions and markets reached a critical stage creating for the first time a 'world economy',[37] one of whose hallmarks was a global market in basic foodstuffs.[38] The universal triumph of the commercial economy was widely expected. The scale of migration increased: from Europe, but also from India, China and even Japan. New zones of settlement sprang up: in Siberia,[39] western Canada, Argentina, Brazil,[40] and Manchuria.[41] As temperate lands 'filled up', writers, publicists and prophets turned their attention to 'the conquest of the tropics'.

Behind the advance of the 'world economy' were two powerful agents of 'globalization' – the gradual convergence of prices, incomes and consumption most visible in the Atlantic economy.[42] The first was the efficiency gains made possible in transport and communications by the spread of railways, steam navigation and the telegraph, the vital transmitter of market prices around the world. Railways could lower the cost of freight by up to 80 per cent,[43] transform the potential of inland regions and reshape their economic (and political) geography with electrifying speed.[44] Railways made bulk exports viable on a grand scale. They opened new regions to intensive settlement. In the Americas and North Asia they were the funnel for mass immigration. But the precondition for this huge expansion of infrastructure, and the second great agent of globalization, was a massive rise of foreign investment, increasing in the British case alone by more than three times between 1880 and 1913.[45] The export of capital played a further vital role in the development of a world economy. It helped ease the shortage of foreign exchange, the barrier to trade between countries without complementary needs, and widen the scope of the multilateral payments system – the electrical circuit of the world economy.[46] Two critical changes, especially visible in the British case, enhanced the scale and impact of foreign capital. After the 1870s returns on earlier investment overseas were large enough to supply new demands for funds abroad: now overseas capital could meet the needs of its own expansion.[47] Secondly, perhaps as a result, late Victorian London saw the florescence of a hyperactive financial network, feverishly shifting capital and profits between far-flung locations in Afro-Asia and the Americas as opportunity or mania dictated.[48] Here, too, was an engine of economic change apparently capable of enforcing social and political transformation at breakneck speed – nowhere more so than in the new eldorado on the Rand.

Of course the larger scale of trade and investment and the closer integration of economic regions was also due in part to the rapid growth of new industrial economies in Europe and North America. The British faced stiffer competition in manufactured exports. German capital, as well as French, now competed for loans in East Asia and the Middle East.[49] But these effects were magnified by the special trajectory of late-nineteenth-century economic globalism. Firstly, America's 'grain invasion' of Europe, still only partly industrialized, exposed the rural producers and landed classes of the Old World to social disaster. The reaction was a sharp turn towards tariff protection among the continental states.[50] Secondly, the new 'global' economy was superimposed on a world in which colonial rule was still widespread and where colonialism was regarded as a legitimate, if not always practical, means of promoting the national interest. It was hardly surprising that colonial expansion appeared attractive, especially in the depressed 1880s, as relief for the stresses of globalism. So for the British, who rejected tariffs, the new shape of the international economy was simultaneously hopeful and threatening. In the worst scenario, if they were excluded from foreign markets by tariffs or colonialism, and challenged in their own by more up-to-date competition, the outlook was commercial attrition.

Geopolitics moved in parallel. Before 1870, European politics were connected to those of the rest of Eurasia and the 'Outer World' mainly by the triangular rivalry of Russia, France and Britain. To this fact, coupled with the relatively limited scope of European rule outside Europe and the undeveloped state of overland communications, can be attributed much of the freedom of manoeuvre enjoyed by the three imperial powers in their colonial and semi-colonial spheres. Where the interests of all three collided, as in the Near East, no decisive advantage could be achieved except in the unlikely event of single-handed military triumph. But after 1871, this triangular system became quadrangular, or even (if Italy is included) hexagonal. It was inevitable that powers in the European states-system should exploit where possible the extra-European weaknesses of their rivals. Henceforth this game would have more players. Germany, in particular, had a powerful incentive to use non-European issues to prop up its new-found role as the arbiter of European diplomacy. As economic competition outside Europe grew sharper and the fear of protectionism rose, European activity in the extra-European world was bound to invoke diplomatic intervention and great power reaction much more frequently than in earlier periods.

Left unmodified, this might have driven the tensions of European diplomacy to a dangerous level. The local struggles of European traders, settlers, missionaries, explorers and other interlopers were always prone to rouse vested interests at home and spark an explosion of 'public' support. Even masters of *Realpolitik* like Bismarck or Lord Salisbury could find themselves jerked into forward movement by the shock this administered to their political systems.[51] The prospect that great power governments would be dragged willynilly into imperial wars by the machinations of colonial buccaneers and their disreputable backers excited and appalled contemporary opinion. In reality, the threat of unbridled imperial antagonism was reduced by the conservatism of all the great European powers; the reluctance to jeopardize their domestic arrangements by a foreign war; and above all by the shrewd calculation that the risks of a European armageddon could hardly be justified by imperial gain. Even under hexagonal imperialism, competitive coexistence remained the rule. Of course, there was always the chance that a grand European coalition would be formed against a power deemed guilty of excessive aggrandisement, and impose the principle of equitable compensation embodied in the theory and occasional practice of the Concert of Europe. But in the 1890s, as the alliance system in Europe grew more rigid, coalitions against a single great power became less likely. The fear of being dragged into general war by the colonial adventures of an alliance partner exerted a further constraint on diplomatic activism in the imperial sphere.[52] Even after 1900 (when Lenin insisted that a redivision of the world was under way) there was little sign of a new partition, let alone one imposed by force. Britain, France, Germany and Russia settled their *colonial* differences by negotiation, however bad-tempered.

This was just as well. The political side-effects of an expanding international economy and the increased capability of European states and private interests to project their influence into distant regions worsened the instability of many non-European societies. The Near East had long been a cockpit on Europe's doorstep. After the Eastern crisis of 1877–78, the problem of its eventual partition was a constant preoccupation of European chancelleries. But since no agreement could be reached on the peaceful share-out of its cadaver, the Ottoman Empire was condemned to be sick but forbidden to die. No single power, or even alliance, could face the retaliation that would follow unilateral seizure of the sultan's territorial assets. The price of this hiatus was an intense armed vigilance. After 1895 and the crushing demonstration of China's fragility inflicted by Japan, a second war of diplomatic position broke out. Pre-emptive occupation, compensatory occupation, concession-hunting, loan-contracting and consortium-building were its weapons. But, as in the Near

East, no European power was strong enough to enforce its will or scoop the pool of Chinese trade.

The Ottoman and Ch'ing empires were the most dramatic examples of a wider phenomenon: the urgent need of many states in Afro-Asia and the Outer World to self-strengthen by administrative and technical modernization or succumb to a lethal combination of external pressure and internal discontent. The 'race against time'[53] into which some Afro-Asian societies had been forced before 1870 now seemed universal. The result was a fusillade of regional crises as polities in Africa, Southeast Asia and the Pacific tottered towards implosion. Volatile successor-regimes, European freebooters and hyperactive proconsuls waited in the wings, ready to impose solutions that took little account of great power relations or the constraints of grand strategy. The frontiers of competition grew wider; the arithmetic of compensation more demanding; the protocols of bargaining more arcane. By the end of the 1890s it was a commonplace that the dual impact of economic and geopolitical change had turned the world into a closed system in which events on the remotest periphery reverberated at the centre of world politics in Europe.[54]

As the European power that had built up the largest portfolio of colonial and semi-colonial interests before 1870, Britain was the most vulnerable to relative decline if hexagonal diplomacy, stiffening competition and geopolitical instability were to affect larger and larger areas where British influence (however superficial) had once ruled by default. For the British, however, the problem could not readily be solved by selecting the zones where commercial advantage or strategic necessity were greatest. As prime agents of economic globalization, British commercial interests had a growing stake in the opening of new markets. A loud domestic chorus was ready to protest against the losses to be expected from foreign occupation on the one hand or anarchy on the other. The weight of the 'overseas sector' in commercial, financial, religious and scientific enterprise was greater than in earlier periods, and its influence more easily exerted through publicity. That would have counted for less had not a second factor acted on British politics with the force of gravity. Unlike the larger continental powers, the British rejected tariffs as an antidote to the grain invasion of the later nineteenth century. They accepted the social consequences of greater exposure to the international economy.[55] Mainstream opinion acknowledged that autarky was not an option, and that Britain was bound to choose the open sea not the closed door. Heavier dependence upon foreign foodstuffs and overseas trade meant a deepening engagement with global politics and economics. It meant taking more seriously than ever the fact, emphasized by geographers, of Britain's centrality in a 'globe-wide world' unified by maritime traffic.[56] It meant accepting, in a world in which globalism and imperialism were yoked together, that the uneasy Victorian experiment in Afro-Asian despotism practised in India might have to be repeated in many lesser rajs.[57]

Defending and *expanding* a free trade empire, formal and informal, against all comers was a nerve-wracking task against imperial competitors who enjoyed much easier access to the extra-European world than before 1870. There were moments when fear of isolation, catastrophic defeat or financial attrition induced something like near panic.[58] But over the period as a whole between 1880 and 1914, geopolitical conditions proved surprisingly benign. The caution and conservatism of European statesmen, and the unexpected resilience of the two main East Asian states were the vital context in which Lord Salisbury and his successors were able to mount a highly successful diplomatic campaign to defend *and enlarge* the mid-Victorian inheritance.

Salisbury held firm views about the likely course of world politics. Like most observers, he expected a small number of 'world states' to dominate the scene. He thought the independence of extra-European states would be undermined by 'pacific invasion'. He regarded Afro-Asian societies as poorly equipped for political survival or material progress, and dismissed most as 'dying nations'.[59] The real question was how the resulting instability could be prevented from damaging Britain's international position or sharpening tensions to the point of war. Salisbury adopted two methods to ward off these dangers. Where possible he favoured an agreed partition of territories and spheres to neutralize the trouble-making of sub-imperialists and their paymasters at home. Where necessary, he strove to maintain the regional balance by the flexible choice of diplomatic partners and limited, *ad hoc*, combinations against aggrandizing rivals – as in the Near East and East Asia.[60] The consolidation of Britain's position in Egypt (1898–1904) and South Africa (over which Russia, France and Germany considered and rejected an anti-British coalition)[61] were the trophies of success. With so many established bridgeheads in the extra-European world, Salisbury was able to exploit, more than any continental statesman, the divisions of European politics: the watchful antagonism of the European powers; their fear of an upset in the continental balance; their aversion to a general war. After 1900, his protégés recovered their nerve and adapted his method to the new dimensions of *Weltpolitik* through an alliance with Japan and the colonial ententes with France and Russia. British world power *might* have suffered a relative decline since the days of Palmerston. But no other power proved strong enough to unravel the global partition (and its informal equivalents) from which the British had made such disproportionate gains. That was the lesson of Russia's military disaster in 1904–05, and of Germany's diplomatic defeat at Algeciras (1906) and over Agadir (1911). British leaders had reason to conclude that it would take the overthrow of the European states system, with all its checks and balances, to demolish the geostrategic defences they had so laboriously constructed.[62]

Edwardian Britain was thus a successful (though not carefree) adaptation to the strenuous conditions of globalism after 1880. In economics as well as politics, there were opportunities to exploit as well as competitors to fear. By remaining a free-trade state, the British had sacrificed their agriculture and encouraged the export of capital, perhaps at the cost of industrial innovation and efficiency. But as the volume of trade rose sharply in the later 1890s, they reaped a rich reward. The neo-Europes in the Americas and Australasia – the heartlands of London's commercial empire – now grew rapidly as demand for their commodities soared. British trade, investment, shipping and services profited from the boom. Huge surpluses were accumulated in the balance of payments, helping to fund a spectacular growth in Britain's foreign lending which doubled between 1900 and 1913.[63] By the eve of the First World War, one-quarter of British output was being sent abroad; and perhaps a third of British wealth now lay there.[64] This economic success had a wider meaning. It underwrote the compromises of Edwardian imperialism. It eased the frictions of domestic and colonial politics. It helped meet the cost of naval armaments and the outbuilding of Germany whose *Weltpolitik* was contained if not suppressed. It deflated the tariff reformers' case against free trade – whose preservation was Britain's strongest card against the collective resentment of other world powers. Last, but not least, it accelerated the heavy concentration of British trade, investment and shipping in the safe havens of the Western hemisphere.[65] For the survival of the British world-system, this great 'swing to the West' was to be of momentous importance.

In the last resort, however, this happy international conjunction depended upon the fragile stability of the European states-system with its volcanic periphery in the Balkans. In August 1914, the British intervened in the European crisis to preserve the continental balance on which so much of their geostrategic advantage depended. The result was a massive loss of blood and treasure,[66] but also striking confirmation of the inherent strength conferred by Britain's portfolio of maritime, commercial and imperial assets: the means by which the resources of America and the 'outer world' were mobilized for the struggle in Europe and the Middle East.[67] Britain suffered: her old imperial rivals were devastated. The German empire disappeared; the Russian empire shrank; the British empire expanded to its maximum extent. With Europe in disarray after 1918, its old states-system no longer seemed the pivot of global order. The best guarantee of that now seemed to lie in the co-operation of the Anglo-Saxon powers, Britain and America, joint rulers of the waves and the exchanges. To an old arch-enemy watching glumly from the sidelines, the meaning of it all was clear enough. 'So the old pirate-state, England, has...succeeded in letting Europe tear herself to pieces and...secured a victory which accords with her material interests'. Tirpitz took comfort in prophecy: 'England's day of judgment will have its birth in this very success.'[68]

IV

Despite the stresses and strains of 'competitive coexistence', British imperialism had prospered in the open global economy of 1870–1914. The British had fashioned a hybrid system of formal and informal imperialism that seemed compatible with global conditions and regional pressures: an expanding commercial empire of free trade; a self-governing settler empire sheltered by naval power; an Indian Empire of rule *and* free trade; and a dependent empire inflated into a defensive *glacis*. After 1920, despite the economic strains of post-war transition, the burden of war debt and the dislocation of markets, there seemed a good prospect of returning to an 'enhanced' normality. The disruptive imperialisms of Germany and Russia had been eradicated by defeat and dissolution. The 'Eastern Question' had been solved by the partition of the Middle East. France was preoccupied with her European security. Japan had been co-opted reluctantly into the Anglo-American 'system' in East Asia. By the later 1920s, the spectre of Bolshevik anti-imperialism no longer seemed so threatening with the collapse of its alliance with Chinese nationalism, while the inflow of American capital helped to underwrite the restoration of political and economic stability in Europe. With the Locarno 'system' in Europe, the Washington 'system' in East Asia, and a League of Nations whose trusteeship ethos was notably indulgent to the old colonial powers, the decentralization of the British Empire seemed safe enough: a programme carried through in India (1919), Ireland (1921), Egypt (1922), with the 'white dominions (1926–31) and through the apparatus of mandates and treaties in the

Arab Middle East (1922–30). The 'third British Empire' seemed in tune with the post-war global order.[69]

Of course, this cheerful scenario rested on the expectation that the open global economy, so vital to British prosperity and to the balance of their world-system, would regain its prewar vigour and permit a full recovery from the losses of war. By 1931, this prospect had vanished in financial chaos. The implications were drastic: a fall of 8–9 per cent in the volume of world trade,[70] but a reduction of more than 25 per cent in prices, a reduction felt with particular severity by commodity producers and rural economies. The political consequences were seismic. In Europe, a radical move towards open repudiation of the postwar order; the drive towards economic bilateralism and barter, pulling Eastern Europe into a closed economic zone dependent on Germany;[71] the sharpening of ideological warfare as economic failure raised hopes, and fears, of social revolution. In East Asia a parallel transformation could be glimpsed. The financial partnership and economic complementarity that had eased Japan's acceptance of the Washington system dissolved. American capital exports dried up; the American market for Japanese silk closed down.[72] Militarism, anti-communism, and the search for autarky exercised increasing influence in Japanese politics and over Tokyo's diplomacy. The three-cornered struggle for influence in China led to open war against the Kuomintang government in 1937 and prompted the blunt rejection of a Europe-centred imperial order in the programme for a 'Greater East Asian coprosperity sphere' in 1938.[73] Even if by 1938 the volume of trade (though not its prices) had recovered the level of ten years before, economic globalism had gone into reverse. Large swathes of the world seemed destined to withdraw into the closed (or only partly open) commercial systems of Germany, Japan and the Soviet Union.

These tendencies were bound to inflict great damage on Britain's commercial 'empire' and its large political superstructure. British wealth rested upon providing goods and services for the international economy to a far greater extent than that of any other major power. The delicate web of political relations spun around the world by imperial influence as much as rule depended upon the sense of mutual self-interest especially in the commercial sphere. Indeed, much British prestige derived from the universalist appeal of liberalism, free trade and representative government. Amid the fierce ideological storms of the 1930s, the fragile entente between liberalism and empire (long sustained by liberal faith in empire as a stage towards global community) began to give way.

The most obvious symptom of British weakness was the debility of their international trade. Even in 1938, Britain was the world's largest trader, ahead of the United States.[74] But much of that trade depended upon the prosperity of commodity-producing countries, worst hit by the fall of prices, and their return purchases of British manufactures. Britain's balance of merchandise trade was bound to suffer. But that was not all. In 1913, Britain's excess of merchandise imports was comfortably paid for by the income drawn from investment overseas. In 1938, the combined total of investment income and the invisible income from overseas services like shipping and insurance barely covered the cost of imports, and in some previous years the balance had only been met by a significant export of gold.[75] As a result, rearmament in the fraught 1930s had to be slowed to ease the strain on the balance of payments. There was other collateral damage. Amid the general repudiation of war debts that took place in 1931, the British government cancelled its obligations to the United States. However necessary, it was a costly blow to British credit where it mattered most. In India, where half Britain's total land forces were garrisoned and paid,[76] the weakness of public finances, exacerbated by political unrest, threw the burden of modernizing the army back on to the Imperial centre in London. Amid the shrinkage of the global economy, all circles were vicious.

This is the global context in which we have to set the paralyzing anxiety with which British leaders confronted the collective threat to their world-system posed by Germany, Italy and Japan, and, as some believed, the Soviet Union: four revisionist powers each in search of its own version of a new world order. The dream of Anglo-American hegemony vanished like a dream in the aftermath of 1931.[77] The British turned back to Europe since the European balance was the alternative precondition of their imperial security. But here their indispensable ally, France, was a broken reed. Shorn of their prewar Russian ally and prey to ideological division, French governments were even less willing than the British to guarantee the postwar settlement and contain the expansion of Germany and Italy. The 'neo-Salisburian' statecraft on which the British had relied to balance the risks of their world-system was all but bankrupt. Amid an outlook so bleak, war seemed the only certainty.

Yet prewar pessimism scarcely prepared the British for the devastating blow that the war inflicted on their world position. Blitzkrieg in 1940 shattered the last remnants of the old European order. The destruction of France prised open the British Empire like an oyster. The Atlantic and the Mediterranean ceased to be lines of imperial communication and turned into avenues of enemy attack. The 'swing-door' of empire in Egypt became the frontline of imperial defence. Worse still, the Vichy government made no resistance to the forward move of Japan into Indo-China, the launching pad for the assault on European colonialism in Asia. When Germany turned on Russia, and Japan on the British, Dutch and Americans, globalism entered its greatest crisis. By early 1942, two vast Eurasian empires were in the making, each capable, or so it seemed, of driving deep into the Outer World: Germany through Egypt; Japan through Southeast Asia.

The British were saved in part by their own efforts, in part by cashing in the stored-up wealth of their age of expansion. But the survival, for the time being, of their empire should also be seen as a product of the inscrutable dynamics of the 'closed system' of world politics under which no great power could be oblivious to major changes in the allocation of territory and resources, however remote. An expanding world economy and increasing integration between regional economies tended on balance to soothe the inevitable friction between great power interests in all too close proximity. When those conditions were reversed by moves towards 'geo-economic' partition, the tensions latent in a dynamic closed system were bound to rise. At almost their last gasp, the British were kept afloat by this ironic twist of globalism. American willingness to court the enmity of Germany, long before Pearl Harbor, sprang from the calculation that Axis control of Britain's empire would damage American world interests, perhaps irreversibly.[78] As the second largest beneficiary of the open economy, Washington had to decide whether to defend it alongside the British or in the last ditch alone.

The global hegemony of Germany and Japan was blocked at the battles of Midway, Alamein and Stalingrad in 1942–43. Churchill's canny influence on Allied strategy ensured that Britain's imperial recovery was secured alongside the reconquest of Europe and the defeat of Japan. But by the war's end the British depended overwhelmingly upon American aid to replenish their wealth[79] and restore their world position. Churchill's famous declaration that he had 'not become the King's first minister to preside over the liquidation of the British Empire' is sometimes dismissed as the empty rhetoric of an unrepentant Victorian imperialist. In fact, Churchill's statecraft, adumbrated in wartime, co-opted by Attlee and Bevin, and sealed in the diplomatic revolution of 1948–49, was a ruthless attempt to exploit the economic and geostrategic possibilities of the postwar world to preserve the appearance and some of the substance of prewar power.

For a decade, global conditions seemed favourable to this enterprise. The failure to make a European peace, the mutual antagonism of the emerging superpowers, and the limits on their military capacity maximized Britain's leverage as the third world power. The disorganization of East Asia and the Chinese revolution of 1949 wrecked the promise of Sino-American partnership and extended the lease of European colonialism in (parts of) Southeast Asia.[80] Crucially, the continuing dislocation of the global economy and the threat of its total breakdown could now be exploited by London (after the crisis of 1947) to protect the remainder of its financial and commercial empire against American penetration.[81] The British raced to develop their closed colonial bloc in Afro-Asia. The illusion that Britain could restore much of its prewar role as the industrial and financial partner of the non-industrial world persisted through the 1950s.[82] In this mirage of continuities it was possible to think that neither the 'loss' of India, nor ejection from Egypt, nor the concessions to colonial nationalism would prevent the imperial association, suitably decentralized, from being a serviceable vehicle of British world power.[83]

In practice, the permissive (if stressful) conditions of the aftermath were too transient to allow any such revival of British imperialism. By the mid-1950s the superpowers had consolidated their grip on lesser and client states[84] and were extending their influence into the hinterlands of Afro-Asia. As the competition for influence grew sharper, old forms of empire-building became obsolete. But new-style empires of informal influence did not come cheap. They could only be sustained by dynamic economies with the means to 'sponsor' new states and feed their voracious appetite for arms and aid – the American path; or (as in the Soviet case) by siege conditions at home and a command economy to service imperial needs. For the British, however, there was little choice by the 1950s but to try to re-enter the open international economy, newly reconstructed by American power, at whatever cost in economic uncertainty.[85] Informal imperialism was now the only option. But the cumulative strains of an extra-European 'world-role' and intra-European rivalry were loaded onto a postwar economy starved of investment and stripped of the overseas assets which had sustained it even in the years of depression. In the twenty years of crisis that followed, the familiar outline of British world power faded slowly away. Globalism and British imperialism had finally parted company.

V

If this rapid sketch of the global setting of British power bears scrutiny, it may offer a modest addition to the usual repertoire of imperial history. Firstly, it reinforces the insight of Robinson and Gallagher long ago that the course of British imperialism is not to be understood as a linear progression towards a predestined future. Instead, the British throve or failed as they took the main chance offered by the shifts of the world's economy and the drift of its politics. They had to adapt their 'domestic' affairs – including the shape of their empire – as best they could to these unpredictable global permutations. Meanwhile the full implications of that protean concept, the 'imperialism of free trade', have yet to be worked out. The uneasy coexistence in the British system between an empire of trade and an empire of rule remains at the heart of the imperial puzzle. Secondly, it gives added weight to the emphasis laid by Cain and Hopkins upon Britain's commercial and financial expansion in the late nineteenth century and to their insistence upon its role as a prop of empire deep into the twentieth – long after the general climate had turned against the British experiment in global power.[86] Finally, it strengthens the impression that once globalism had set in after 1870 British power was at the mercy of the unstable relationship between the four indispensable elements of their world-system: Britain's own strength and status as a great European power; the resources of the City's informal empire of commerce; the military and commercial assets of India – the arm of their Asian power; and the manpower, markets and 'Britannic loyalty' of the white dominions.[87] In the late nineteenth century, it had been easy enough to hold together this bizarre centrifugal construct. Up to 1939, it had survived well enough to weather the crises of the 'globe-wide world'. But by 1960 only the husk was left. World-system shrivelled to 'empire-commonwealth'; empire-commonwealth to the vacuities of a 'world-role'; the 'world-role' to Europe. Where next?

Notes

1   For the extension of the original argument of the 'imperialism of free trade' into the twentieth century, J.A. Gallagher, *The Decline, Revival and Fall of the British Empire* (Cambridge, 1982).

2   D.C.M. Platt, 'The Imperialism of Free Trade: Some Reservations', *Economic History Review*, 2s, 21 (1968), 296–306; M. Lynn, 'The Imperialism of Free Trade and the Case of West Africa', *Journal of Imperial and Commonwealth History* 15 (1986), 22–40.

3 M. Daunton, '"Gentlemanly Capitalism" and British Industry 1820–1914', *Past and Present* 122 (1989), 119–58; G. Ingham, 'British Capitalism, Empire, Merchants and Decline', *Social History* 220, 3 (1995), 339–54.

4 I.R. Phimister, 'Corners and Company-mongering: Nigerian Tin and the City of London 1909–1912' *JICH*, 28, 2 (2000), 23–41.

5 A.N. Porter, ' "Gentlemanly Capitalism" and Empire: the British Experience', *JICH*, 18, 3 (1990), 265–95.

6 A.G. Hopkins, 'Informal Empire in Argentina: an alternative view', *Journal of Latin American Studies*, 26 (1994), 469–84.

7 J. Gallagher and R.E. Robinson, 'The Imperialism of Free Trade', *Econ Hist Rev*, 2s, 6 (1953), 1–15.

8 For a recent attempt, J. Darwin, 'Imperialism and the Victorians', *English Historical Review* 112 (1997), 614–42.

9 A.G. Hopkins, 'Back to the Future: from national history to imperial history', *Past and Present* 164 (1999), 198–241.

10 See Kenneth Pomeranz, *The Great Divergence* (Princeton, 2000), 53–4; D.A. Washbrook, 'Britain and India in the Pre-history of Modernity', *Journal of Economic and Social History of the Orient*, 40, 4 (1997), 421.

11 The classic account is R. Davis, 'English Foreign Trade 1700–1774', *Econ Hist Rev*, 2s, 15 (1962).

12 K.B. DuBoff, *Accumulation and Power: an Economic History of the United States* (New York and London, 1989), 14–15.

13 J.H. Moore, *The Emergence of the Cotton Kingdom in the Old South: Mississippi 1770–1860* (Baton Rouge, 1988), 16.

14 Ulrich B. Phillips, *A History of Transportation in the Eastern Cotton Belt to 1860* (New York, 1908), p. 54. Dorothy R. Adler, *British Investment in American Railways 1834–98* (Charlottesville, 1970).

15 European migration to the Americas in the 1830s was four times the figure for the 1820s. D. Eltis, 'Free and Coerced Transatlantic Migration: some comparisons', *American Historical Review* 88, 2 (1983), 278.

16 See P. Temin, *The Jacksonian Economy* (New York, 1969).

17 Thus China's import of opium increased fourfold 1838–1860. H.B. Morse, *The Trade and Administration of the Chinese Empire* (New York and London, 1908), 337.

18 S. Roberts, *The Squatting Age in Australia 1835–47* (Melbourne, [1935] 1964), ch. 1.

19 H. Reynolds, *The Other Side of the Frontier* (pbk. edn. Ringwood, Vic., 1982), 84.

20 P. Adams, *Fatal Necessity: British Intervention in New Zealand 1830–1847* (Auckland, 1977).

21 Carolyn Hamilton (ed.), *The Mfecane Aftermath* (Johannesburg, 1995).

22 Thus, the tonnage of Western shipping at Canton increased by 23 times between 1719–25 and 1833. See L. Dermigny, *La Chine et l'Occident: le commerce à Canton 1719–1833* (Paris, 1964), II, 520.

23 Britain was the first country to permit absolute freedom of movement. M.A. Jones, *Destination America* (pbk. edn, London, 1977), 13.

24 Potential emigrants from subsistence economies were 'too poor to move'. K.H. O'Rourke and J.G. Williamson, *Globalisation and History* (Cambridge, MA, 1999), 130.

25 R.A. Stafford, 'Geological Surveys, Mineral Discoveries and British Expansion 1835–71', *JICH* 12, 3 (1989), 5–32; Stafford, *Scientist of Empire* (Cambridge, 1989), 205.

26 Stafford, *Scientist*, 213–18.

27 For its receptiveness to humanitarian pressure in the 1830s, J.A. Gallagher, 'Fowell Buxton and the New Africa Policy, 1838–42', *Cambridge Historical Journal* 10 (1950), 36–58.

28 P. Schroeder, *The Transformation of European Politics 1763–1848* (Oxford, 1994), 726–55.

29 See, for example, Elgin to Clarendon, 29 July 1857, in D. Bonner-Smith, *The Second China War 1856–60* (Naval Records Society, 1954), 218.

30 P. Winn, 'Britain's Informal Empire in Uruguay', *Past and Present* 73 (1976), 104, n.20.

31 H. Blumenthal, *Franco-American Relations 1830–1871* (Chapel Hill, 1959), 43.

32 Maori armed resistance continued into the 1880s. J. Binney, *Redemption Songs: a Life of Te Kooti* (Auckland, 1995) ch. 12.

33 Winwood Reade, *The Martyrdom of Man* (26th impression, London, 1928), 242.

34 E.D. Steele, 'Palmerston' in K.M.Wilson (ed.) *British Foreign Secretaries and Foreign Policy* (London, 1987).

35 R. Shannon, *Gladstone: Peel's Inheritor 1809–1863* (pbk. edn., 1999), 222–23; 333.

36 For this term, E. Luttwak, *Turbo Capitalism* (London, 1998).

37 League of Nations, *The Network of World Trade* (Geneva, 1942), 9.

38 A.J.H. Latham and L. Neal, 'The International Market in Wheat and Rice 1868–1914', *Econ Hist Rev* 36, 20 (1983), 260–75.

39 D. Treadgold, *The Great Siberian Migration* (Princeton, 1957).

40 See J.P. Fogarty, 'The Comparative Method and 19th Century Regions of Recent Settlement', *Historical Studies* 19, 76 (1981), 412–29.

41 Even before the Chinese revolution in 1911, three-quarters of the population of Manchuria was made up of recent Chinese immigrants. For subsequent immigration, I. Bowman, *The Pioneer Fringe* (NY, 1931), 281.

42 See O'Rourke and Williamson, *Globalisation*, pp. 2–3 for a concise statement.

43 As in British India, O'Rourke and Williamson, 42.

44 As emphasized by Halford Mackinder and Leo Amery in 1904. See P. Kennedy, *The Rise and Fall of British Naval Mastery* (London, 1976), 183–4.

45 R.C.O. Matthews, C.H. Feinstein and J.C. Odling-Smee, *British Economic Growth 1856–1973* (Oxford, 1982), 128.

46 League of Nations, *Network*, 84.

47 S. Pollard, 'Capital Exports 1870–1914, Harmful or Beneficial?', *Econ Hist Rev* 38 (1985), 489–514. Britain's net overseas assets rose from £1 billion in 1873 to £4.2 billion in 1913, a rise of £3.2 billion. Over the same period, Britain's overseas investment earnings totalled £4.04 billion, more than enough to cover the increase. See B.R. Mitchell, *Abstract of British Historical Statistics* (Cambridge, 1962), p. 334.

48 The Stock Exchange *Yearbooks* in the 1890s reveal a rapid rise in the number of companies registered for enterprise overseas.

49 P. Cain and A.G. Hopkins, *British Imperialism 1688–2000* (second ed., London, 2002), chs. 12, 13.

50 D. Blackbourn, *Fontana History of Germany: the Long Nineteenth Century 1780–1918* (London, 1997), 315–18, for a recent discussion.

51 For Bismarck, O. Pflanze, *Bismarck and the Development of Germany*, Vol 3: *the Period of Fortification 1880–1898* (Princeton, 1990), 123–5. Like Salisbury, Bismarck hoped to avoid the cost and trouble of ruling these colonial spheres.

52 For the mutual anxiety of Britain and France at the time of the Russo-Japanese war, G. Monger, *The End of Isolation* (London, 1963), 128–9, 139.

53 J. Lonsdale, 'Scramble and Conquest in African History' in R. Oliver and G.N. Sanderson (eds) *Cambridge History of Africa* VI: *From 1870 to 1905*, Cambridge, 1985).

54 J. Bryce, *The Relations of the Advanced and Backward Races of Mankind* (Oxford, 1902) 8–9; H.J. Mackinder, 'The Geographical Pivot of History', *Geographical Journal* 23,4 (1904), 422.

55 J. Harris, *Private Lives, Public Spirit: Britain 1870–1914* (pbk. ed. Harmondsworth, 1994), 4–6.

56 H. Mackinder, *Britain and the British Seas* (London, 1902), 12–13.

57 Egypt was the test-case: hence its controversial role in British politics and the importance of propaganda tracts like A. Milner, *England and Egypt* (London, 1892).

58 See J.Gooch, *The Prospect of War* (London, 1981), 79–106.

59 Salisbury used this term in a speech to the Primrose League in May 1898.

60 R. Robinson and J. Gallagher, *Africa and the Victorians* (London, 1961) chs. 8, 10, 12; L.K. Young, *British Policy in China 1895–1902* (Oxford, 1970).

61 For this episode, Baron Meyendorff (ed.) *Correspondance diplomatique de M. De Staal*, vol. 2 (Paris, 1929), 441,450; N. Rich, *Friedrich von Holstein*, vol. 2 (Cambridge, 1965), 617.

62 For the argument that Britain's entente policy was chiefly motivated by imperial concerns, K.Wilson, 'British Power in the European Balance 1906–14' in D. Dilks (ed.) *Retreat from Power* (London, 1981), 41.

63 From around £2000m in 1900 to £4000m in 1913. Cain and Hopkins, *British Imperialism*, 161.

64 Matthews *et al.*, *British Economic Growth*, 433, table 14.3; O'Rourke and Williamson, *Globalisation*, 208.

65 By 1913, the Americas took 20 per cent of British exports, supplied a third of British imports, accounted for more than half of British overseas investment, and employed perhaps three-quarters of British oceanic shipping.

66 For the estimate of wealth lost, Matthews *et al.*, *British Economic Growth*, 129.

67 A. Offer, 'The British Empire 1870–1914: a Waste of Money?' *Econ Hist Rev* 46, 2 (1993), 234–35; generally, Offer, *The First World War: an Agrarian Interpretation* (Oxford, 1989).

68 A. von Tirpitz, *My Memoirs* (Eng. trans, London, c. 1926), vol. 1, 287.

69 A. Zimmern, *The Third British Empire* (3rd edn., Oxford, 1934), 75.

70 League of Nations, *Network*, 16.

71 For the development of a German *Grossraumwirtschaft* in Eastern Europe after 1934, A. Basch, *The Danube Basin and the German Economic Sphere* (London, 1944), chs. xi, xvi; E.A. Radice 'The German Economic Programme in Eastern Europe' in M. Kaser (ed.), *The Economic History of Eastern Europe 1919–1975* (Oxford, 1986), II, 300–1.

72   League of Nations, *Network*, 61–2.
73   F.C. Jones, *Japan's New Order in Asia: Its Rise and Fall 1937–45* (London, 1954). For German abandonment of China to Japan, see J.P. Fox, *Germany and the Far Eastern crisis 1931–38* (Oxford, 1982), 55 ff.
74   Matthews *et al.*, *British Economic Growth*, 435.
75   Mitchell, *Abstract*, 334–5.
76   Approximately one-third of the British army was kept in India.
77   See B. McKercher, *Transition of Power; Britain's Loss of Global Pre-eminence to the United States 1930–1945* (Cambridge, 1999) ch. 4.
78   McKercher, *Transition*, 293–98.
79   The Second World War cost Britain 28 per cent of total net assets. Matthews *et al.*, *British Economic Growth*, 129.
80   See D. Brotel, 'Indochina (Vietnam) between National Independence and Colonial Continuity' in G. Krebs and C. Oberland (eds) *1945 in Europe and Asia* (Munich, 1997).
81   Cain and Hopkins, *British Imperialism*, 628–9.
82   This was the view of the Radcliffe committee on monetary reform in 1959.
83   See J. Darwin, *Britain and Decolonisation* (London, 1988).
84   A. Deporte, *Europe between the Superpowers* (New Haven, 1986).
85   Cain and Hopkins, *British Imperialism*, 637 ff.
86   Ibid., passim.
87   J. Darwin, 'A Third British Empire: the Dominion Idea in Imperial Politics' in W.R. Louis and J. Brown (eds), *The Oxford History of the British Empire*, Vol. 4: *The Twentieth Century* (Oxford, 1999), ch. 3.

* I have benefited from the advice of Dr Ian Phimister to whom I am most grateful. Errors of fact and interpretation are mine.

4
Empire, Imperialism and the Partition of Africa

Ian Phimister

Peter Cain and Tony Hopkins wrote:

> From the perspective of... [our study of British Imperialism], there is an argument to be made for reducing the attention customarily paid to the partition of Africa because the importance of the continent, as measured by trade and financial flows, did not give it a high ranking among Britain's international trading partners or even among regions that felt the force of her imperialist ambitions.... However, given that partition... is so firmly entrenched in the literature as the classic case of late nineteenth century imperialism, there are compelling historiographical reasons why we have situated our own interpretation in the context of the existing literature.[1]

Profoundly dissatisfied with explanations for Africa's partition which have emphasized variously the significance of strategic concerns; the crucial role played by proto-nationalism; or the problems besetting Britain as 'an ageing, defensive power struggling to fend off new challenges to her interests', Cain and Hopkins instead argued that:

> the impulses motivating [British] policy can be traced to the metropole, and particularly to the expansion after 1850 of... gentlemanly occupations and values... Indeed Britain's actions in partitioning Africa followed the contours of this development: the main weight of her interests lay in Egypt and southern Africa, where City and service interests were most prominently represented, and it was there that Britain showed the greatest vigour in promoting her claims.[2]

More precisely, Britain's occupation of Egypt was 'closely linked to restoring the health of public finance'...; while the occupation of southern Africa was 'also a result of Britain's growing stake in the region, where her investments had risen substantially following the discovery of minerals'. In the latter case, though, Cain and Hopkins were at pains to acknowledge that:

> the Anglo-Boer War was not fought at the behest of the mineowners any more than it was fought to secure a naval base or to realise the dreams of an ambitious pro-consul. The decision was made because Britain was an expanding power which sought to create in Africa a dynamic economic and political satellite of the kind already in evidence in Australia, Canada, New Zealand and, it should be added, Argentina. Kruger's plans for achieving greater political independence cut across the trajectory of British policy by threatening to confine Britain's influence to the Cape and by perpetuating uncertainties about the long-term future of the mining industry.[3]

So far as tropical Africa was concerned:

> in the absence of a powerful City interest, the Foreign Office had to rely on chartered companies, which in turn required subsidies...in exchange for political services. Organisations such as the Royal Niger Company and the Imperial British East Africa Company represented gentlemanly capitalist interests in a dilute form...In West Africa, mercantile pressure groups also joined with British Chambers of Commerce representing manufacturers who were keen to preserve markets for their goods. But this example is an exception that proves the rule: policy in Britain's principal spheres of interest...was not made by the manufacturing lobby and was influenced by it only to a limited extent. Even in West Africa, manufacturing interests made headway only because their demands were consistent with free trade....

Far from British policy, then, or rather policies, as there 'could be no "one Africa" policy...since the continent was not united',[4] being 'essentially restrained and reactive',[5] the rapid expansion of the financial and service sector of the economy in London and the south-east meant that Britain in Africa was an 'advancing not a retreating power'.[6]

Seven years have passed since the argument summarized above first appeared in fully worked out form,[7] certainly time enough for an assessment to be made of the extent to which gentlemanly capitalism does actually provide 'a systematic account of a momentous historical event'.[8] In what follows, this chapter will examine the part played by Britain in the Scramble for Africa in the light of subsequent publications and recent research. Amongst the former are essay reviews of *British Imperialism* itself; general overviews of Africa's partition or of British overseas expansion; and specialist monographs and reviews devoted to particular aspects of British involvement in Africa during the nineteenth century.[9] The latter comprises as yet unpublished research on the City of London and the coming of war in South Africa between 1895 and 1899. Not surprisingly, the verdict is mixed; less predictably it may point to a contradiction of sorts at the core of imperialism.

I

Of all the examples of 'gentlemanly capitalist' interests shaping British intervention in Africa, the case of Egypt seems to be the strongest. According to Robinson and Gallagher, Britain occupied Egypt in 1882 because the breakdown of law and order following the overthrow of the compliant regime of the Khedive by proto-nationalists threatened Britain's strategic interest in the Suez Canal, the crucial importance of which was to safeguard the route to India.[10] Cain and Hopkins will have none of this. They argue instead that British policymakers were driven to defend Britain's substantial economic interests. These comprised some 80 per cent of Egypt's exports and 44 per cent of her imports by 1880. More importantly, they also constituted significant holdings of Egyptian Government stock by City investors who believed that they carried an implied guarantee by Britain. It was these investments which the British thought were threatened by the nationalist deputies of the Chamber of Notables. When Lord Granville, the Foreign Secretary, was advised in March 1882 that the Chamber would not give up their claim to manage parts of the Budget, he came to the reluctant but unavoidable conclusion that 'it must end by their being put down by force'.[11]

This is not a version of events which has been much disputed in recent years. Apart from Afaf Lutfi al-Sayyid-Marsot's non-committal listing of the possible causes of British intervention, the reference for which is Hopkins's own article on the subject,[12] the only serious challenge came from Andrew Porter a decade ago. He attacked the argument put forward by Hopkins in 1986[13] for failing 'to embrace...[the] very broad range of British interests which is still missing in...accounts of Egypt's occupation, and which the gentlemanly capitalist framework fails to provide'.[14] Neither of these charges was explicitly addressed in

British Imperialism, and it appears to be a disagreement which turns primarily on very different readings of Bruce Johns's work on British business interests in Egypt.[15] What is significant for Porter is the picture of 'an indecisive and ill-informed Government' whose 'hesitant adjustments of policy to a changing economic relationship' caused 'the convergence of imperial and private interests',[16] while for Cain and Hopkins the importance of Johns's research is the proof that 'the City's involvement reached to the highest levels'. Lord Rothschild himself actively 'represented the interests of British investors... [as did] the Corporation of Foreign Bondholders, which mobilized *The Times*, the financial press, and the considerable number of members of parliament (besides Gladstone) who had a financial stake in the Egyptian economy'.[17] It is this latter interpretation which receives most support in Colin Newbury's chapter in Volume III of the *Oxford History of the British Empire* on the Partition of Africa. Britain's demarcation of Egypt in 1882 as a British sphere by unilateral naval and military action, writes Newbury, 'had its origins in both the internationalisation of the khedive's insolvency and the methods pursued by foreign agencies to cure that condition'.[18] Starting from Lord Salisbury's acknowledgement that Britain's stake in Egypt was largely commercial, this interest grew to the point where:

> in a wave of Gladstonian justification and City satisfaction, Parliament ultimately approved the official underwriting of a 'special interest' in trade through the Canal, investment of 'capital and industry', and protection of British nationals.

It was 'these motives for the defeat of [the nationalist] Urabi's forces at Tel-el-Kebir in September [1882] which left Britain the task of patching up "the great disintegration"'.[19]

II

Further south, however, the role played by 'gentlemanly capitalism' appears to have been very much weaker. Indeed, if there is one region where Cain and Hopkins stretch the utility of the concept of 'gentlemanly capitalism' to breaking point, it is tropical Africa. This is the case not least because their earlier studies, separately[20] and together,[21] seem to offer a more satisfactory account of the diffuse influences shaping British (and other European) interventions in West Africa, one which ascribed a much less pushful role to the financial interests of the City.

Indeed, it was by placing Cain and Hopkins's earlier works in an international context that the present writer attempted in 1995 to explain the process and pattern of Africa's partition.[22] It took as its starting point Eric Hobsbawm's observation that:

> the major fact about the nineteenth century is the creation of a single global economy, progressively reaching into the most remote corners of the world, an increasingly dense web of economic transactions, communications, and movements of goods, money and people linking the developed countries with each other and with the undeveloped world.[23]

Of particular importance was the further fact that the pace and nature of change accelerated in the last 30–40 years of the century. This period, according to Barraclough, transformed itself to such an extent that 'the age of coal and iron was succeeded after 1870 by the age of steel and electricity, of oil and chemicals'.[24] Industrial capital's accelerated development, sometimes called the 'Second Industrial Revolution', more precisely identified as the transitionary phase between competitive and monopoly capitalism, was quintessentially an uneven process. It profoundly upset existing economic and social balances both between countries and within them. Generally speaking, the new industries were most in evidence in Germany and the United States. By 1900, these two countries had carved out an increasing share of the world's trade for themselves largely at Britain's expense.

Britain's relative industrial decline after 1870 was influenced not only by increased competition from other countries, however, but also by the fact that her own protracted process of industrialization had been extremely uneven, subordinated in the latter part of the nineteenth century to the City of London's commercial and financial interests. Consequently, from the 1870s onwards, as Cain and Hopkins famously stressed, 'while Britain's dominance of international finance increased, her industrial sector began to decline relative to her major competitors. Free trade and invisible exports, the twin supports of financial supremacy, played their part in emphasizing and underwriting the decline of industry.'[25]

This industrial decline was all the more serious because it occurred in the context of what contemporaries called the 'Great Depression' of 1873 to 1890. Once again, the effects of the Depression were not uniformly felt, but while there were periods of recovery, the general tendency of prices was downwards. In this deflationary situation, increased competition for markets sent a wave of protectionism sweeping across Europe and North America between 1875 and 1892. Only Britain remained committed to free trade. It did so not because of any sentimental attachment to past practice when Britain had been the 'workshop of the world', but because the operations of the City depended on the unfettered movement of capital and commodities. As a result, British industry, already disadvantaged, according to some scholars, by a basic distortion in British capital markets, was denied protection on its home ground. British imports of manufactured goods increased from 3 per cent of total imports in 1850 to 25 per cent in 1900. Nor were British manufacturers best placed to compete in the markets of advanced industrial countries. Excluded by the often better quality of German and American products, as well as by tariff barriers, British exports to Europe and the United States fell by 19 per cent in value between 1874 and 1900. For all these reasons, 'industrial interests in Britain shifted, around 1880, into decisive support for the acquisition of new markets in Asia and Africa'.[26]

But neither the shifting balance of economic and political power in the northern hemisphere nor intensified competition for markets during the Depression determined that Africa would be partitioned. Processes and events in Africa itself were important, influenced as they were by external forces. After 1870, the price of vegetable oils, West Africa's main export crop, fell dramatically. It did so not only because the opening of the Suez canal in 1869 provided Southern Asian producers with easier access to European markets, but also because of expanding world production of mineral oils. The ensuing trade depression quickly made itself felt along the West African coast and hinterland. Local rivalries intensified as disputes raged over 'the allocation of shares in the export trade, over the prices to be asked and given, and over the distribution of reduced profits'. These rivalries in turn were accentuated by European merchants, as they were drawn into African politics, particularly in their role as creditors. And increasingly all of these tensions and struggles adversely affected the flow of trade.[27]

In these circumstances, some European traders began calling upon their respective governments to restore 'law and order'. The smooth operation of trade, they argued, depended on political stability. They were joined by others whose falling profit margins made them want to restructure the market so as to eliminate African middlemen. The introduction in the 1850s of regular steamship lines between Europe and West Africa had already added to the problems facing established merchants by lowering freight rates and making it easier for newcomers to enter the trade, and when competition intensified during the Depression, the interruptions to the regular flow of trade caused by the dissolution of the indigenous West African economy and society, were the last straw. European merchants began demanding

> political action up to and including colonial annexation, as a means of checking or suppressing commercial competition and, by reducing the political independence of African middlemen, forcing them to accept lower prices.[28]

The 'character, intensity and influence of mercantile pressures' for metropolitan intervention not only varied from locality to locality in West Africa itself,[29] but also met with very different responses from the governments of France, Britain and Germany. Of all the major powers trading in West Africa, France was least able to absorb the new competitive strains. Because the convergence of merchant demands with the broader impact of the Depression was particularly marked in France, her merchant lobby received a sympathetic hearing from successive administrations. With key sectors of French civil society increasingly willing to countenance military campaigns, and with Europe and North America's technological lead over the rest of the world widening almost daily, wars of colonial conquest promised to be cheap and easy. 'By 1870 the local [West African] deterrents to penetration were no longer serious', Flint has noted.[30]

Starting from their existing Senegalese enclave in 1879, the French began to advance across western Sudan. In its latter stages, the French scramble for African territory, even if accelerated by Britain's occupation of Egypt in 1882, and justified, like its British and German counterparts in terms of Social Darwinism, was primarily sustained by 'renewed industrial depression and heightened tariff barriers [which] generated a French will to claim any domain which could be brought within the tariff system of the French Empire'.[31] The colony's governor commented:

> At a time when France is trying to increase her volume of business with Senegal, to develop the resources of her colony and to create new outlets in the very centre of Africa, it does not seem to me possible that all this effort should be made for the profit of a foreign industry.... In such a country the theory of free trade cannot be put into practice.[32]

By contrast to French policy, Britain's initial response to the clamour of her own merchants for intervention in West Africa was cautious and conservative. Although Britain's trading interests were by far the largest of any European state involved in West Africa, merchant cries for help were largely ignored. However, once France began swallowing large chunks of West Africa, this raised the spectre of British trade being excluded by high tariff barriers from a widening zone of French territory. Only then did British policy begin to change direction.

This slow and reluctant change of policy reflected the limited importance of industrial capital in contemporary British political economy. Its interests were often important enough to cause London to react to external changes but it was rarely sufficiently powerful to initiate action. Government policy, crucially influenced by the financial and service interests of the City of London, remained committed to free trade. In this context, and recognizing that there was no realistic possibility of free trade being jettisoned in favour of Protection, industrial interests in Britain added their voice to merchant demands for state intervention. Businessmen, according to Cain, 'began to take an interest in anticipatory annexation of overseas markets. The main fear was that large areas of the world might otherwise be occupied by rival powers with protectionist inclinations.'[33] 'Protectorates are unwelcome burdens', wrote one senior member of the Foreign Office, 'but in this case it is...a question between British protectorates, which would be unwelcome and French protectorates, which would be fatal. Protectorates of one sort or another, are the inevitable outcome of the situation.'[34]

Britain's pronounced reluctance during the 1880s to do anything more than was strictly necessary to safeguard her existing commercial interests was exemplified further south in West-Central and in East Africa. In neither region were significant British interests involved. Their export trade, however, was more diversified, including cloves from Zanzibar and ivory and wild rubber from the coastal hinterlands. Here the key is that although the price of vegetable oils collapsed after 1870, the price of cloves remained stable and the prices of rubber and ivory actually increased. They ran counter to the general trend of the Depression. This, as Munro noted, had the effect of attracting newcomers to these regions, 'who saw in their relative commercial vitality...a potential for the creation of commercial empires'.[35] Chief amongst the interlopers attracted to West-Central Africa was Leopold II of Belgium. Obsessed with the idea of controlling what he hoped would be the riches of the Congo Basin, Leopold actively promoted European exploration of Central Africa during the second half of the 1870s. In East Africa, Leopold's British counterpart was William Mackinnon, a shipowner whose vessels plied between Aden and Zanzibar. Mackinnon had earlier wanted to lease the Sultan of Zanzibar's mainland territories in order to develop the interior's trade, but this particular scheme was blocked in 1877 when the British Government opted for the continued exercise of indirect influence through the local potentate. The ensuing uneasy equilibrium was disturbed at the start of the 1880s when Leopold's efforts to make commercial treaties with local rulers ran up against the activities of the French explorer, Savorgan de Brazza. When France ratified de Brazza's treaties in 1882, this set off alarm bells in Whitehall and the Wilhelmstrasse. Both Britain and Germany were worried that the protectionist French were about to carve out another huge colony, this time in Central Africa. But because neither country had vital economic interests at stake, they were reluctant to make pre-emptive annexations of their own. For broadly similar reasons, they would have preferred the vast area which later became the Congo Free State left open to everyone's trade. '[The]...main interest of Britain was that the Congo should be free to the peaceful enterprise of all the world,' so Hyam and Martin claim. 'Basically, Britain had enough to do and wished the Congo to lie fallow.'[36]

While key aspects of the argument made above, notably the conse-quences of the City's attachment to Free Trade, can be found in Hopkins's *Economic History of West Africa* and in Cain's *Economic Foundations of British Overseas Expansion*, they sit uneasily with Cain and Hopkins's subsequent insistence in *British Imperialism* on the proactive part played even here by gentlemanly capitalism. Attempts to bring Goldie and Mackinnon within the gentlemanly fold by hailing them as 'gentlemen in the making...[because they were] on the make',[37] are a little strained, to say the least. As Geoffry Ingham has complained, it presents 'obvious problems of historical interpretation...[to] subsume this aspect of British expansion under the "gentlemanly" rubric'.[38] That British policy in tropical Africa was more restrained and reactive than Cain and Hopkins now allow is also suggested by Newbury's conclusion that it was French expansionism and protectionism after 1879 which called into question established British policy in West Africa.[39] Obliged to rethink her position as the French military advance moved eastwards from Upper Senegal, Britain's room for manoeuvre was further circum-scribed during the Berlin Congo Conference of 1884/5. Although her rights along the Niger were recognized, Britain failed to get her own way over the Congo. Forced by Germany to abandon her support for Portuguese claims to West-Central Africa, Britain reluctantly recognized the sovereign existence of Leopold's personal fiefdom once the Congo Free Trade Area was guaranteed.

In East Africa, where no such guarantees obtained in the aftermath of Germany's unexpected seizure of Tanganyika, Britain's hand was again forced by foreign competition. Granted a royal charter for his Imperial British East Africa Company in 1888, Mackinnon was belatedly unleashed. But whether Britain's occupation of Kenya and Uganda can be ascribed to the imperatives of gentlemanly capitalism however 'diluted' is another matter. While commercial rather than strategic considerations were certainly uppermost in British thinking, John Darwin has suggested that interest turned into intervention only because the local bridgehead – 'the hinge or "interface" between the metropole and a local periphery' – was 'sufficiently strong and its domestic lobby forceful enough to outweigh the diplomatic and military hazards of a forward policy'. In East Africa, 'as so often elsewhere, Salisbury found himself struggling to regulate the effects of private expansionism, to parry its domestic lobbying and to balance the weight of British interests on the spot against the wider diplomatic pressures to which London was exposed'.[40] By arguing that 'even when only half exerting herself, Britain was still able to outdistance her new foreign competitors',[41] Cain and Hopkins may have underestimated the range of pressures brought to bear on Whitehall even as they attribute more constancy and purpose to German colonial policy than there actually was.

III

The sheer scale of Britain's financial and commercial involvement in southern Africa generally, and in the gold mines of the Transvaal in particular, dwarfed her interests everywhere else on the continent. At the end of the nineteenth century, Britain supplied about two-thirds of the region's imports worth £15 million per annum, while total investment in the gold mines stood at some £74 million, of which Britain accounted for an estimated 70 per cent. Surely here, if anywhere in Africa, gentlemanly capitalism reigned supreme? J.A. Hobson, of course, notoriously thought that British intervention was 'driven by a conspiracy of financiers', but this is not a line of argument which finds any favour with Cain and Hopkins. Instead they opt for an interpretation which is curiously close to the one formulated by Robinson and Gallagher in *Africa and the Victorians*; that is, 'the inpouring of trade and capital [into the Rand] combined with a[n Afrikaner] nationalist reaction to crack British paramountcy'. What caused Lord Salisbury and his Cabinet 'to try and force the [South African] republic into a settlement at the risk of war was their fear of losing British South African loyalty;

their hope of impressing Afrikanerdom with a sense of imperial strength; and their determination to halt the decline of their paramount influence'. Assuming, above all, that Kruger's republic would dominate Britain's South African colonies and determine the region's future unless it was forced into a compromise settlement, Salisbury's government 'committed itself at last to dictate terms at all costs'.[42] This is essentially the same position adopted by Cain and Hopkins.

> The power and potential of the Transvaal had greatly expanded [as a result of the discovery of gold], and the prospect of a Canadian solution to Britain's problems in South Africa was now threatened by the emergence of a rival possibility: the creation of a 'United States of South Africa' under Afrikaner control.[43]

But in following Robinson and Gallagher in this regard, Cain and Hopkins make much the same error as their predecessors. Both sets of authors appear to believe that the threat posed to British supremacy was the rise of Kruger's Afrikaner republic. Yet this is manifestly *not* what worried Selborne when he penned his influential Memorandum in March 1896. Described by Robinson and Gallagher as 'perhaps the best evidence of the fundamental considerations which inspired Chamberlain and Selborne henceforward and which in the end dragged the ministry into the Boer War',[44] and accepted as such by just about every scholar who has worked on the war, its full version warrants careful scrutiny. As demonstrated below, this is significantly different from the truncated version printed in *Africa and the Victorians*. That Selborne took as his 'postulate...[the fact] that the Transvaal is going to be by far the richest, by far the most populous part of South Africa, that it is going to be the natural capital, state and centre of South African commercial, social and political life' is clear enough. He was further of the opinion that 'if South Africa remains as now a congeries of separate States, partly British Colonies and partly Republics, it will inevitably amalgamate itself into a United States of South Africa'. But what was likely to precipitate this 'cataclysmic' outcome was not the present 'Afrikaner-dominated republic'. On the contrary, observed Selborne:

> if the Transvaal were always going to remain a Dutch Republic, I admit that this danger would not be so imminent. Racial jealousies might temporarily postpone the effects of commercial interests. But...the Transvaal cannot permanently remain a Dutch Republic.

There has never been a census; but the best information obtainable gives a maximum of 25,000 male Boers and a minimum of 50,000 Uitlanders, of whom $\frac{3}{4}$ are British. Before Jameson's criminal blunder the Uitlanders were said to be pouring into the Transvaal at the rate of 500 males per week. Just think what would be the result of 10 or of 20 years of an immigration maintained at one fifth or one tenth of this rate! Therefore according to all the experience of history, this country so powerful in its future wealth and population *must be a British Republic if it is not a British Colony; and I cannot myself* see *room for doubt but that a British Republic of such great wealth and so large a population* situated at the geographical centre of political South Africa would assuredly attract to itself all British Colonies in South Africa.[45]

Whether viewed from Whitehall or the City, British financial and commercial interests on the Rand were flourishing before the war.

The existence of the Republic did not prevent British exporters from enjoying most of its trade... It mattered little to the British manufacturer and merchant whether the Rand trade passed through colonial ports or through Delagoa Bay. Neither did the investor demand to see pro-British politicians governing the Rand, before he would put his money in it.'[46]

Indeed, this awkward fact had impressed itself upon British policy-makers in the period before the Jameson Raid as well as afterwards. As the then High Commissioner, Sir Hercules Robinson, had explained to Chamberlain in November 1895, however much Randlords and uitlanders might object to Kruger's government, they had little desire to see the Transvaal inside the British Empire: 'They dislike[d] the native policy of England – they dislike[d] the meddling of the House of Commons and of the philanthropic societies.'[47] It was the looming prospect of a 'capitalist republic', British but outside the Empire, which worried the Colonial Secretary. Chamberlain concluded:

Whatever defects may exist in the present form of Government of the Transvaal, the substitution of an entirely independent Republic governed by or for the capitalists of the Rand would be very much worse for British interests in the Transvaal itself and for British influence in South Africa.[48]

While Robinson and Gallagher recognized how this concern crucially influenced British attitudes in the months immediately preceding the Raid, their misreading of Selborne's post-Raid deliberations led them to think that the threat perceived thereafter by Selborne and Chamberlain was one posed by an Afrikaner republic rather than the spectre of a British one. But at the same time, Robinson and Gallagher appreciated that whatever challenge Kruger did embody, it was not to the City of London or the gold mining industry as a whole. From this it followed that 'intervention in the Transvaal was hardly needed to turn it either into a market or a field of investment'.[49] This being so, they concluded, the causes of the war must lie elsewhere. Selborne, however, was contemplating a deeper paradox – it was the very success of British and foreign investment which might require imperial action to be taken.

IV

What does the 'balance sheet' of British Imperialism and Africa look like in view of the preceding three sections of this chapter? That gentlemanly capitalism can account satisfactorily for the British occupation of Egypt in 1882 seems well established. When the scramble for tropical Africa is considered, however, its explanatory power appears to be limited. The region where the City's financial interests were virtually non-existent is also the one where the concept of gentlemanly capitalism is weakest. Cain and Hopkins themselves, notes Darwin, seem

> uncertain how far British intervention was driven by decision-makers at home, by a new breed of 'mega-merchants' on the spot, by pressure groups appealing to the 'national interest' or by the sub-imperialism of pocket pro-consuls.[50]

Nor is the wider context given as much attention as it might be. As one historian wrote in 1903:

> The world is…more than ever before, one great unit in which everything interacts and affects everything else, but in which also everything collides and clashes.[51]

It is one thing for Cain and Hopkins to demonstrate that past portraits of British decline have been overdrawn; quite another for their argument not to accommodate the unparalleled transformation of global conditions which witnessed the rise of Germany and the United States in the last quarter of the nineteenth century. Paul Kennedy has observed:

> The transfer of industrial technology to the United States, Imperial Germany, later Russia and Japan, created new centres of economic and strategic power where previously none had existed. British industry was no longer supreme, its commerce was hit by rival manufactures and foreign tariffs, its naval supremacy was ebbing away, its empire was much more vulnerable.[52]

In these radically changed circumstances, a 'far less confident' Britain was 'taking imperialist measures to ward off decline'.[53] It is an observation which could be extended to cover France as well. Surely it is no coincidence that the two powers least transformed by the 'Second Industrial Revolution' were also the ones who seized most of tropical Africa? So pronounced was the impact of this shift in the balance of power on France that a powerful case could be made for the Partition as a whole owing more to French commercial calculations and the Quai d'Orsay than it ever did to British concerns, whether those of the City of London or those of the 'official mind of British Imperialism'.

So far as this chapter is concerned, what some of these problems suggest is that Cain and Hopkins might have been better advised to resist the temptation of situating their interpretation in the context of the Partition's established historiography. All too often, the result has been debate at cross purposes. As they themselves acknowledged, the logic of their overall argument is to downplay the significance of the Scramble for tropical African territory. Generally speaking, the region did not attract the interest of the City. The latter's attention was focused on Canada, Australasia and 'informal empire' in Latin America and elsewhere. The further difficulty, of course, is the perennial one of definition. What is meant by 'imperialism' and/or by 'empire'? Nonetheless, it may be possible to identify two intertwined processes at work. The first of these constitutes the core of Cain and Hopkins's analysis. Characterized by massive financial flows, British Imperialism went from strength to strength in this period – that is, after c. 1870. One or two important exceptions aside, however, the dynamic expansion overseas of 'gentlemanly capitalism' did not turn on territorial annexation. By contrast, vested British interests in tropical Africa, usually those most threatened by the changes associated with the Second Industrial Revolution, looked to colonial acquisitions to bolster their position. This second process witnessed a huge increase in the size of the British Empire in Africa, but it was characterized by caution as much as calculation; by peripheral as often as metropolitan impulses; by defence rather than offence. Granted that Cain and Hopkins are primarily concerned with imperialism, and their critics are largely interested in empire, perhaps Cain and Hopkins should simply have conceded ground of so little concern to them instead of fighting on such unfavourable terrain in the first place.

Arguably, these issues find their most complicated expression in Southern Africa, where the interests of 'informal imperialism' appear not always to have coincided with those of territorial empire. Well aware that late-nineteenth-century South African history bristles with snares for the unwary, Cain and Hopkins attempted to follow what seemed to be the most judicious historiographical path. But by taking this route, they may have lost sight of how to deploy the concept of 'gentlemanly capitalism' to best advantage. Although they assert at one point that 'where City and service interests were most prominently represented [as in Southern Africa]...it was there that Britain showed the greatest vigour in promoting her claims',[54] in practice the role which they grant gentlemanly capitalism in the region is unexpectedly modest. In doing so, they may well have sold the concept short. To start with, their argument is unnecessarily confined to the Cape and the Transvaal. After all, Southern Rhodesia and by extension Northern Rhodesia, were acknowledged by contemporaries as exemplifying the 'relationship between a good or bad share market on the one side and a British Colony in the stage of tender infancy on the other'. 'Rhodesia', declared one newspaper in 1898, 'is a country which, almost avowedly is intended to be built up, or at least forced upward, by aid of gold mining and land dealing on the £1 share limited liability principle.'[55] Much more importantly, in the hotly debated case of the gold mining industry of the Transvaal, the weight of the City of London's interests was no less for having been misjudged by later observers. If the reading of the Selborne Memorandum suggested earlier in this chapter is correct, it opens up the prospect of seeing the Transvaal before 1899 in a new and intriguing light. Given the degree of dominance enjoyed by British trade, as well as the Transvaal's marked dependence on the City for investment, loans and other financial services, by most criteria the South African Republic was already part of Britain's informal empire. This suggests that the relationship between economic imperialism, informal empire and territorial empire is not only ambiguous, as many scholars have realized.[56] There were circumstances in which it was antagonistic.

Notes

1   P. Cain and A. Hopkins, *British Imperialism, 1688–2000* (London, 2002), 335–6.
2   Ibid., 337.
3   Ibid.
4   Ibid., 311.
5   Ibid., 361.
6   Ibid., 338.
7   For earlier versions, see Cain and Hopkins, 'The Political Economy of British Expansion Overseas, 1750–1914', *Economic History Review*, 1980, 33, 4; idem, 'Gentlemanly Capitalism and British Expansion Overseas, II: New Imperialism, 1850–1914', *Economic History Review*, 1987, 40, 1.
8   Cain and Hopkins, *British Imperialism*, 337.
9   See, particularly, G. Ingham, 'British Capitalism: Empire, Merchants and Decline', *Social History*, 1995, 20, 3; G. Krozweski, 'Rethinking British Imperialism', *Journal of European Economic History*, 1994, 23, 3; I. Phimister 'Africa Partitioned', *Review*, 1995, 18, 2; J. Darwin, 'Imperialism and the Victorians: the dynamics of territorial expansion', *English Historical Review*, 1997, 22, 447; C. Newbury, 'Great Britain and the Partition of Africa, 1870–1914', in A. Porter (ed.), *Oxford History of the British Empire. Vol. III. The Nineteenth Century* (Oxford, 1999); and R. Dumett (ed.) *Gentlemanly Capitalism and British Imperialism. The New Debate on Empire* (Harlow, 1999).
10 R. Robinson and J. Gallagher, *Africa and the Victorians. The Official Mind of Imperialism* (London, 1961), 120. See also Darwin, *Britain, Egypt and the Middle East. Imperial policy in the aftermath of war 1918–1922* (London, 1981), 5–6.
11 Cain and Hopkins, *British Imperialism*, 313, 315. See also Cain, 'Hobson Lives?, Finance and British Imperialism 1870–1914', in S. Groenveld and M. Wirtle (eds), *Government and the Economy in Britain and the Netherlands since the Middle Ages* (Zutphen, 1992).
12 A.L. al-Sayyid-Marsot, 'The British Occupation of Egypt from 1882', in Porter (ed.) *Oxford History of the British Empire*, 654.
13 Hopkins, 'The Victorians and Africa: a Reconsideration of the Occupation of Egypt, 1882', *Journal of African History*, 1986, 27, 2.
14 Porter, '"Gentlemanly Capitalism" and Empire: the British Experience since 1750?', *Journal of Imperial and Commonwealth History*, 1990, 18, 285.
15 B.R. Johns, 'Business, Investment and Imperialism. The relationship between economic interests and the growth of British intervention in Egypt 1838–1882', University of Exeter, unpub. PhD, 1982.
16 Porter, '"Gentlemanly Capitalism" and Empire', 285.
17 Cain and Hopkins, *British Imperialism*, 315.
18 Newbury, 'Great Britain and the Partition of Africa', 632.
19 Ibid., 634.
20 Notably Hopkins, *An Economic History of West Africa* (Harlow, 1973); and Cain, *Economic Foundations of British Overseas Expansion 1815–1914* (London, 1980).
21 Cain and Hopkins, 'Gentlemanly Capitalism and British Expansion Overseas, II: New Imperialism'.

22 What follows in the rest of this section is a much shortened and revised version of Phimister, 'Africa Partitioned', 362–71.

23 E. Hobsbawm, *The Age of Empire, 1875–1914* (London, 1987), 62.

24 G. Barraclough, *An Introduction to Contemporary History* (Harmondsworth, 1967), 44.

25 Cain and Hopkins, 'Gentlemanly Capitalism and British Expansion Overseas, II: New Imperialism', 4.

26 Cain and Hopkins, 'Political Economy of British Expansion Overseas', 482.

27 Hopkins, *Economic History of West Africa*, 148. See also R. Law (ed.), *From Slave Trade to 'Legitimate' Commerce: the Commercial Transition in West Africa* (Cambridge, 1995); and M. Lynn, *Commerce and Economic Change in West Africa. The Palm Oil Trade in the Nineteenth Century* (Cambridge, 1997).

28 J.F. Munro, *Africa and the International Economy 1800–1960* (London, 1976), 72. See also Lynn, 'From Sail to Steam: the Impact of the Steamship Services on the British Palm Oil Trade with West Africa, 1850–1890', *Journal of African History*, 1989, 30.

29 Ibid. For differing assessments of the significance of this pressure, see R. Austen, *African Economic History: Internal Development and External Dependency* (London, 1987); W. Hynes, *The Economics of Empire: Britain, Africa and the New Imperialism, 1870–1895* (London, 1979); and B. Ratcliffe, 'Commerce and Empire: Manchester Merchants and West Africa, 1873–1895', *Journal of Imperial and Commonwealth History*, 1979, 7.

30 J. Flint, 'Britain and the Partition of West Africa', in Flint and G.Williams (eds), *Perspectives of Empire: Essays Presented to Gerald. S. Graham* (London, 1973), 101. For discussion of the key technological issues involved, see especially R. Headrick, 'The Tools of Imperialism: Technology and the Expansion of European Colonial Empires in the Nineteenth Century', *Journal of Modern History*, 1979, 51; and his *Tools of Empire* (Oxford, 1981).

31 Munro, *Africa and the International Economy*, 73. See especially Newbury and A. Kanya-Forstner, 'French Policy and the Origins of the Scramble for West Africa', *Journal of African History*, 1969, 10; and Newbury, 'The Tariff Factor in Anglo-French West African Partition', in P. Gifford and W. Louis (eds), *France and Britain in Africa* (New Haven, 1971).

32 As cited in Newbury, 'Trade and Authority in West Africa', in L. Gann and P. Duignan (eds), *Colonialism in Africa: I, History and Politics of Colonialism* (Cambridge, 1969), 93.

33 Cain, *Economic Foundations of British Overseas Expansion*, 52.

34 As cited in Flint, 'Britain and the Partition of West Africa', 108.

35 Munro, *Africa and the International Economy*, 75.

36 R. Hyam and G. Martin (eds), *Reappraisals in British Imperial History* (London, 1975), 150–1. See also S. Forster *et al.* (eds), *Bismarck, Europe and Africa* (Oxford, 1988); P. Kennedy, *The Rise of the Anglo-German Antagonism 1860–1914* (Boston, 1980); and H. von Strandemann, 'Domestic Origins of Germany's Colonial Expansion under Bismarck', *Past & Present*, 1969, 42. For the part played by Leopold II, see especially J. Stengers, 'King Leopold's Imperialism', in R. Owen and R. Sutcliffe (eds), *Studies in the Theory of Imperialism* (London, 1972).

37 Cain and Hopkins, *British Imperialism*, 308.

38 Ingham, 'British Capitalism', 345.

39   Newbury, 'Great Britain and the Partition of Africa', 636.
40   Darwin, 'Imperialism and the Victorians', 629.
41   Cain and Hopkins, *British Imperialism*, 338.
42   Robinson and Gallagher, *Africa and the Victorians*, 458.
43   Cain and Hopkins, *British Imperialism*, 327.
44   Robinson and Gallagher, *Africa and the Victorians*, 434.
45   Bodleian Library, Selborne Papers, Colonial Office Memorandum, 26 March 1896. The italicized portion is omitted from the section quoted in *Africa and the Victorians*.
46   Robinson and Gallagher, *Africa and the Victorians*, 458.
47   Robinson to Chamberlain, 4 Nov. 1895; as cited in Robinson and Gallagher, *Africa and the Victorians*, 422.
48   Ibid., 428–9.
49   Ibid., 458.
50   Darwin, 'Imperialism and the Victorians', 616.
51   As cited in Barraclough, *Introduction to Contemporary History*, 53.
52   Kennedy, 'Continuity and Discontinuity in British Imperialism 1815–1914', in C. Eldridge (ed.), *British Imperialism in the Nineteenth Century* (London, 1984), 38.
53   Ibid.
54   Cain and Hopkins, *British Imperialism*, 337.
55   *Rhodesia Herald*, 14 Oct. 1898.
56   Most recently, Ingham, 'British Capitalism', 345; and Krozweski, 'Rethinking British Imperialism', 628. See also Phimister, 'Corners and Company-mongering: Nigerian Tin and the City of London, 1909–1912', *Journal of Imperial and Commonwealth History*, 2000, 28.

5
Gentlemanly Imperialism and the British Empire after 1945

Gerold Krozewski

Most of the attention on *British Imperialism*[1] has justifiably focused on its treatment of the nineteenth century. Given the breadth and scope of the study, the authors had to condense the period of the postwar empire onto a few pages.[2] As for the period after 1945 as a whole, the original two-volume edition has found some wider resonance among writers onto British political and current affairs,[3] and has been acknowledged in a survey essay of the City of London.[4] From among those isolated critical essays of the volumes extending into the post-1945 period, one has dealt with a region neglected in the study, namely Malaya,[5] while another has approached the argument from the perspective of Britain's economic performance.[6] Both have therefore not engaged with the argument in its overall political dimension of linking society, politics and policy in the context of Britain's overseas and imperial relations.

In focusing on the period between 1945 and the early 1960s, when Britain eventually withdrew from most of its colonial empire, this essay will discuss the concept of 'gentlemanly capitalism', as employed as the backbone of Cain and Hopkins's study of imperialism.[7] Elsewhere, I have offered a broad appreciation of their volumes,[8] and a detailed argument about the politics of Britain's external economic and imperial relations unrelated to 'gentlemanly imperialism'.[9] In the following, I will sketch Cain and Hopkins's conception of 'gentlemanly imperialism', and provide a critical assessment of its applicability to the period, before engaging with historical and methodological aspects of their argument. The conclusions will raise, albeit briefly and tentatively, some broader conceptual issues of research on British imperial relations after 1945.

Constituent elements and underpinnings

First, put in the simplest terms for the sake of analysis, *British Imperialism* advances a continuity thesis on a socioeconomic formation in Britain, which begins in the nineteenth century and stretches into the post-1945 period.[10] The period after 1945 attracts the authors' attention because they argue that one can identify similar impulses in Britain's overseas relations as in earlier periods of British imperial expansion, namely influences of crucial financial relationships connected to a 'gentlemanly capitalist' elite in Britain. The authors, therefore, aim to establish the continuing relevance of their argument beyond the period for which it was developed. The study (and Hopkins separately in an article published after the first edition of the books) advances another, more specific continuity argument, albeit less emphatically, with regard to the 1950s and 1960s, namely that British policy attempted to maintain some informal control over the colonies after their independence.[11] Conceptually, this argument resembles earlier historical interpretations of a continuity between informal and formal empire in Britain's imperial relations, albeit inversed and transplanted into the mid-twentieth century.[12]

Second, the study analyzes the impulses rather than the effects of imperial rule (as indeed do the classical theories of imperialism). Impulses are apparently defined in terms of the general underlying motivations of policymakers as representatives of a socioeconomic group which is identified as the extension of a 'gentlemanly capitalist' stratum of British society.[13] Incidentally, it is also assumed that these impulses, portrayed as synonymous with the importance of the City of London in the British polity, continue to be relevant to British external relations at least until the Thatcher period, irrespective of the existence of a colonial empire.[14] In this context, the argument is mainly about policy impulses. The structural aspect, well developed for the late nineteenth century, takes second stage in the twentieth century. However, there is some ambiguity as to whether the study is intended to offer an argument about Britain's postwar imperial policy *per se*, or simply emphasizes influences of the particular nineteenth-century legacy of the British state related to foreign relations, since the narrative also summarizes changes in Britain's global economic relations and policies. In principle, one could conceive of an argument which structurally relates society to state and empire, simply as one about the characteristics of the British polity and the ensuing implications for Britain's external relations rather than as one about British policy in particular regions and periods.[15]

Third, the incorporation of the postwar period in a study of imperialism is an exception. Hitherto, research of the empire during this period has been conducted within the framework of essentially self-contained studies of decolonization. Research published within the paradigm of the dependency school advances a more or less explicit argument about an imperial design. But this research sharply contrasts with Cain and Hopkins's conception of imperialism, which focuses on impulses in the centre and makes no claims about welfare benefits or the exploitation or underdevelopment of the periphery in a territorial north–south divide as is the case of dependency studies.

A critique of 'gentlemanly imperialism' and its assumptions with regard to the 1940s and 1950s requires to clarify what Cain and Hopkins's continuity thesis precisely means, what it implies, and how it relates to imperialism as they define it. This raises questions about the claim, scope and explanatory power of their argument. The second continuity thesis simply raises questions about the historical evidence. But before turning to this critique, I should set the scene from the perspective of my own research.

The 'financial theme' and imperial relations

Cain and Hopkins are right in claiming that British imperial policy (and to a certain extent colonial policy) during the period after 1945 can only be fully understood by drawing on economic and especially financial relationships. In this very general sense, I am in agreement with the argument advanced in their book. If one assumes that continuity simply means that financial relationships played a role during the period and, moreover, that imperialism is a control relation, then one can accept that there was a continuity in British imperialism down to the Suez crisis of 1956, which is also the watershed identified by specialists of decolonization.[16] This point could be substantiated extensively with historical evidence, far more than *British Imperialism* provides in the limited space available. As I have argued elsewhere, archival sources underscore the importance of sterling relationships during the period as well as their role in the key policy debates assessing political control in British foreign and imperial relations.[17] For the present purpose, I will simply pinpoint some principal elements, which are also relevant to the conceptual suggestions at the end of this article.

Domestic and external factors imposed priorities on British policy emphasizing financial relationships. These issues include the problem of the British balance of payments during postwar reconstruction and designs of welfare capitalism; the sterling exchange crises, which posed challenges for the management of the pound; and Anglo-American relations, given the twin problem of re-establishing an equilibrium in the world economy between the dollar and sterling areas and the striving for liberal multilateralism in a new international economic order.[18] Therefore, discriminatory policies were implemented with regard to the dependent sterling area's commodities, which proved vital in relations with the dollar area for 'dollar saving' and 'dollar earning'. As a result, the economic role of the colonies for Britain increased during the late 1940s and early 1950s, triggered by the convertibility crisis of 1947.[19] The resulting policies cannot be interpreted as merely reflecting wartime approaches which had not yet been phased out. Rather, this point ushered in a distinct policy approach towards British imperial and external economic relations. In the absence of colonial control, the discriminatory trade policies, necessitated by Britain's position in the international economy, would not have been feasible and the colonial contribution to Britain's balance of payments less marked. As a matter of coincidence, policies were complemented by other factors, such as boom periods for some commodities (for example, with regard to rubber, less so cocoa) and the fact that the imports of consumer goods could be restricted more easily in some colonies than in the independent sterling area. Colonial economic policy was an intrinsic part of the overall management of British external economic relations. Decisions concerning import restrictions and 'dollar ceilings' were taken in the main interdepartmental committees under the aegis of the Cabinet Office or co-ordinated in the short-lived Ministry for Economic Affairs, whereas the role of the Colonial Office was, on the whole, limited to assessing administrative needs and the political feasibility of economic policies.[20]

British relationships with the empire underwent considerable change during the period both in structural and policy terms for a variety of reasons. The need, feasibility and desirability of discriminatory management and direct control diminished in the course of the 1950s. The dollar gap was closing and liberal multilateralism imposed its own dynamic on policy-making, as did the challenge from the European Common Market. No further extension of discrimination was feasible and it was proving politically costly, especially in areas in which direct political control was crucial, such as with regard to import controls. Developmental objectives on the periphery and in Britain proved ultimately irreconcilable, which ended the 'common cause' advocated earlier. The relevance to cosmopolitan sterling relationships of colonial commodities was questioned, given changes in trade flows and the expected fall in commodity prices. As a result, north–south relations became far less relevant for the British economy than previously had been the case, and the empire passed into oblivion almost unnoticed. States on the periphery also changed during the period, which in some territories, though not in every case, made British policy designs increasingly difficult to execute as the 1950s wore on.[21]

The continuity thesis: some critical observations

With regard to the nineteenth century, the authors have closely inte-grated their analysis of domestic socioeconomic transformations with that of changes in British policy and structural changes in Britain's global relations. However, my reading of their argument on later periods is that 'gentlemanly capitalist' relationships continued to impel the course of imperial policy, even after 1945, in a way that goes beyond merely emphasizing a continuity of the relevance of financial factors to British external and imperial relations. From this perspective, the argument becomes problematic because it assumes that imperialist impulses relating to an explanation based on the context of the nine-teenth century are applicable to the postwar period. To illuminate these issues, a set of questions related both to methodology and the historical context need to be discussed.

The argument about the genesis of 'gentlemanly capitalist' imperialism in the nineteenth century derives its strength precisely from the discus-sion of the sociological dimension, namely connections and inter-actions between civil society and the state at a time of important shifts in state formation and the emergence of nation states – discussed in diverse intellectual contexts from Gramsci to Weber and Schumpeter.[22] It is illuminating, moreover, how the peculiar polity and state shaped Britain's foreign relations, even if some critics have expressed doubts about the precise links established between British society, the state and policy. As studies of the comparative sociology of the state have amply demonstrated, individual societies gave rise to specific forms of states and institutions.[23] These factors, in turn, influenced a country's external relations.

Nonetheless, one could argue that the study's strength of an analysis of social change in Britain in the late nineteenth century, proves to be its weakness with regard to the twentieth century. From the perspective of an investigation of British foreign and imperial relations and policies after 1945, the way 'gentlemanly capitalism' is construed *conceptually* reflects the authors' *historical* analysis of nineteenth-century Britain rather too closely. The concept feeds on an interpretation of the decline and alleged transformation of the landed aristocracy in Britain related to the financial and service sectors of the economy which set priorities in Britain's overseas relations. In this context 'gentlemanly imperialism' is a temptingly parsimonious concept. But one has to question whether it is meaningful in its timeless application of historical continuity.

Simply put, the suggested link between British society, the state and external relations appears as a projection into later periods based on a historical argument about the late nineteenth century. The argument takes insufficiently into account that these main constituent elements have all undergone considerable change since. Therefore, I would argue that the continuity thesis is relevant to the period of empire after 1945 only insofar as it is synonymous with the role of the financial sector in the British polity and the long-lasting legacy of British institutions, which took shape in the late nineteenth century. However, I would also argue that this is, strictly speaking, not a continuity of 'gentlemanly capitalism' as a social formation but rather shows a certain relevance of relations it has shaped. Otherwise, one would have to assume that 'gentlemanly imperialism' could accommodate generically different relationships in different periods, which would turn the concept into a mere synonym of financial relationships, divesting it of its original meaning.

Three related methodological points are worthwhile discussing with regard to the historical evidence on the empire after 1945 when assessing the applicability of the Cain and Hopkins argument. First, it is regrettable that the structural analysis of the British polity is rather underdeveloped. In particular, the state remains stagnant or is excluded as an entity of analysis in its own right. Secondly, while the argument is ultimately about British policy rather than structural aspects of foreign and imperial relations (quite unlike the classical theories of imperialism), one could argue that the changing structural context and constraints of international relations influenced British policy to a greater extent than is evident from the study. Third, policy is directly related to impulses emanating from the social background of policymakers, intent directly related to outcome, which, at certain points, and contrary to the authors' stated intentions, runs the risks of making the argument open to criticism of social-psychologism.[24]

Even if one accepts that a 'gentlemanly elite' was still strong in the rank and file of the civil service and among members of government in the mid-1940s and 1950s, these actors operated in a different context from that in the late nineteenth century, and politicians were confronted with a much more broadly based electorate. States had become more elaborate and diversified constructions as had the international state system, and the link between British society and the state had become considerably transformed since the nineteenth century. The state designed by, or at least aspired to by Labour leaders in the late 1940s, such as Attlee, Bevin, Dalton and Cripps (to some extent influenced by Harold Laski) had little to do with the state of Britain's free trading 'gentlemanly capitalists', – except for the undeniable but also obvious fact that it inherited Britain's global economic connections from the latter's legacy. Labour's management of the empire became associated with welfarism effectively giving rise to a version of 'socialist imperialism'. The British state and empire were seen as part of a protectionist international order where economic planning and controls were tailored to the needs of the nascent welfare state.

Besides, the prominent imperialist politicians in the Labour party were distinctly 'ungentlemanly' – and rather closer to that Radical imperial reformer of yesteryear, Joseph Chamberlain.[25] A comparison with Chamberlain is made in the study but rather too rapidly fused with the 'gentlemanly imperialism' theme.[26] Many influential Labour leaders, though not Ernest Bevin,[27] may well have come from relatively prosperous social backgrounds, which may well show who made it into the British political elite and who did not, irrespective of a particular party affiliation; but (even if they originated from the elite related to the financial and service sectors) one could hardly argue that their state-management of the empire was prompted by their affinity to City interests rather than an opportunity sought to support welfarism driven by the necessity to remedy balance of payments imbalances.

Under the Conservative governments of the 1950s the principles of a liberal British state and liberal multilateralism became dominant. But this is hardly evidence of the continuity of 'gentlemanly capitalism' as a social formation, be it in its impact on the state (and policy) or on the City of London (and policy). Cain and Hopkins's assessment of the period appears to be somewhat trapped by their concept of 'gentlemanly capitalism'. The move forward into the post-imperial age looks (almost literally) like a move backward into a golden age. This argument is tempting from the viewpoint of an analysis of the psychological make-up and the motivations of civil servants. A certain imagery was pervasive among policymakers, who occasionally compared the sterling area to an English gentleman's club, which implied a similarity of interest and purpose of its members as well as an informal co-ordination of policies under British leadership. It is indicative, for example, how Britain rationalized sterling area arrangements and the approach towards central banking on the periphery as a line of defence for the pound.

But, one does not need to endorse the state's immunity from civil society to observe that changes in state organization and institutions in their historical context played a mediating role between civil society and policy in the twentieth century and particularly after 1945 rather than society *per se* being the driving force behind policy. Cain and Hopkins would need to bring 'the state back in' not because their argument advances a causation which relates politics to society (the original target of advocates of the so-called relative autonomy of the state), but because their causation overemphasizes and also oversimplifies the role of agency, and because they attribute too much explanatory power to their historical conception.[28]

In this connection, it is imperative to point out that the realms of the British state, City of London, sterling area and sterling empire, though obviously related, also need to be kept distinct as entities of analysis to enhance our understanding of the specific nature of Britain's imperial and external economic relations and policies during the period. This point can be made, for example, with regard to the relevance of political control in the empire. For the City of London, a control relationship in the existing empire did not matter. However, it mattered for the state and the management of the sterling area until the point when policymakers realized (tentatively from about 1956 and definitely after Suez) that a redefinition of north–south relationships in general was in the making.[29] Incidentally, this is also the reason why the second continuity thesis of *British Imperialism* needs to be qualified. Policymakers did dream of a reinvigorated British cosmopolitanism based on sterling after 1960, but precisely for this reason they did not aim to revitalize the old empire in an informal way. Attempts at informal influence in the 1960s were defensive.[30] British policy towards the pivots of the discriminatory sterling area, Malaya and West Africa, was shaped in a different global context before and after the juncture of 1957–60, though some relationships with these regions took until the late 1960s to reflect this change.

In explaining British imperial policy, an argument focusing on the institutional dimension does have its place.[31] The specific nature of the British state and institutions had an impact on imperial and external economic policy. The institutional and technocratic legacy influenced British policy and implied a general continuity in terms of policy predilections, for example, when it came to prioritizing the empire or Europe, or a cosmopolitan or domestic orientation in sterling policy. Indeed, technocrats from the Treasury and the Bank of England had considerable influence on policy, occupying a prominent position in the policy process as representatives of their respective institutions in interdepartmental committees. In the economic realm of policymaking, politicians and even government ministers were often not sufficiently informed, knowledgeable, or involved, given the sheer quantity of tasks at hand, to supervise or influence important decisions beyond the overall approach to policy. In external economic relations, moreover, exogenous factors imposed themselves too frequently to secure a coherent course of policy. So, discriminatory policies towards the empire derived as much from the influence of technocrats as from politicians, even under the Labour government, though the former saw discriminatory sterling area management as a temporary measure in contrast to many Labour politicians. One could perhaps say that the technocrats' ambition was to assist in making the politician's dreams for British recovery come true. It is also a fact that policymakers did hanker after Britain's past glory and attempted to emulate principles of past policy, though their perception was not always accurate.

Nonetheless, interpreting British policy against the background of the institutional bias of the British state is not the same as suggesting that a 'gentlemanly capitalist' social stratum impelled external economic policy. Nor is it, of necessity, the same as attributing an important place to the influence of the City of London in external economic policy. These are necessary areas of analysis for arguments about British external relations (and factors often neglected by imperial historians), but they need to be kept analytically distinct, and alone they are insufficient to explain policy in a specific historical period. Cain and Hopkins's argument on British imperialism enriches our understanding of how the British polity evolved in a certain way and why financial relations became so important for the British polity. However, the legacy of past relationships, *per se*, does not amount to an explanation of policy. There was a rationale of state management related to, but also distinct from, the City which is not distinguished clearly enough in the study's account and conceptualization. While the City certainly influenced the state's leverage, the state's management of external economic relations was different in nature from simply representing City interests, which were hardly homogenous anyway. It would be misleading to interpret the management of the British state's external and imperial economic relations as the aggregate response to the cumulation of individual entrepreneurial pressure groups, financial or other. This is especially true for the post-1945 empire (unlike in the case of France, for example), though the investigation of British business in the empire is of course of interest in its own right and was an important influence in specific regions.[32] Otherwise, the focus on government policy, rather than entrepreneurial pressure, in the summary account of the period accurately reflects the structural peculiarities of British imperial relations at the time as well as the well-known divide between Parliamentary interest groups and government in the British policy process.[33]

The specific structural international context within which policy was formulated would also need to be more carefully analyzed. The intricate debates between and among representatives of the political elite, the civil service and the City of London were importantly influenced by this setting. The sterling crises of the 1940s and 1950s needed to be tackled one way or another, all the more so, given Labour's welfare objectives. Here, the state evidently mattered as a factor in its own right separate from the influences of social forces or economic doctrine. The Macmillan government's move towards commercial and financial liberalization in the late 1950s, in part, reflects the constraints of Britain's financial sector, which circumvented government policy if it suited its interests, as the emergence of the Eurodollar market before *de jure* convertibility shows. But Macmillan's failure to extricate Britain from established sterling relationships is also evidence of the fact that sterling's role in the international economy was an inescapable structural constraining factor for the British state, as the international context, namely Europe and the United States, forced itself on the policy agenda whether policymakers liked it or not.[34]

On the whole, the study's conception of empire is attuned to 'gentlemanly capitalist' impulses, which may also account for the fact that British policy is portrayed as having been successful rather than subject to constraints. In my view, it is difficult to see how one could reconcile an interpretation of British policy during the period with claims of the continuity thesis of 'gentlemanly imperialism', except in an extremely loose, and therefore in explanatory terms weak fashion. Nonetheless, even if the general account offered in *British Imperialism* cannot do full justice to the systemic dimension, the study rightly emphasizes the empire as a system (which policy aimed to influence). Regional case studies of late colonialism and some general studies of decolonization often assume that British policy operated 'bilaterally'. This is implausible, even in such obviously central cases as India, and was clearly not the case in the framework of the discriminatory sterling area.

Finally, I should mention a point which is particularly evident from the perspective of the post-1945 empire but applies to the Cain and Hopkins thesis as a whole. My critique of the way in which the authors conceive of the state in connection with policy is also relevant to the definition of imperialism employed in their study. As mentioned earlier, theirs is not an abstract theoretical argument about imperialism. Imperialism is studied as a historical phenomenon in a specific country, Britain, and tested in case studies on the periphery. Conceptually, *British Imperialism* relies on an argument about metropolitan impulses to illuminate overseas expansion. The 'imperialistic' nature of this expansion is then defined as the infringement of the sovereignty of states on the periphery which thus becomes part of the overall argument.[35] Therefore, while the state in Britain is neglected in the analysis of the twentieth century, the state re-emerges as the very measuring device which makes Britain's foreign relations 'imperialistic'. This definition of imperialism accommodates a broad spectrum of relationships, from British influence exerted on like-minded social formations, such as in Argentina, to direct colonial rule. It should, however, be noted that, although, according to this conception, metropolitan impulses are testable in case studies, the basic assumptions of 'gentlemanly capitalism' (being about the transformation of British society) are only testable in Britain. These impulses need not, of necessity, be reflected in individual overseas territories. A critique from a regional standpoint taking Cain and Hopkins to task for not being able to identify 'gentlemanly capitalists' in some part of the empire at a given point in time would do little damage. To falsify their argument, one would need to show that expansionist impulses mediated through a system of co-ordinated relations were irrelevant to policy in a particular region.

Nonetheless, the authors' definition of the 'imperialistic' nature of expansion is based on a somewhat static concept of the state on the periphery. The argument fails to take into account that notions of state sovereignty are fluid. Moreover, states existed in a variety of forms at the time of colonial expansion and were, in part, a colonial construction. Colonial states changed not least in response to local social and political constraints. Besides, it is difficult to determine what infringement of sovereignty precisely means. The authors' argument about imperialism is not defined in terms of a control relation, and therefore insufficiently supported by an argument about structural change on the periphery and in the international context. In an accessory publication on Argentina published after the first edition of *British Imperialism* Hopkins has shifted the argument towards a definition of control influenced by a concept of structural power in international relations introduced by Susan Strange and similar to Platt's usage of imperialism. However, the foreword to the one-volume edition of Cain and Hopkins's study does not follow up this argument.[36]

Elements for an alternative perspective

In relation to the points raised so far in this essay one can attempt to broaden the perspective towards sketching a historical conceptualization of the period, thus shifting the explanation away from 'gentlemanly' impulses. The key problems which have to be addressed are what characterized Britain's external and imperial economic relationships and distinguished them from other cases, what defined complementarities between Britain and other regions of the world, within and outside the empire, and what were the shifts that occurred in these complementarities. As a further step it could be explored where and how centres of power protected, retained or even gained manoeuvrability, or carved out niches of political control as an alternative to, or in support of structural power. This might be one conceivable perspective of integrating different regional research initiatives and, if cautiously employed, also different explanatory approaches. The historical experience of Britain and the empire after 1945 prompts a number of tentative observations in these areas.

In the early postwar years, Britain's relative structural power (to continue adapting Susan Strange's conceptual framework) vis-à-vis the United States was limited. This was one reason for the antagonism over Britain's endorsement of liberal multilateralism. The peculiar setting of the needs of reconstruction and British welfare objectives, the prominence of commodities in international trade, and specific conditions in the colonies in terms of resources, social relations of production and political structures, conferred an indispensable role in terms of direct political control to the empire and colonial states in the discriminatory management of the sterling area.[37] Britain's state-led discriminatory management was facilitated by various political constellations, namely US concurrence with discriminatory policies in order to keep the international economy afloat, given the imbalances between the dollar and sterling areas in the international economy. At the same time, the 'old' independent Commonwealth was still an important outlet for British investment. In the late 1950s, however, one observes a trend towards economic redeployment in investment and trade in an increasingly competitive liberal international economy, the more stringent prioritization of British policy along these lines, and perhaps a radical shift away from a long-standing nationally organized management of external economic relations prevalent since the mid-nineteenth century.[38] As is well known, the period was specific from the international relations perspective, given the gradual move towards freer trade and capital flows and a shift away from commodity trade towards inter-industrial trade. Alongside these changes, regional shifts occurred between the war period and the early 1960s, first in the priorities of Britain's discriminatory sterling relations from the independent towards the dependent sterling area and from India to Africa and Southeast Asia, and subsequently, in the liberalizing international economy, within the sterling area towards the Middle East, and outside it, towards Europe and North America.

One could employ complementarity[39] in a systemic conception of international relations as a simple analytical tool to sketch out how regional economic settings interconnected or conflicted with each other. Complementary relationships were inherently unstable and difficult to influence by policymakers. For reasons related to the specific conditions of the period, the hitherto rather marginal colonial empire in Africa and Asia (except India) was for a brief period complementary within, and one essential pillar of a discriminatory trade-cum-financial triangle in support of Britain's balance of payments. Meanwhile, the 'old' Commonwealth merely remained a supplementary realm for Britain, while complementary relationships with Britain decreased in importance. Australia boosted its industrialization not least due to the benefits it derived from the sterling area's dollar pooling, eventually focusing on a closer association with US and East Asian markets. In other areas, peripheral development objectives meant a move towards protectionism. Both ultimately led to important changes in trade flows away from traditional sterling area patterns, and these changes and perceived trends also prompted new policy approaches in the late 1950s, for example with regard to aid arrangements and the access to loans.[40]

Complementarity had an important political dimension related to structural and formal control. As pointed out, political control mattered in the state-planned discriminatory sterling management allowing colonial import and export policies to be shaped to meet the contingencies of the British balance of payments, thereby supporting Britain's recovery – even if the feasibility of control was as often as not a matter of coincidence rather than design. In the international context, political control in the colonies was primarily a counterpoise against the undermining of the sterling system by the United States, but intended to lend support to Britain's external economic relations elsewhere too. For example, with regard to Anglo-Japanese relations in the early 1950s, economic planning in British colonies was tuned to the level of Japanese sterling balances, cutting colonial textile imports from Japan when necessary, or increasing them and negotiating their availability for sterling.[41] Nonetheless, not only could formal control not be maintained in the long run, it was also hardly worth maintaining, given shifts in complementarity. Under liberal multilateralism formal control mattered less and structural power proved to be the determining factor in international relations, which, one could argue, also triggered a transformation in Britain's political relationships with the empire.

Further insight might be gained by broadening the view towards a comparison with other European empires. Polities are indeed peculiar, as the British case shows, but the underlying question here is the role of the impact on imperial relations and policies of the social order at the expense of that of the state and international structural context in a specific historical period. In some cases, there were important similarities between colonial empires in terms of the relationships between the centre and periphery and in policy designs. Balance of payments constraints existed in other empires too, and the British example of running a currency area prompted some imitation elsewhere, as it had done in the 1930s. For example, the Portuguese escudo zone, in a way similar to the dependent sterling area, was designed to support the centre's balance of payments.[42] As for the franc zone, motivations are less clear and the actual policies were rather different from the British. One is inclined to attribute the zone's establishment to the privileged access of particular business elites to the state during a modernization drive, which however was typical for the period between the mid-1950s and 1960s.[43] Yet, other imperial powers had rather less to rely on than Britain in terms of commodities and also different priorities; after all, none had to manage a currency of international exchange. Differences between empires may well also have been due to the fact that Britain was better able to resort to a discriminatory management in the sterling area and operated under different constraints, given its structural position in the world economy, rather than being exclusively attributable to any specific political, social or institutional legacies.

Conclusion

The principal strength of Cain and Hopkins's study lies in illuminating possible connections between British civil society, the state and a global system of external relations during a formative period of the nineteenth century. The authors are right in pointing out institutional and ideological legacies of the policy discourse related to a specific socioeconomic elite in Britain. But projected into the future the explanatory power of 'gentlemanly imperialism' is limited. While the financial theme is imperative in understanding Britain's imperial relationships during the period, it is not a simple reflection of 'gentlemanly capitalism'. Whether one interprets the historical construction in terms of structure or the individual social affiliation and motivation of policymakers (and both is possible in different sections of the book), if applied to a long historical period it becomes too malleable a concept to be meaningful in explaining relationships beyond the period for which it was originally conceived. A conceptualization of British imperial relations after 1945 needs to draw to a greater extent than *British Imperialism* on the specificity of the historical context. An analysis propelled by an argument about a historical legacy is not fully persuasive, notably because it is offered at the expense of an analysis of the influences of the imperial and international economic system, British state and instititutions, and regional complementarities or antagonisms in the specific historical period. In all these complex and interconnected areas important changes need to be discussed in more detail, not only the social legacies emphasized.

Notes

1 P.J. Cain and A.G. Hopkins, *British Imperialism, 1688–2000* (London, Longman, 2nd edition 2001). The original edition appeared in two volumes: P.J. Cain and A.G. Hopkins, *British Imperialism: Innovation and Expansion, 1888–1914* [vol. 1] and *British Imperialism: Crisis and Deconstruction, 1914–1990* [vol. 2] (London, Longman, 1993). References below are to the second (one-volume) edition, which has been augmented with a new foreword and afterword but not been revised.
2 See Cain and Hopkins, *British Imperialism*, ch. 26, especially pp. 620–40.
3 Will Hutton, *The State We're In* (London, Jonathan Cape, 1995).

4   Paul Thompson, 'The Pyrrhic Victory of Gentlemanly Capitalism: the Financial Elite of the City of London, 1945–90', *Journal of Contemporary History*, 32 (3), 1997, pp. 284–5.

5   Nicholas White, 'Gentlemanly Capitalism and Empire in the Twentieth Century: the Forgotten Case of Malaya', in *Gentlemanly Capitalism and British Imperialism: the New Debate on Empire*, edited by Raymond E. Dumett (London, Longman, 1999), 175–95.

6   Angela Redish, 'British Financial Imperialism after the First World War', in idem, 127–40.

7   'Gentlemanly Capitalism' has importantly also been invoked in studies of the City of London. For extensive recent references on the post-1945 period from this angle, see Paul Thompson, 'The Pyrrhic Victory of Gentlemanly Capitalism', *Journal of Contemporary History*, 32 (3), 1997, 283–304, and 32 (4), 1997, 427–40.

8   Gerold Krozewski, 'Rethinking British Imperialism', *Journal of European Economic History*, 23, 3 (1994), 619–30.

9   Gerold Krozewski, *Money and the End of Empire: British International Economic Policy and the Colonies, 1947–1958* (Basingstoke and New York, Palgrave, 2001 (now Palgrave Macmillan)).

10 See Cain and Hopkins, *British Imperialism*, 'The Survival of the Gentlemanly Order', pp. 620–2.

11 See ibid., pp. 640, 677 and A.G. Hopkins, 'Macmillan's Audit of Empire, 1957', in *Understanding Decline; Perceptions and Realities: Essays in Honour of Barry Supple* (Cambridge, CUP, 1997), 234–60.

12 See the essay by Ronald Robinson and Jack Gallagher, 'The Imperialism of Free Trade', *Economic History Review*, 2nd series, VI (1953), 1–15, which has attracted a considerable following among an increasingly self-contained group of imperial historians.

13 See, in particular, Cain and Hopkins, *British Imperialism*, pp. 53–5.

14 Ibid., pp. 640–4.

15 For example, based on the arguments developed in ibid., chs 3 and 4.

16 See, for example, John Darwin, *Britain and Decolonisation: the Retreat from Empire in the Post-War World* (Basingstoke, Macmillan, 1988 (now Palgrave Macmillan)), pp. 211–14, 222–35.

17 For reasons of brevity, I take the liberty of referring below to my own published work on the subject rather than directly to archival sources.

18 For structural aspects, see my *Money and the End of Empire*, ch. 3; for pertinent policy aspects, see ch. 4.

19 Ibid., chs 4 and 5.

20 For the policy process, see ibid., pp. 11, 17–18, 20, 66.

21 See ibid., chs 6 and 8.

22 See, for example, Joseph Schumpeter, 'The Sociology of Imperialism', in *Joseph A. Schumpeter: the Economics and Sociology of Capitalism*, edited by Richard Swedberg (Princeton, Princeton University Press, 1991); Max Weber, *Economy and Society* (New York, Bedminster Press, 1968); C. Buci-Glucksmann, *Gramsci and the State* (London, Lawrence and Wishart, 1978).

23 See, for example, B. Badie and P. Birnbaum, *The Sociology of the State* (Chicago, Chicago University Press, 1983).

24 Compare, for example, Cain and Hopkins, *British Imperialism*, p. 59 with pp. 620–1, also pp. 10–11.

25 For an incisive argument about the Chamberlain period, see E.H.H. Green, *The Crisis of Conservatism. The Politics, Economics and Ideology of the British Conservative Party, 1880–1914* (London, Routledge, 1995), esp. chs 2 and 7.

26 See Cain and Hopkins, *British Imperialism*, p. 625.

27 See, for example, Peter Weiler, *Ernest Bevin* (Manchester, Manchester University Press, 1993), ch. 1.

28 See the well-known debates regarding Skocpol's arguments, notably P.R. Evans, D. Rueschemeyer and T. Skocpol (eds), *Bringing the State Back In* (Cambridge, CUP, 1985); and for an assessment of the theoretical debates, Bob Jessop, *State Theory. Putting Capitalist States in Their Place* (Oxford, Polity Press, 1990), ch. 10.

29 See my *Money and the End of Empire*, pp. 112, 160–1.

30 A good example is the controversy during the currency negotiations with Malaya in 1960: see ibid., p. 180; for the general argument, see ibid., pp. 171–4.

31 See, for example, B. Elbaum and W. Lazonick, 'An Institutional Perspective of British Decline', in *The Decline of the British Economy*, edited by B. Elbaum and W. Lazonick (Oxford, OUP, 1986), 1–17.

32 For a recent comparative study, see R.L. Tignor, *Capitalism and Nationalism at the End of Empire: State and Business in Decolonizing Egypt, Nigeria, and Kenya, 1945–1963* (Princeton, Princeton University Press, 1998).

33 See B. Badie and P. Birnbaum, *The Sociology of the State*, part 3, ch. 2; Zara Steiner, 'Decision-making in American and British Foreign Policy: an Open and Shut Case', *Review of International Studies*, 13 (1987), 1–18.

34 See for these constraints *Money and the End of Empire*, ch. 8, and for the period of the Labour governments, ch. 4.

35 See Cain and Hopkins, *British Imperialism*, pp. 53–4.

36 Compare Susan Strange, *States and Markets: an Introduction to International Political Economy* (London, Pinter, 1988), ch. 2 and part III (esp. ch. 5, pp. 88–105), with A.G. Hopkins, 'Informal Empire in Argentina: an Alternative View', *Journal of Latin American Studies*, 26, 4 (1994), 469–84. Compare also the discussion of the definition of imperialism in D.C.M. Platt, 'The Imperialism of Free Trade: Some Reservations', *Economic History Review*, 2nd series, 21 (1968), 296–306.

37 For this argument, see my *Money and the End of Empire*, pp. 196–9.

38 For this argument, see B.J. Cohen, *The Geography of Money* (Ithaca, NY, Cornell University Press, 1998).

39 The term has been invoked in research on the sterling Commonwealth: G. Zappalà, 'The Decline of Economic Complementarity: Australia and the Sterling Area', *Australian Economic History Review*, 34, 1 (1994), 5–21.

40 See my *Money and the End of Empire*, chs 6 and 8.

41 See ibid., pp. 43, 67–8, and from the complementary perspective of Japan, Kaoru Sugihara, 'International Circumstances Surrounding the Postwar Japanese Cotton Textile Industry', *Discussion Papers in Economics and Business* (Discussion Paper 99–06, Graduate School of Economics and Osaka School of International Public Policy (OSIPP), Osaka University, March 1999).

42 The key study of the escudo system is João Estêvão, *Moeda e sistema monetário colonial* [Money and the Colonial Monetary System] (Lisbon, Escher, 1991).

43 See Jacques Marseille, 'La balance des paiements de l'outre-mer sur un siècle, problèmes méthodologiques', in *La France et l'outre-mer. Un siècle de relations monétaires et financières*, Colloque tenu à Bercy les, 13, 14 et 15 novembre 1996 (Comité pour l'histoire économique et financière, Ministère de l'Economie, des Finances et de l'Industrie, Paris, 1998), 3–26, and idem, *Empire colonial et capitalisme français. Histoire d'un divorce* (Paris, Albin Michel, 1984), ch. 15.

Part II

Gentlemanly Capitalism and Informal Empire in East Asia

6
Gentlemanly and Not-so-Gentlemanly Imperialism in China before the First World War

Niels P. Petersson

Considered in the setting of global – or simply international – history, British gentlemanly imperialism was only one among many, not always 'gentlemanly' forms of imperialism.[1] Taking as an example informal imperialism in China before the First World War, this chapter will focus on the interaction of various 'imperialisms', aligned at times nationally, at other times sectorally, and on the concepts that underlie these various forms of imperial expansion.[2] Gentlemanly capitalism could have a perceptible and distinctive effect at the 'point of imperial impact' only if specific factors in the international and peripheral environment were aligned in a certain way. The circumstances under which gentlemanly capitalism could 'filter through' to overseas territories that were not under British rule were very specific and, as will be seen, short-lived.[3]

China before 1905: gentlemanly imperialism on the defensive

The agenda of British gentlemanly imperialism in China as described by Cain and Hopkins was to uphold China's territorial integrity and financial stability. Gentlemanly imperialism was thus bound up with a framework of *informal* European predominance. That framework seemed threatened when power politics and expansionism came to East Asia around 1895 and Russia, France and, fitfully, Germany, pursued policies implying dismemberment, 'pacific penetration', and the creation of spheres of influence.[4] China's weakness and reluctance to embrace reform combined with increasing rivalry amongst the powers created an atmosphere in which British policy came to appear less gentlemanly and more imperialist – despite the very specific interests and motives behind British policy, it was, in method and aim, hardly distinguishable from what other powers did, however different their interests and motives may have been.

The tendencies of these years crystallized in the 1898 'scramble for concessions' (started by Germany's decision to occupy Jiaozhou Bay), in the course of which all the powers acquired railway concessions and naval bases in China. The 'scramble' shows gentlemanly imperialism on the defensive, though rather aggressively: Britain acquired several large railway concessions. These were geographically dispersed so as to prevent the partition of China or the creation of exclusive, commercially closed 'spheres of influence'. But in the heat of battle, this objective was often subordinated to the more immediate one of making a good showing in a game of imperialist rivalry – a situation with a dynamics of its own where structural causation may fail to provide an adequate explanation of the course of events.[5] The crucial initiative in defence of the 'open door' was, interestingly, taken by the United States, not by Britain.

During the scramble, Britain was successful, but in ways not necessarily compatible with the interests of gentlemanly capitalists. Britain's railway concessions had been conceived as private enterprises; China having granted the concessions, the terms for financing, constructing and operating the lines remained to be agreed upon between the Chinese and private investors. But the gentlemanly capitalists of the City were not interested – however desirable railways might be from the point of view of trade, they certainly were not seen as good investment.[6] British policy in China remained on the defensive, and even supported Chinese economic nationalism which appeared as a welcome check on the ambitions of rivals like France with her policy of *pénétration pacifique*. Sir Ernest Satow, British minister in Beijing (1900–06), wrote: 'We have heard a good deal of la conquête paisible de la Chine par le chemin de fer and that is what I am trying to oppose . . . it is necessary for us to be vigilant on behalf of China.' More positively, British diplomats encouraged British railway firms to co-operate, first with each other, and then increasingly with French financiers who showed primarily a financial, not industrial or political, interest in Chinese railways (and therefore could not count on much political support in Paris). In 1905, the Anglo-French railway entente was concluded, supplementing existing co-operation agreements between British and German firms.[7]

On the whole, however, the years around the turn of the century were marked by an aggressive and competitive expansionism which made it difficult to actually exploit the opportunities perceived by gentlemanly capitalists when China's need for foreign capital first became acute in the aftermath of her 1895 defeat. As long as the 'open door' seemed constantly under threat, loans and railway concessions were bound up with rival imperial strategies and their attractiveness from a business point of view remained limited – political influence had to be bought at the price of lower interest rates and/or greater insecurity.

The Boxer Uprising of 1900 and the Russo-Japanese War of 1904–05 considerably modified the international situation as well as conditions within China and thus opened up new possibilities for gentlemanly imperialism. The Boxer intervention can be regarded as the culmination of China's weakness and European interventionism. But instead of toppling the seemingly fragile system of informal European predominance, it served to strengthen it by showing clearly that additional territory or privilege acquired in China would not be easy to digest. Paul Claudel, the French writer and at that time a consular officer in China, said that the most important lesson of the Boxer events was to make everyone understand the 'double impuissance' of both Europe *vis-à-vis* China and China *vis-à-vis* Europe.[8] Russia and Japan, the only powers to pursue openly expansionist policies after the Boxer Rebellion, eventually clashed and exhausted themselves in war. Russian and Japanese expansionism thus was temporarily stopped. As for the other powers, both Germany and France felt their strategic positions in East Asia were weakened and exposed to Japanese threats. The Boxer Rebellion had already taken the expansionist edge out of French and German policy; now, both powers felt that, strategically, they were on the defensive.[9] Thus, at a stroke, several major threats to British interests in China, and to gentlemanly capitalism, had been removed. Once again, it seemed possible to think in terms of an imperialism of free trade and development: 'The focus of competition for advantages in China between the powers now shifted from division to development, and the advance was led by bankers instead of gunboats.'[10]

The Russo-Japanese war also had an important effect upon China – an effect that has been described as a patriotic awakening, and one that was clearly perceived by all the foreigners present in China at that time. A new generation of politically mobilized Chinese were now convinced that an Asian nation could beat a great European power, and that modernization and constitutional government were the road to success.

The golden age of gentlemanly imperialism in China: changing perspectives and changing realities

The years 1905–11 thus became something like the golden age of gentlemanly imperialism in China. A British-inspired programme of foreign-financed infrastructure development (more precisely, railway construction)[11] was the central socioeconomic, political and diplomatic issue during these years. Why was gentlemanly capitalism apparently so successful in imposing its agenda in these years? I think the answer lies in a conjunction of forces and developments at the international and peripheral levels.

To some extent a new departure...

Late in 1905, the Foreign Office under the new Foreign Minister, Sir Edward Grey, embarked upon a comprehensive review of British interests and strategies in China. Until now, Whitehall had, in economic matters, simply supported the demands of the mercantile community, provided they did not collide with political interests.[12] Now, Grey and his collaborators consciously strove to turn into reality a gentlemanly imperialist vision of development, combining considerations of 'high politics' with a programme of economic development and modernization. As a result, Britain's China policy became something like the conscious pursuit of a gentlemanly capitalist agenda. Railways remained a central part of British policy, but there was no longer any need to use them to counter other powers' expansionism; instead, they were conceived of in terms of economic development and political stabilization. The Foreign Office was prepared to support China's efforts to take the development of her railways into her own hands:

> His Majesty's Government will...encourage and welcome [China's] efforts to develop the resources of the country under her own auspices, and on terms which will give her the help of foreign capital and experience when required, without being derogatory to her sovereignty or her independence.[13]

Basically, Grey proposed to offer concessions in practical matters while upholding the imperialist framework built around the 'unequal treaties'.[14] In that sense, Grey was perfectly right in describing his new policy as '*to some extent* a new departure'.[15]

British gentlemanly imperialism

British gentlemanly imperialism in China was distinguished from other forms of expansionism by its comparative breadth of view and perspective. For British diplomats, foreign-financed railway construction was not just a profitable investment or an opportunity to sell the products of heavy industry, it was a development tool – the vehicle of Progress, with a capital 'P'. In the first place, railways would induce economic modernization, facilitating trade and enabling the interior provinces to exploit their mineral resources and to bring to market their agricultural produce. The Chinese would earn more and spend at least part of that on imported European goods and appliances. British diplomats and merchants worked on the assumption that 'every mile of railway adds to the trade of China and to the general good' (the two obviously being more or less synonymous, and equally indispensable for the progress of civilization). They subscribed to the ideology of gentlemanly capitalism as described by Cain and Hopkins – opening up to the world market and setting free market forces is seen as both the means to and the ends of a modernization effort described in terms of the progress of civilization.[16]

British diplomats did not entrust Progress to the intervention of an invisible hand. Railway construction for them was not only to facilitate economic development, but also to create the political conditions under which such a development would be possible. To quote from an FO memorandum written in 1908:

> the tendency of railways must be to make the dismemberment of China more difficult...the power of the Central Government would be much increased, and the country would be more closely knit together and better capable of withstanding foreign aggression and dealing with internal disturbances.[17]

Foreign-financed railway construction thus was expected to start a virtuous circle of economic growth and political stability.

The British were convinced that railways in China, even if formally 'under the control of the Chinese Government' could not be built and operated efficiently – and thus would not be the development tool they were designed to be – without strong European participation: 'the Chinese are by themselves incapable of successfully building and working a considerable railway owing to the immense amount of dishonest profits that would be made during the process.'[18] That explains why the Foreign Office was reluctant to follow up the idea of a 'new departure' with specific proposals to give the Chinese more of a say in the railways they were supposed to build and to pay for.[19] British diplomats supported the principle of 'foreign control of foreign capital' which they saw as indispensable for the success of their liberal development programme and for the maintenance of Chinese financial stability. Furthermore, the Foreign Office wished railway bonds to be attractive to private investors so that China would not depend on politically motivated lenders. It was this reasoning more than a desire to cater to the interests of the HSBC, the 'chosen instrument' of British financial diplomacy in China, that explains the British attitude in railway negotiations. While British diplomats took care of what they saw as the political part of the question, they felt that, as to the rest, 'the financiers may be trusted to know their own interests best'.[20] However, a detailed examination of the close co-operation of British diplomats and HSBC bankers in railway negotiations certainly confirms that British officials and 'gentlemanly capitalists' shared a common outlook and closely co-operated even on the day-to-day evolution of policymaking.

British railway policy in China fused motives and interests from finance, trade and diplomacy into 'a grand development strategy designed by Britain to reshape the world in its own image':[21] China would become strong enough to withstand the pressure of Britain's rivals bent on acquiring territory and commercial privilege; the Beijing government would gain the strength needed to keep in check internal forces opposed to any sort of co-operation with 'imperialism'; China's economy and thus her demand for foreign goods would grow; and multinational railway finance would give other powers a stake in China's development under the auspices of gentlemanly capitalism. Finally, British presence and policy in China would be given special legitimacy by the pursuit of this programme – by promoting railway construction, Britain rose above selfish interests and was doing a service to Civilisation: 'All these railways will make a marvellous difference in China and one feels that one is doing real good in putting them through.'[22] With 'the awakening spirit amongst the Chinese' making it increasingly 'unlikely that railways [would] in the future be utilized as instruments of conquest by any Power', Sir John Jordan, British minister in Beijing (1906–20), and the officials in London felt confident that they could concentrate on development instead of rivalry and seek the co-operation of other powers and of the Chinese government to put into practice the policy of the 'new departure', as it made 'little difference who constructs the railways so long as they are built'.[23]

Co-operative financial imperialism

The success or failure of British gentlemanly imperialism in China now depended on good relations with the other powers, and on the co-operation of China. Let's turn to the powers first, taking as examples those whose bankers and diplomats were the first to align themselves with Britain, *viz.*, France and Germany. How did these two come to join forces with gentlemanly imperialism?

The French government was late in adapting its China policy to a changing situation. In 1905–06, French consular officers had been just as aware of change in China as their British and German colleagues, but apparently their reports did not inspire any new reflections at the diplomatic and policymaking level. Of course, France was not involved in the unresolved financial and commercial issues that forced the other powers to keep their approach up to date, and policymakers had to concentrate their attention on France's highly precarious international position. Thus Jordan expressed a common judgement when he wrote that French policy was 'behind the times and...blind to the changes that are going on in China'.[24] This changed in 1907–08. Diplomatically, the Quai d'Orsay sought to promote accommodation between French interests and those of Britain, Japan and Russia (the 'Far Eastern Agreements' of 1907). In addition, various initiatives that until now had marked French policy in the eyes of foreign observers as one of 'spheres of influence' (despite the formal rejection of that principle by Delcassé as far back as 1899) were abandoned. To name a few, France cut her informal ties to Sun Yat-sen's revolutionaries and concentrated on establishing good relations with the Beijing Government;[25] cut back the funding of schools, post offices and shipping lines designed to prop up her influence in Southern China,[26] and – amid acrimonious self-critique – abandoned an ill-fated attempt to take over the management of China's maritime arsenal in Fuzhou.[27]

Finally, Paris renounced the use of railway policy to generate export opportunities for French heavy industry and employment for the graduates of French schools in China. There was, indeed, no other choice after the failed attempt to prevent the repurchase of the Franco-Belgian Beijing–Hankou railway by China. The Government in Paris had hoped to retain some measure of control over the line and especially over the purchase of railway material, either by renewing the concession or by attaching stringent conditions to a loan that China would need to repurchase the line. But, in the end, a group with purely financial interests formed by the French Banque de l'Indochine and Britain's HSBC lent China the necessary money, without attaching any conditions as to the employment of staff or the purchase of *matériel* from specific European countries. China gained full control of the line, its managements, and its profits.[28] Paris lost the railway, but gained an insight into Chinese intentions and into the effects of competition among European industrial and financial interests.

The Quai d'Orsay adapted its policy to the spirit of the times by focusing on development. The practical problem to solve now was, 'dans quelles conditions on arriverait à favoriser l'essor d'un grand mouvement à la fois industriel et commercial, développant réellement les ressources latentes, au profit de ceux qui se consacreront à une pareille tâche'. Much against her will, France had had to abandon hopes of gaining cultural influence and protected industrial markets through railway construction in China; her new policy in China now would be a financial imperialism based on the strength of the Paris capital market, international *détente* and co-operation, and China's insatiable need for loans: 'c'est en somme l'argent qui serait la marchandise la plus demandée [en Chine], celle que l'on pourrait importer avec le plus de profit.'[29]

The French became possible partners for British gentlemanly imperialism after being forced by developments within China, by a changing international situation and by the internal contradictions of the policies hitherto pursued to reject policies incompatible with British aims. French bankers, diplomats, and policymakers did not, however, share the world view and structural base of gentlemanly imperialism. French policy was not a development strategy; it tried to provide small investors with safe investment opportunities under European control. Financial imperialism was, for the French, chiefly a way of using the joint pressure of the powers to improve the conditions for capital exports to China.

German policy was again very different. Like the British, the Germans clearly perceived China's new economic nationalism and the impossibility of imposing their demands by force, and, again like the British, they felt that flexibility and a conciliatory attitude were called for. Minister Alfons von Mumm recommended that Germany withdraw from power politics in East Asia and concentrate on economic interests.[30] This implied, on the one hand, developing the trust and sympathy he felt were needed to promote German commercial interests, and, on the other hand, creating European solidarity to keep in check Chinese economic nationalism.[31] German policy more or less followed these recommendations.[32]

Thus, Germany succeeded in shaking off the image of the 'most hated power in China' that she had acquired by seizing Jiaozhou and starting off the 'scramble'. German industry, being competitive and well served by agents on the ground and active merchants, demanded only to be spared political complications.[33] The role of diplomacy under these circumstances was chiefly to remind the Chinese periodically of the fact that Germany did *not* seek to intervene in transactions between German industry and her Chinese customers, be they private or official.[34] China's decision to adopt a Krupp canon as her army's standard equipment was facilitated not by German diplomatic lobbying, but by the ostentatious abstention of German diplomats from joining their colleagues in adverse comment on political and administrative developments in China.[35] Schools and cultural initiatives were to play a supporting role in this export-centred policy relying on advertising rather than power politics.[36]

The most important effects of Berlin's new policy were felt in loan matters. Being prepared to offer railway loans with only minimal requirements as to the employment and powers of European executive personnel, the Deutsch-Asiatische Bank managed to establish itself among the leading European banks in China and decisively undermined the principle of 'foreign control for foreign capital' defended by the other banks. For that, minister Count Rex felt entitled to the 'sincere thankfulness of all politically aware Chinese'. Jordan angrily noted that his German colleague sometimes acted 'almost more Chinese than the Chinese themselves'. One can, however, be sure that he did so rather reluctantly and for purely tactical reasons.[37]

Concentrating on purely economic aims[38] implied, for German diplomacy, a readiness to meet China's wishes, an unfaltering opportunism, and the search for short-term economic advantage over Germany's rivals and partners. It also implied a complete – and sometimes conscious – neglect of long-term perspectives. Rex, for example, demanded to 'create interests' in China in times of disorder and insecurity, in a typical way regarding 'interests' as justifications for claims to influence, and not influence as a means to promote interests.[39] German financiers of course were more cautious than Count Rex – after all, it was their money that diplomats wanted to convert not into profit, but into political influence, which paid no dividend. Thus, there was no common ideology shared by financiers and officials in Germany as there was in Britain. However, even German financiers did not develop the long-term considerations that are so prominent in British bankers' concern for the creditworthiness and financial stability of China.[40] There was virtually no reflection in Germany on the conditions for development in China or on the role European capital could be assigned in that process.

While the French sacrificed the interests of industrial exporters to those of financial imperialism, the Germans pursued a strategy based on the industrial exporter's characteristic short-term orientation. The long-term issues of interest to financiers and investors who would tie up their money for decades hardly received any attention. Having given up power politics – in response to strategic considerations, but also to public opinion which judged Jiaozhou a failure – and seeking export markets, the Germans were potential partners for gentlemanly imperialism. But, like the French, they did not share the basic assumptions of gentlemanly capitalism, and their policy was motivated by different considerations and supported by different forces.

With the abatement of great power rivalry, in the words of René Girault, 'le partage des affaires' became a more attractive prospect than 'le partage du monde', and modernization and development came to play a central role in European imperialism in East Asia. The industrial exports of Germany and capital exports of France depended on rapid infrastructure modernization in China. The British knew that economic growth and political stability in independent Asian states diminished strategic threats and allowed the integration of Asia into an order of international political and economic relations with London as the global financial centre. French adaptation to the spirit of the times, German weakness and opportunism, China's 'awakening', and Russia's and Japan's paralysis resulted in 'co-operative financial imperialism' (the term is Jürgen Osterhammel's), the international framework within which Britain could pursue the development programme of gentlemanly imperialism.[41]

The periphery: railway imperialism

Foreign-financed railway construction[42] became the most important aspect of China's economic modernization in the early twentieth century, whether viewed from the perspective of European diplomacy and finance or from that of Chinese domestic politics and political economy. In China, the central government, local elites and intellectuals saw railway construction as a tool of economic growth and national regeneration, though these groups sharply differed on who should build, finance and control China's railways. The powers meanwhile wished to develop the concessions acquired in 1898 and to start further railway projects. In 1899–1911, China raised £30.7m worth of foreign loans, 90 per cent of which was for railway construction. Nearly all of China's railways in operation before 1949 were built in these years.[43] During the years 1906–09, multilateral agreements involving China,

Britain, France, Germany, and, later, also the USA were concluded for the European-financed construction of five major Chinese railway lines. The chief issue in the negotiations preceding these agreements was described by one of the protagonists, Charles Addis of Britain's Hongkong Bank (HSBC), as that of reconciling 'the conflicting claims of China for the Chinese and foreign control for foreign capital'.[44] Competition between different European financial, political and industrial interests set free by the retreat of power politics forced European diplomats and bankers to compromise on several important points, including the control lenders could exercise over construction, operation, and, most importantly, purchase of *matériel*. By renouncing some of the privileges extracted by force during the 'scramble', the Europeans transformed their concessions into real and potentially profitable businesses, while China obtained foreign capital on terms acceptable even to some of her more patriotic statesmen. Jordan described the process as follows: 'Chinese aspirations for more liberal treatment could no longer be disregarded...Chinese public opinion...rendered necessary a choice between two alternatives, namely, further concessions on our part or indefinite delay of railway expansion...the first of these alternatives was adopted.'[45]

From the beginning, the gentlemanly imperialist vision of development had implied some readiness to compromise with peripheral interests, though in practice intra-European competition and Chinese resistance had been necessary to achieve it. Anyway, the curious mixture of imperialism, world market integration, and modernization which made up the development programme of gentlemanly imperialism in practice meant that market forces and financial considerations at least in day-to-day matters gradually took precedence over imperialist privilege guaranteed by treaty. While the imperialist framework of course remained in place, it could in practice no longer be used to exact tangible privileges.

Once European bankers and diplomats had defined their interests in a way compatible with gentlemanly imperialism and international co-operation had developed, 'peripheral' factors were of primary importance for the success of gentlemanly imperialism. The peripheral partners for co-operative financial imperialism in China were to be found in the central government in Beijing which needed railways to strengthen its position *vis-à-vis* provincial governments, to raise revenue and to promote economic development. China's authoritarian, centralist modernizers and the powers practising co-operative financial imperialism were natural allies.[46] But could the programme of foreign-financed railway construction be made acceptable to provincial elites and the general public who adhered to the doctrine of 'civilized anti-foreignism' and wanted to keep strategic assets such as industry and railways out of foreign reach?[47] The fate of the Huguang railway loan agreement may serve to illustrate the influence of such peripheral factors. This loan was sought by Chinese statesmen on their own initiative and on their own terms, in order to finance the construction of the important line Guangzhou–Hankou–Chengdu. It represented 'the crystallization of a new policy toward China'.[48] It also brought into being a banking consortium uniting all the relevant banks and supported by the major powers. Its terms granted China unprecedented freedom from control over the funds she borrowed. Its fate shows the limits of the gentlemanly imperialist development programme.[49]

With the Huguang loan, the Europeans hoped, China was binding herself to those powers who were interested in her economic development instead of hindering her progress through territorial ambitions, as the German *chargé* Count Luxburg put it.[50] In order to implement the railway policy agreed upon with the powers, the Beijing government in May 1911 seized control over all major railway lines hitherto controlled by provincial interests and private investors. This was, for Jordan, 'beyond doubt the boldest and most statesmanlike pronouncement that the Chinese Government has made on any question of policy in recent years'.[51] It was also, as Jordan and at least some Chinese ministers knew, highly risky.[52] In the end, provincial opposition forces found in the central government's railway policy the long-awaited issue necessary to fuse all kinds of grievances into a revolutionary movement, so that a localized army uprising could turn into a revolution toppling the Qing dynasty. Foreign-financed railway construction, far from securing Beijing's authority and spurring on economic development, led to the downfall of that government and to a period of instability which was as harmful to China's international position as to her economic prospects.

This also meant the end of the 'golden age' of gentlemanly imperialism. The conditions on which co-operative financial imperialism had depended now gradually eroded. While negotiating about a £25m 'reorganization loan', the powers were still nominally bound to co-operate and to seek a solution which would achieve both the long-term financial stabilization of China and the protection of the lenders' interests. Britain was especially active in pursuing this policy which aimed at preserving the gentlemanly-imperialist framework and reintegrating the new regime into it as smoothly as possible. But the desperate need of Chinese administrations at all levels for money created tempting opportunities for concession-hunting and for the acquisition of exclusive privilege, in the face of which co-operation among the powers was not easily preserved. The Quai d'Orsay, for example, secretly supported the shady Banque Industrielle de Chine which sought to obtain industrial concessions in China by offering loans on (financially) easy terms and thus broke the ranks of the consortium enjoying the official support of the powers, including France. The German foreign ministry meanwhile turned a blind eye to the activity of commercial firms like Carlowitz & Co. who gave local Chinese administrations large 'advances', supposedly to finance future purchases of machinery. While France and Germany thus undermined stabilization efforts by an opportunistic search for short-term industrial or financial success, the Foreign Office's struggle to preserve the existing system by giving exclusive support to the HSBC and firmly discouraging rival financial institutions from providing China with alternative sources of money came under increasing domestic criticism: the HSBC was denounced as being under the influence of German interests, and industrialists and financiers alike complained about being barred from competing for business in China. As to China, she now clearly lacked the minimum of strength and stability necessary for integration into the framework of co-operative financial imperialism.[53]

Thus, nationalism and protectionism became increasingly prominent not only in China but in Europe as well. The result was a revival of policies pursued before 1900 – policies that were generated by 'ungentlemanly' forces such as greedy merchants, disreputable financiers and protectionist industrialists; that were directed towards 'ungentlemanly' aims incompatible with political stability, sound finance, and the 'open door'; and conducted in an 'ungentlemanly' manner, involving bribes, diplomatic pressure, reckless lending, short-termism. The 'golden age' of gentlemanly imperialism came to an end, and, by early 1914, things had partially reverted to where they had been in the last years of the nineteenth century: British gentlemanly capitalism now was but one force among others and could no longer set the overall course for European imperialism, while, at the same time, facing the disintegration of a regime in China which had been both able and willing to co-operate with gentlemanly capitalism. This suggests that gentlemanly imperialism demanded too much from China: based as it was on long-term considerations, it had much stronger domestic policy implications for the society subjected to it than had other forms of Western domination. No wonder then that gentlemanly imperialism relied on an authoritarian government and on the stifling of forces demanding greater democracy and government accountability.[54] The gentlemanly-imperialist development programme failed because the market-based relationships proposed to substitute for more openly imperialist ones were just as unpopular in China as imperialism itself and because most powers were only temporarily prepared to co-operate with a policy they clearly saw as merely a second-best solution.[55]

Conclusion

British gentlemanly imperialism had to operate within a three-level structure. 1) *Metropolitan*. European governments, banks and companies pursued their own strategies resulting from the alignment of various domestic forces with their own specific agendas and outlook. 2) *International*. At the international level, these forces competed and sometimes co-operated with forces emanating from other countries; their alignment opened up possibilities for expansion or set limits to it. 3) *Peripheral*. Social, political, economic and cultural forces on the periphery favoured or hindered certain forms of imperial expansion.

The interplay of forces at these three levels only rarely allowed for strategies defined in one place to filter through unaltered, or for metropolitan forces like gentlemanly capitalism to have a clearly distinguishable influence on global history. Only during the years 1905–11 did gentlemanly imperialism manage to give direction to the forces at the international level and seem to find partners on the periphery. Just as Britain had been forced to behave more imperialistically and in a less gentlemanly manner during the 'scramble' and after 1911, France and Germany were, in these years, more or less left with co-operative financial imperialism as the only possible policy under prevailing circumstances. In order to get a clear picture of the forces interacting in the shaping of 'global history', we need an international or transnational history of empire. Cain and Hopkins have recently suggested a perspective which might be useful in this respect: they proposed to distinguish 'structural power' (establishing processes, building structures and disseminating values) from 'relational power' (direct influence on specific decision-making processes).[56] Asking which forces shape structures and procedures and how strong structures and procedures are as opposed to relations may help us internationalize the history of imperialism.

British policy within the framework of co-operative financial imperialism was distinguished from that of other powers by the conscious pursuit of 'structural power'.[57] Gentlemanly imperialism implied an ideology that defined and at the same time legitimized a European role in Asia. European and Asian interests, modernization, the market, and imperialism were described as sensibly related to each other and as parts of a coherent whole. Such an outlook – however eurocentric or hypocritical it may appear today – was at least capable of guiding action and adaptation in a way that cruder expansionist ideologies were not. It supported a policy directed, in a very modern way, at securing 'global leadership on the cheap' by holding out the promise of prosperity through free markets.[58] Increasingly, such a policy had to be pursued in the face of a – likewise very 'modern' – resistance against a world order dominated by the market and by Western ideas and values. Here, the notion of 'structural power' helps us to see that this resistance was not only, as has frequently been asserted, the beginning of a global 'revolt against the West',[59] but also the expression of forces *within* the West opposed to free trade, finance, liberalism, internationalism, and the rules and procedures required to uphold them. In this respect, the extent to which the influence of gentlemanly capitalist interests on British policy and their overall success depended upon forces from outside Europe like the United States deserves further study. At any rate, the forces responsible for the failure of European co-operative financial imperialism in China are, to a significant extent, the same that, on the level of global history, brought about the collapse of the pre-1914 European world order – nationalism, protectionism, a general dissatisfaction with a liberal world order, and a widespread readiness to seek to exploit, rather than reform, this order's contradictions.

Notes

1 I thank Professor Lynn Zastoupil for his comments on the style as well as the substance of an earlier draft of this paper, and Professors Peter J. Cain and Antony G. Hopkins for their comments on the version presented at the conference.

2 For the concept of 'imperialisms', see R. Girault, *Diplomatie européenne et impérialismes* (Paris, 1979), 148, 177f.; W.J. Mommsen, 'Europäischer Finanzimperialismus vor 1914. Ein Beitrag zu einer pluralistischen Theorie des Imperialismus', in: W.J. Mommsen, *Der europäische Imperialismus. Aufsätze und Abhandlungen* (Göttingen, 1979), 85–148; also B. Barth, 'Internationale Geschichte und europäische Expansion: Die Imperialismen des 19. Jahrhunderts', in: W. Loth and J. Osterhammel (eds), *Internationale Geschichte. Themen – Ergebnisse – Aussichten* (Munich, 2000), 309–27.

3 For the purpose of this paper it may be useful to distinguish gentlemanly capitalism, a specific alignment of social forces characteristic of British society, from gentlemanly imperialism, the specific expansionist movement based on these forces.

4 P.J. Cain and A.G. Hopkins, *British Imperialism*, Vol. 1: *Innovation and Expansion, 1688–1914* (London/New York, 1993), 424. For a general overview, see J. Osterhammel, *China und die Weltgesellschaft. Vom 18. Jahrhundert bis in unsere Zeit* (Munich, 1989); J. Osterhammel, 'Britain and China, 1842–1914', in A. Porter (ed.), *The Oxford History of the British Empire*, Vol. III: *The Nineteenth Century* (Oxford/New York, 1999), 146–69. For issues concerning the powers and problems of modernization in China, see my *Imperialismus und Modernisierung. Siam, China und die europäischen Mächte, 1895–1914* (Munich, 2000).

5 For the diplomacy of the 'scramble', see B. Barth, *Die deutsche Hochfinanz und die Imperialismen. Banken und Außenpolitik vor 1914* (Stuttgart, 1995); E.W. Edwards, *British Diplomacy and Finance in China, 1895–1914* (Oxford, 1987); G. Kurgan-Van Hentenryk, *Léopold II et les groupes financiers belges en Chine: La politique royale et ses prolongements, 1895–1914* (Brussels, 1972); E-tu Zen Sun, *Chinese Railways and British Interests, 1898–1911* (New York, 2nd ed. 1971); L.K. Young, *British Policy in China, 1895–1902* (Cambridge, MA, 1968).

6 Edwards, *Diplomacy*; Lee En-han, *China's Quest for Railway Autonomy, 1904–1911: a Study of the Chinese Railway-Rights Recovery Movement* (Singapore, 1977); Sun, *Chinese Railways*.

7 Satow to Lansdowne, 22.5.1905, Public Record Office, London (PRO), 30/33/14/13; Edwards, *Diplomacy*, 59–65 and ch. 4.

8 Paul Claudel, *Sous le signe du dragon*, Paris 1957 (6th ed.), 128.

9 Memo Defence of Indo-China (1904), Archives Nationales-Centre des Archives d'Outre-Mer, Gouvernement Général de l'Indochine, 26673; *cf.* the report by the German military attaché in Paris, 13.8.1904, Bundesarchiv Berlin, China 72; Satow to Lansdowne, 14.4.1905, PRO FO 17/1671; N.P. Petersson, *Deutsche Weltpolitik in der französischen Einflußsphäre. Deutsche und französische Aktivitäten in Südchina*, M.A.-thesis Tübingen 1994, 87–9. For Germany: W. Stingl, *Der Ferne Osten in der deutschen Politik vor dem Ersten Weltkrieg (1902–1914)*, 2 vols (Frankfurt, 1978), 460–90, 502 f., 531; U. Ratenhof, *Die Chinapolitik des Deutschen Reiches von 1871 bis 1945. Chinas Erneuerung, Großmachtrivalitäten in Ostasien und deutsches Weltmachtstreben* (Boppard, 1987), 197, 209; K. Hildebrand, *Das vergangene Reich. Deutsche Außenpolitik von Bismarck bis Hitler 1871–1945* (Stuttgart, 1995), 236 ff.

10 Edwards, *Diplomacy*, 59–65 and ch. 4; E.W. Edwards, 'The Far Eastern Agreements of 1907', in: *Journal of Modern History* XXVI (1954), 340–55; K. Hildebrand, 'Europäisches Zentrum, überseeische Peripherie und neue Welt. Über den Wandel des europäischen Staatensystems zwischen dem Berliner Kongreß (1878) und dem Pariser Frieden (1919–20)', in: *Historische Zeitschrift* 249 (1989), 53–94; Hildebrand, *Reich*, 222–7, 241 ff.; Ratenhof, *Chinapolitik*, 201 ff., 226 ff.; G. Rozman (ed.), *The Modernization of China* (New York/London, 1981), 226 (quotation).

11 On railway diplomacy in China, see Barth, *Hochfinanz*; D. Brötel, *Frankreich im Fernen Osten. Imperialistische Expansion in Siam und Malaya, Laos und China, 1880–1904*, Stuttgart, 1996; Edwards, *Diplomacy*; F.H.H. King, *The History of the Hongkong and Shanghai Banking Corporation*, 4 vols., Cambridge/New York 1988/89; Lee, *Railway Autonomy*; Sun, *Chinese Railways*; C.B. Davis, 'Railway

Imperialism in China, 1895–1939', in: C.B. Davis/K.E.Wilburn, Jr. (eds), *Railway Imperialism*, New York/Westport/London 1991, 155–74; Hou Chiming, *Foreign Investment and Economic Development in China, 1840–1937*, Cambridge, MA, 1965; R.W. Huenemann, *The Dragon and the Iron Horse: the Economics of Railroads in China, 1876–1937*, Cambridge, MA, 1984. My *Imperialismus und Modernisierung* offers a somewhat more detailed overview and more references than can be given here.

12 Nathan A. Pelcovits, *Old China Hands and the Foreign Office* (New York, 1948). The 'new departure' implied a strong rejection of the views of 'treaty port society' described in R. Bickers, *Britain in China: Community, Culture and Colonialism, 1900–1949* (Manchester/New York, 1999).

13 Grey to Jordan, 7.8.1906, 31.8.1906, PRO FO 371/35.

14 For an overview, see A. Feuerwerker, 'The Foreign Presence in China', in: *Cambridge History of China*, vol. 12, 128–207; J. Osterhammel, 'Semi-Colonialism and Informal Empire in Twentieth-Century China: towards a framework of analysis', in: W.J. Mommsen and J. Osterhammel (eds), *Imperialism and After. Continuities and Discontinuities* (London, 1986), 290–314.

15 Grey to Jordan, 31.8.1906, PRO FO 371/35 (my emphasis). The 'new departure' must be seen in the context of a change of government, a general reappraisal of foreign policy perspectives (A.J.P. Taylor, *The Struggle for Mastery in Europe (1848–1918)* (London, 1957), 427 ff., 438, 437 f.), and a change of diplomatic representatives in Beijing all happening simultaneously. A limited 'new departure' in British policy can be found, at the same time, in India and Egypt as well: R. Hyam, *Britain's Imperial Century, 1815–1915: a Study of Empire and Expansion* (Basingstoke, 2nd ed. 1993), 266–72.

16 Jordan to Campbell, 4.2.1909, PRO FO 350/5. The basic goals of British railway policy in China are described in: Memo Railways in China, 16.1.1908, PRO FO 371/418. See also Edwards, *Diplomacy*, and, for a colonial context, M. Adas, *Machines as the Measure of Men: Science, Technology and Ideology of Western Dominance* (Ithaca, 1989), 222; H. Sieberg, *Colonial Development. Die Grundlegung moderner Entwicklungspolitik durch Großbritannien, 1919–1949* (Stuttgart, 1985); M. Havinden and D. Meredith, *Colonialism and Development: Britain and Its Tropical Colonies, 1850–1960* (London, 1993), 99–111. 'Ideology' is used here in the sense implied by M.H. Hunt's contribution to 'A Roundtable: Explaining the History of American Foreign Relations', in: *Journal of American History* 77 (1990).

17 Memo Railways in China, 16.1.1908, PRO FO 371/418.

18 Ibid. and Jordan to Campbell, 23.7.1908, 17.9.1908, 5.10.1908, PRO FO 350/5.

19 For a short summary of debates on this point within British officialdom, see Jordan to Campbell, 6.8.1908, PRO FO 350/5.

20 D.C.M. Platt, *Finance, Trade and Politics in British Foreign Policy, 1815–1914* (Oxford, 1968), 299. Quotation: Jordan to Campbell, 23.7.1908, PRO FO 350/5.

21 Cain/Hopkins, *British Imperialism*, 23–46 (quotation 46).

22 Jordan to Campbell, 5.3.1908, PRO FO 350/5.

23 For the use of railways as strategic tools, see R. Robinson's introduction and conclusion in Davis and Wilburn, *Railway Imperialism*, esp. 1, 192. See also Edwards, *Diplomacy*, 69, 75, 125. Quotations: Jordan to Grey, 7.10.1909, FO 350/6; Robinson, *Railway Imperialism*, 4.

24   Taylor, *Struggle*, 438–41; Instructions for the new French minister in Beijing, E. Bapst, 3.3.1906, Ministère des Affaires Etrangères (MAE) NS Chine 198; Brötel, *Frankreich*, 570–5; Jordan to Grey, 30.5.1907, PRO FO 371/231; Jordan to Campbell, 24.6.1908, 29.10.1908 (quotation), PRO FO 350/5.

25   J.G. Barlow, *Sun Yat-sen and the French, 1900–1908* (Berkeley, 1979), 67 ff., 77 ff.; M.-C. Bergère, *Sun Yat-sen* (Paris, 1994), 199–215; J.K. Mulholland, 'The French Connection that Failed: France and Sun Yat-Sen, 1900–1908', in: *Journal of Asian Studies* 31 (1972), 77–95, here 90 ff.

26   Beauvais to Pichon, 25.5.1908, MAE NS Chine 219. For more on the change of French strategy in South China in 1907/1908, see Petersson, *Weltpolitik*, 103–7.

27   Petersson, *Imperialismus und Modernisierung*, 233 ff.; Bourgeois to Pichon, 28.2.1907, 28.9.1907; Bourgeois to Bapst, 9.7.1907, MAE NS Chine 634.

28   Brötel, *Frankreich*, 553–8, 571–579; Edwards, *Diplomacy*, 115–22; King, *Hongkong Bank*, 388–94; Kurgan-Van Hentenryk, *Léopold II*, 616–63, 737–46; Lee, *Railway Autonomy*, 219–23; M. Meuleau, *Des Pionniers en Extrême-Orient. Histoire de la Banque de l'Indochine, 1875–1975* (Paris, 1990), 225–8; Sun, *Chinese Railways*, 137–41; Bapst to Pichon, 20.3.1908, MAE NS Chine 200; Jordan to Campbell, 3.4.1909, 24.6.1909, PRO FO 350/5; Memo railway negotiations, 27.4.1908, MAE NS Chine 448.

29   Memo Hankeou Pékin, 20.12.1908, MAE NS Chine 200; Memo entreprises financières en Chine, Dec. 1908, MAE NS Chine 345; Girault, *Diplomatie européenne*, 190 f., 193 f. This 'modernization' of French imperialism is completed with the 1908 reorientation and not, as R.S. Lee suggests in *France and the Exploitation of China, 1885–1901: a Study in Economic Imperialism* (Hongkong/Oxford/New York, 1989), 267–74, with Delcassé's rejection in 1899 of the most contradictory aspects of the strategies pursued by his predecessor Hanotaux.

30   Mumm to Bülow, 29.7.1905, Auswärtiges Amt, Politisches Archiv, Bonn/Berlin) AA China 1/55; military report no. 84, 20.12.1905, AA China 1/57c. Mumm's further reflections on the political situation in East Asia are to be found in a private letter to Chancellor Bülow (3.6.1905, AA China 22/15). See also a report by military attaché v. Claer (27.9.1904, AA China 22/13). For the new departure in German China policy, see also Ratenhof, *Chinapolitik*, 169–227; Stingl, *Der Ferne Osten*, 383–431.

31   Mumm to Bülow, 8.1.1906, AA China 1/58; 10.2.1906, AA China 1/59; 13.4.1905, AA China 22/14; 14.8.1905, AA China 22/15.

32   Memo v. Brandt, 13.2.1906, AA China 1/57c.

33   This policy was based on strategic considerations which seemed to imply, for a time, the conclusion of a triple alliance consisting of Germany, China and the USA. The exploitation of China was somehow supposed to be compatible with an alliance. For this, see Stingl, *Der Ferne Osten*, 614 ff.

34   See, for example, Buri to Bülow, 14.12.1907, AA China 4/16; Rex to Bülow, 8.11.1909, AA China 1/70.

35   The 'gun question' was the reason why Germany did not join Britain and the US in protests against the dismissal of Yuan Shikai in January 1909: Petersson, *Imperialismus und Modernisierung*, 249 f.

36   O. Franke, 'Die deutsch-chinesische Hochschule in Tsingtau, ihre Vorgeschichte, ihre Einrichtung und ihre Aufgaben', in: O. Franke, *Ostasiatische Neubildungen*.

Beiträge zum Verständnis der politischen und kulturellen Entwicklungsvorgänge im Fernen Osten (Hamburg, 1911), 200–17; F. Kreissler, *L'action culturelle allemande en Chine. De la fin du XIXe siècle à la Seconde Guerre mondiale* (Paris, 1989), 65, 127–71; K. Mühlhahn, *Herrschaft und Widerstand in der 'Musterkolonie' Kiautschou. Interaktion zwischen China und Deutschland, 1897–1914* (Munich, 2000), 236–55; Stingl, *Der Ferne Osten*, 601–9.

37   Rex to Bülow, 25.3.1909, AA China 4/19; Rex to Bülow, 4.4.1907, 9.4.1907, 16.4.1907, AA China 4/3; 21.5.1907, 3.6.1909, AA China 4/20; Jordan to Campbell, 17.4.1907, PRO FO 350/4; Jordan to Grey, 1.6.1907, PRO FO 371/313; 1.1.1910, PRO FO 371/866.

38   Stingl, *Der Ferne Osten*, 611.

39   Knipping to Bethmann Hollweg, 15.11.1910; Rex to Bethmann Hollweg, 28.11.1910, AA China 1/74; Barth, *Hochfinanz*, 300, 405–8.

40   Barth, *Hochfinanz*, 153 ff, 290 f.

41   Girault, *Diplomatie européenne*, 177–94; Cain and Hopkins, *British Imperialism*, 148–60; Osterhammel, *China*, 223.

42   On railway diplomacy, see the works listed in note 11 above.

43   Hou, *Foreign Investment*, 24 f., 29. For John Jordan, railways were 'a positive obsession': Jordan to Campbell, 6.8.1908, PRO FO 350/5.

44   Quoted in R.A. Dayer, *Finance and Empire: Sir Charles Addis, 1861–1945* (London, 1988), 53. The terms of these agreements are analyzed in King, *Hongkong Bank*, 345–51 and Osterhammel, *China*, 214–21. All important agreements are printed in J.V.A. MacMurray, *Treaties and Agreements with and Concerning China, 1894–1919*, 2 vols. (New York, 1921). The lines concerned were three concessions dating from the 1898 scramble (Guangzhou–Hongkong, British; Tianjin–Pukou, British–German; Shanghai–Ningbo, British); the already operating line Beijing–Hankow (Belgian–French) repurchased by the Chinese government with a foreign loan; finally the lines Guangzhou–Hankow and Hankow–Chengdu (Huguang-railways) for which no concession agreement existed.

45   Jordan to Grey, 26.3.1909, PRO FO 371/636.

46   Hou, *Foreign Investment*, 31–49; King, *Hongkong Bank*, 434; Lee, *Railway Autonomy*, 208 f.; Mommsen, 'Finanzimperialismus', 89, 91, 99; Osterhammel, *China*, 207–26.

47   Robinson, 'Conclusion', 175. For the term 'civilized anti-foreignism', see Lee, *Railway Autonomy*.

48   Sun, *Chinese Railways*, 90.

49   On the other hand, there remained imperialist privileges, such as the stipulation to employ engineers of a certain nationality. And the railway loans were parts of strategies of imperial expansion, even after many of the imperialist teeth had been drawn. King, *Hongkong Bank*, 434; Hou, *Foreign Investment*, 31–49; Osterhammel, *China*, 207–26.

50   Luxburg to Bethmann Hollweg, 1.5.1911, AA China 4/26. For the context, see Jordan to Grey, 10.3.1911, 13.4.1911, 20.4.1911; Addis to FO, 19.4.1911; Addis to Grey, 19.4.1911, PRO FO 371/1080; Luxburg to Bethmann Hollweg, 8.4.1911, AA China 4/26.

51   Jordan to Grey, 10.5.1911, PRO FO 371/1080; Jordan to Campbell, 24.5.1911, 24.7.1911, PRO FO 350/7. For the loan agreement and related documents, see MacMurray, *Treaties*, 866–99.

52 Jordan to Grey, 22.5.1911, PRO FO 371/1080; Jordan to Campbell, 22.4.1911, 15.5.1911, PRO FO 350/7; Jordan to Grey, 18.9.1911, PRO FO 371/1081. The perception of risk and importance of timing are also stressed by J.H. Fincher, *Chinese Democracy: the Self-Government Movement in Local, Provincial, and National Politics, 1905–1914* (London/Canberra, 1981), 116.

53 For a more detailed account of the disintegration of co-operative financial imperialism in China, see my *Imperialismus und Modernisierung*, ch. 8.

54 For the weakness of the 'collaborators', see Sun, *Chinese Railways*, 113–19; S.A.M. Adshead, *Province and Politics in Late Imperial China: Viceregal Government in Szechwan, 1898–1911* (London/Malmö, 1984), 84. For evidence from the German side, see Rex to Bethmann Hollweg, 25.10.1910, AA China 1/73; 3.2.1910, 4.2.1910, AA China 4/23; 7.1.1911, AA China 1/74; 7.1.1911; Luxburg to Bethmann Hollweg, 26.5.1911, AA China 4/26. As to the extent of the modernization programme, see D.R. Headrick, *The Tentacles of Progress: Technology Transfer in the Age of Imperialism, 1850–1914* (New York, 1988); King, *Hongkong Bank*, 382, 251–6; Mommsen, 'Finanzimperialismus', 91, 99.

55 The aversion of Chinese Reformers across the political spectrum to capitalism is described by Chi Wen-Shun, *Ideological Conflicts in Modern China: Democracy and Authoritarianism* (New Brunswick, 2nd ed. 1992), 293 f., 325 and J.E. Schrecker, *The Chinese Revolution in Historical Perspective* (New York, 1991), 124.

56 P.J. Cain and A.G. Hopkins, 'Afterword: the Theory and Practice of British Imperialism', in: R.E. Dumett (ed.), *Gentlemanly Capitalism and British Imperialism: the New Debate on Empire* (London/New York, 1999), 196–220, here 204 f.

57 Sir Eyre Crowe explicitly says so in his famous 1907 memorandum: Britain, he argued, had to pursue a policy '[that] is so directed as to harmonize with the general desires and ideals common to all mankind and . . . is closely identified with the primary and vital interests of a majority, or as many as possible, of the other nations': *British Documents on the Origins of the War 1898–1914*, ed. by G.P. Gooch and H. Temperley (reprint: New York, 1967), vol. 3, 357–420, here 402 f.

58 Of course, a socially dominant position of gentlemanly capitalism is the background to explaining this attitude. Quotation: J. Sachs, 'Global Capitalism: Making It Work', in: *The Economist*, 12.9.1998, 21–5.

59 Just a sample: L. Woolf, *Imperialism and Civilisation* (London, 1928), 13 f., 65 ff.; G. Barraclough, *An Introduction to Contemporary History* (Harmondsworth, 1967); I. Clark, *Globalization and Fragmentation: International Relations in the Twentieth Century* (Oxford, 1997), 12 ff.

7
British Imperialism and Decolonization: a Chinese Perspective

Shunhong Zhang

Historians of different opinions have showed great interest in P.J. Cain and A.G. Hopkins's two volumes, *British Imperialism: Innovation and Expansion 1688–1914*, and *British Imperialism: Crisis and Deconstruction 1914–1990*, since their publication in 1993. Many reviews with comments for and against Cain and Hopkins's concept of gentlemanly capitalism and interpretation of British imperialism have appeared. The most comprehensive response so far has been the collective work entitled *Gentlemanly Capitalism and British Imperialism*, which includes eight essays and a general introduction by the editor commenting on Cain and Hopkins's arguments. This study work also includes an afterword by Cain and Hopkins themselves.[1] It seems that 'gentlemanly capitalism' is becoming a viable concept in the historical debate on British imperialism, despite the ambiguity surrounding its connotation. Cain and Hopkins's books, however, have not yet attracted much attention from historians in China: as far as I know, no review has appeared in a Chinese-language publication. In this chapter, I shall comment on Cain and Hopkins's *British Imperialism* and elaborate some of my own ideas on British imperialism and decolonization.

The merits of the Cain–Hopkins thesis

The two volumes, which are now available in a new, consolidated edition, are an extension of the authors' previous articles, and present the theory of 'gentlemanly capitalism' in great detail. In reviewing Cain and Hopkins's study, D.K. Fieldhouse offered the following concise summary:

The main argument of the two earlier articles and these two books can therefore, crudely, be summed up in two propositions. First, the central fact of modern British economic development was less indus- trialization than the emergence of a financial and services sector which, unlike manufacturing, for long dominated the international economy and continued, or at least tried, to do so even after Britain had ceased to be a leading industrial power during the early twenti- eth century. Second, this sector was controlled by a network of capi- talists and those in the higher reaches of the public and services sectors, all of whom inherited and exemplified a code of conduct which had been established by the landed aristocracy and gentry. These gentlemanly capitalists dominated public policy, including international relations, because there was no division between busi- ness GCs (Gentlemanly Capitalists) and those in government who made policy decisions. Overseas imperialism expressed a consensual world view of the governing class.[2]

This summary gives a general idea of the books. Here only a few points need to be added. According to Cain and Hopkins, imperial expansion was promoted or determined by metropolitan forces. 'Gentlemanly capitalism' was the most dominant force in Britain and the most decisive factor in the policymaking of British imperial expan- sion. The interests of the 'gentlemanly capitalists' were the priority of governments in formulating British overseas policy. The interests of manufacturers would be sacrificed if they were inconsistent with those of the gentlemanly capitalists. Where a choice had to be made, 'gentle- manly interests invariably took precedence'.[3] The making of British overseas policies was mainly decided by the gentlemanly elite, not by industrial capitalists, as historians have long argued. Industrial capital- ism was never a dominant force in British policymaking. In the late nineteenth and early twentieth centuries, when British manufacturing industries underwent a decline, gentlemanly capitalism grew rapidly. Given that gentlemanly capitalism dominated the policy of imperial expansion, so the periodization of the rise and decline of the British Empire needs to be reassessed in accordance with the growth and decay of the strength of the gentlemanly capitalist order.

Cain and Hopkins undertook considerable work and their books undoubtedly have merits. First of all, their work has opened a new way of looking into the history of British imperialism. The theme of gentlemanly capitalism is certainly a valuable contribution to the study of the history of both Britain and the British Empire – at least in the sense that it has stimulated widespread discussion and further research. It is especially inspiring in understanding the internal class structure and power balance between different groups of capitalists in Britain. It also illuminates the relations between the British government and those social groups labelled 'gentlemanly capitalists'. Cain and Hopkins frequently stress that, in the making of overseas policies, British governments considered first the interests of the gentlemanly capitalists, quite often at the cost of industrial capitalism if the interests of the two were inconsistent. They emphasize, too, that policies designed to secure the benefits of gentlemanly capitalism overseas promoted the competitiveness of foreign or colonial manufacturing industries. This in turn placed pressure upon British industrial capitalists. Such arguments, no matter to what extent they are based on historical facts, have the effect of arousing a reconsideration of the causes of Britain's industrial decline.

The authors' most valuable contribution to the academic development of studies of British imperial history is surely their claim that imperial policies were oriented towards the economic needs of gentlemanly capitalism. This argument admits, indirectly or implicitly, that self-interest was the primary motivation of overseas expansion. This in turn points to bare historical realities which many historians have tended to ignore. Such an analysis, it can be said, is fairly close to the methodology of Marxist historical materialism, even if it is not, *per se*, a Marxist approach, for Cain and Hopkins frequently criticize Marx's views on the Industrial Revolution. This outlook is indeed an advance on the so-called 'peripheral thesis', which claims that the British Empire resulted from instability on distant frontiers.

The weaknesses of the Cain–Hopkins thesis

First of all, as to the definition of imperialism, the statement of Cain and Hopkins is unsatisfactory. They point out that the 'distinguishing feature of imperialism' is that 'it involves an incursion, or an attempted incursion, into the sovereignty of another state'.[4] There is, of course, a rational element in this statement. But their analysis of the nature of imperialism is far from adequate. Indeed, it can be seen that they do not intend to give a full definition of imperialism or a complete analysis of its nature. This is undoubtedly a great defect of their work. The authors also show a tendency to preach the 'civilizing mission' of imperialism. Reading their books, one can frequently come across phrases like 'colonial mission', 'imperial mission' and 'civilizing mission'. Furthermore, by focusing their research mainly on 'gentlemanly capitalism', they ignore other significant aspects of imperialism.

The crucial nature of imperialism is that one state oppresses, exploits and enslaves another. Imperialism means war, political oppression and economic exploitation. If we are to consider the nature of imperialism, we need to look into all its major manifestations. Otherwise, it would be difficult to see the whole picture. Cain and Hopkins have examined little more than one aspect of the economic dimension of the problem. The picture of imperialism they present to the reader is certainly partial. The contradictions and conflicts caused by imperialism are rarely referred to. In their view, British imperialism is much linked with world development and the promotion of civilization and living standards. They state that: 'The empire was a superb arena for gentlemanly endeavour, the ultimate testing ground for the idea of responsible progress, for the battle against evil, for the performance of duty, and for the achievement of honour.'[5] This is far removed from the historical facts. Empire-building went virtually hand in hand with numerous evils. Imperialism, no matter whether it was British, American or any other, was not 'gentlemanly' or 'gentle' at all.

Cain and Hopkins's explanations of the causes of imperialism are equally inadequate and, in a sense, one-sided. It cannot be denied that manufacturing industries were a substantial sector of the British economy for a long time, at least in the nineteenth century. The needs of these industries were important, and surely often the chief impulses behind British imperial expansion. Colonies were not only places where British manufacturers could obtain raw materials, but also places where they could find markets for their products. It is an established fact that colonies were regularly urged to produce raw materials for the needs of Britain's manufacturing industries.

British imperial expansion was pushed not merely by the interests of so-called 'gentlemanly capitalism' which, as Cain and Hopkins have described, was mainly the finance and services sector. These interests certainly played an important role in the formation of British imperial policies and in the expansion of the Empire, but so too did the interests of manufacturers and other social groups. Cain and Hopkins's views are a bit too extreme, overemphasizing the influence of 'gentlemanly capitalism' and playing down the significance of industrial capitalism in British imperial expansion.

Britain's diplomatic and military efforts to open the door into China were no doubt intended mainly to find markets for British products. For instance, the Macartney embassy, the first British embassy to reach

China, was sent to the Qing Court to promote British commercial interests. As the history of this peculiar mission – a dramatic event in the history of Sino-Western relations – has been well researched both by Western and Chinese historians,[6] it is not necessary to discuss it here in any detail. It will be sufficient to mention Macartney's requests to the Qing Court to reveal the main purpose of the mission. Before the embassy left Beijing, Lord Macartney handed a note to the Court of Qing that included six requests. They were: to allow the English merchants to trade to Zhoushan (Chusan), Ningbo (Ningpo), and Tianjin (Tientsin); to allow them to have a warehouse at Beijing for the sale of their goods as the Russians had formerly; to allow them to use some small, detached, unfortified islands near Zhoushan; to allow them a similar privilege near Guangzhou (Canton); to abolish the transit duties between Macao and Guangzhou, or at least to reduce them to the standard of 1782; to prohibit the exaction of any duties from the English merchants over and above those settled by the Emperor's diploma.[7] All these requests were concerned with British commercial interests. The embassy also brought with it many samples of British industrial goods, intending to arouse the interest of potential consumers.[8] As it happened, Macartney could not stay in Beijing as the Ambassador and his mission failed to achieve its major goal.

Opium was smuggled into China largely because British manufactured goods could not find a market there large enough to reduce Britain's trade deficit with China. Subsequently, Britain launched the Opium Wars against China to open the market – chiefly for manufactured goods. At the time of the Macartney embassy, the interests of the financial and services sector were obviously not yet that important in the making of Britain's China policies.

Later on, when British financial interests did appear on the stage, the interests of 'gentlemanly capitalism' and industrial capitalism were not necessarily divided or in conflict with each other. For instance, British loans to China in the last years of the nineteenth century enabled Britain to take firmer control of China's tariffs. Control of customs duties helped Britain to monopolize China's imports and exports. This in turn enabled Britain to promote exports of British products to, and exports of raw materials from, China. The efforts of the British government to make loans available for railway construction in China were not beneficial merely to Britain's financial sector. The construction of railways was also intended to promote the interests of British manufacturers by making it easier for them to secure raw materials from the interior of China and to supply British manufactures in return. Loans and railways can be considered part of the attempt to create spheres of influence in China at the close of the nineteenth century. For instance, while making loans to the Qing government in 1898, the British forced it to declare that no concession or lease of land along the Changjiang (Yangtse) River would be made to any other country. This was the first time the Chinese government admitted that the valley of the Changjiang River was a British sphere of influence.[9] The financial relations between China and the Powers at this time have been well researched by historians in China,[10] and it is unnecessary to discuss them here in any detail.

Doubtless, as Cain and Hopkins have argued, economic impulses are the basic cause of imperialism. But conditions for the existence of imperialism are based fundamentally on military power. Without military superiority, no state can impose imperialist control or colonial rule on others. Industrial technologies strengthened British military capabilities. The advance of industries was the basis of British military superiority, just as military superiority was a precondition of British imperial expansion. It was the Industrial Revolution that provided Britain with military superiority over China and rendered it possible for the Victorians to 'open the door' by means of the gunboat.

The fact that different parts of the world developed in an unbalanced way, with some areas being more advanced than others, undoubtedly provided a necessary condition for the emergence and continued existence of imperialism. Imperialism was possible because there were weaker territories for the imperialists to invade, oppress and exploit. It can be said that the effectiveness of imperialism was determined crucially by the power balance of the three sides: 'the imperialist country', 'the object countries' of imperial expansion, and other 'major powers' in the international power structure. In the case of British imperial expansion, 'the imperialist country' was Britain; 'the object countries' were the colonies and semi-colonies in the Americas, Asia, Africa and other parts of the world; the other 'major powers' were mainly European continental powers. The United States, once one of Britain's colonies of settlement, joined the process of colonial expansion later on. Japan was another new 'major power'. Like other Asian countries, Japan had also been besieged by imperialism. In response to the Western challenge, Japan carried out reforms, strengthened herself and quickly joined the ranks of the colonial powers. But after the October Revolution in 1917, the 'major powers' included a new socialist country, the Soviet Union, which became an anti-colonial force in the international power structure. The emergence of a new socialist country constituted a strong challenge to the imperialists and drew much of their attention away from colonial adventures.

At times when capitalism plays a dominant role in international affairs, the rise and fall of imperialism are decided mainly by the power balance among these three elements. At the high point of Western expansion, all the major European states were colonial powers, struggling against each other and endeavouring to establish and expand empires overseas. There was no single 'major power' in the international system to counter-balance or contain colonial expansion. Other non-Western parts of the world were in general the objects of colonialism. Without any check from the anti-colonial 'major powers', the expansionists achieved great success and did enormous mischief to the weaker peoples.

The chief condition for the emergence and expansion of the British Empire was Britain's military superiority over the 'object countries'. In North America, the native Indians were militarily too weak to defend themselves from being invaded and demolished by the colonialists. In South Asia, India, divided and with a weak central government, did not have the military power to hold back foreign invaders and gradually fell under British colonial rule. China, which never became part of Britain's formal empire, but was considered to be a part of her 'informal empire', started to fall into the position of a semi-colony only from the Opium War, when Britain defeated China and imposed the first unequal treaty. In the process of European colonial expansion, people in other parts of the world suffered numerous catastrophes. Their destiny was largely decided by their powers of resistance. As history has illustrated, those with weaker powers suffered more. This also explains why some parts of the world became colonies, some became semi-colonies, and others settlements with the native inhabitants being driven away, submerged or simply annihilated (for example, the Tasmanians).

Just as the emergence and expansion of imperialism were decided mainly by the power balance among the three elements, so was the end of imperialism or colonial empires. The Second World War was a land-mark in the history of the Western empires because it changed this balance of power and led to the rapid disintegration of the British Empire. The war weakened Britain both militarily and economically, at least in a relative sense. The forces of anti-colonial nationalism became much stronger during the war. On the international stage, the Soviet Union emerged as a superpower that advocated the end of colonialism and provided support to national liberation movements across the world.

The Soviet factor in the disintegration of colonial empires has long been ignored or deliberately played down by Western historians.

Reading publications on the end of the British Empire, one will frequently find historians stressing American pressure for British decolonization, while saying little about the influence of the Soviet Union. In reality, the United States was, and still is, one of the closest allies of Britain in postwar times and has enjoyed a strong strategic partnership with Britain in international affairs. It was the Soviet Union and other newly established socialist countries that were the major enemies of colonialism and imposed real pressure to end the colonial empires. The rise of the Soviet Union and other socialist countries made a historic contribution to the rapid collapse of the colonial empires in the postwar era.

It can be said that the Soviet Union was the greatest international force contributing to the collapse of colonial empires. The establishment and development of the Soviet Union led to the spread of communism across the world. Under its influence, communist parties were founded in many colonies and semi-colonies and became a leading force in national liberation movements in many territories. After the Second World War, the Soviet Union emerged as a superpower and played the key role in the formation of the postwar socialist bloc. The existence of the socialist bloc diverted the military resources of the colonial and imperialist powers, thus making the task of suppressing national liberation movements more difficult. The Soviet socialist model was also attractive to many colonial nationalists. Colonial powers were often forced to make concessions to colonial nationalists in order to prevent them from becoming more radical and from turning to the Soviet Union.

The Soviet Union strongly condemned colonialism and offered great assistance to national liberation movements in the colonies and semi-colonies. For instance, when France occupied Lebanon and Syria in May 1945, the Soviet Union condemned the action and demanded that France withdrew her troops. The Soviet Union consistently supported the colonial and semi-colonial national struggle against colonialism and imperialism in the United Nations and through other diplomatic channels. For instance, in May 1948, the Soviet Union established diplomatic relations with the young Indonesian Republic. This was a great support for the Indonesian people in their struggle against Dutch colonial rule. The Soviet Union also directly provided vast amounts of military and economic assistance to many newly independent countries and helped them to maintain their independence.

Thus, the Soviet factor in the disintegration of colonial empires cannot be ignored. It is an indisputable historical fact. The Soviet Union itself collapsed later on, but without the presence of the first socialist country in human history, independence for colonies and semi-colonies would certainly have been delayed; some of them might never have achieved their freedom. Admittedly, the Soviet Union made mistakes in its policy towards developing countries and also pursued its own hegemonic ambitions. Nonetheless, the Soviet contribution to the world national liberation movement cannot be denied and should not be played down. The rapid change in the balance of power after 1945 led Britain to conduct a wholesale imperial retreat. Britain, like other colonial powers, was primarily forced into action by the international situation, and was not willing to confer independence to the colonies, as Cain and Hopkins and many other historians have suggested.

Cain and Hopkins are not very consistent in explaining the causes of the end of the British empire. On the one hand, they admit that Britain retreated from the colonies because 'nationalist aspirations could not be contained at a price that was worth paying, or perhaps at any price'.[11] On the other hand, they claim that 'the empire became progressively less important to Britain's needs and it became easier, even for Conservative policy-makers, to envisage and then to speed the process of decolonization'.[12] This suggests that Britain did not intend to control the colonies and was willing to end the empire. In effect, the whole argument of the theory of 'gentlemanly capitalism' assumes that the Empire ended because it became unnecessary for the gentlemanly capitalists to continue to control the colonies. Either the colonies had become less useful, or it was unnecessary to maintain formal colonial rule to secure Britain's interests.

This inconsistency can be clearly seen in their explanation of the causes of Britain's retreat from India. They note that India had become 'ungovernable' at the point when Britain conceded independence. At the same time, they assert that:

in 1947 the case for 'staying on' was no longer compelling. By then, India had ceased to be one of Britain's largest debtors and had joined the ranks of her creditors instead, while Britain's newer interest in joint ventures in manufacturing and other economic activities pointed to the wisdom of working with the nationalists rather than against them.[13]

The bare truth, however, is that Britain had to leave India irrespective of her interests and no matter how important or how unimportant the interests of 'gentlemanly capitalism' in India were. This was simply because the forces of Indian nationalism had become too strong for the

British to contain. The military force available was unable to deal with the power of nationalism. The British had no choice but to go.

The British Cabinet reached this conclusion when considering India's constitutional position on 10 December 1946:

> The strength of the British Forces in India was not great. And the India Army, though the Commander-in-Chief had great personal influence with it, could not fairly be expected to prove a reliable instrument for maintaining public order in conditions tantamount to civil war. One thing was quite certain viz., that we could not put back the clock and introduce a period of firm British rule. Neither the military nor the administrative machine in India was any longer capable of this.[14]

There was no controversy here: Britain could not continue to rule India. The problem was how to retreat so as to maintain British interests as far as possible. For this reason, the British government had to 'work with the nationalists'; it was forced by circumstances to do so, whether it was willing or not.

Britain's retreat from Burma can be explained in the same way. The British Cabinet was aware that it was imperative to leave the territory:

> All the advice from Burma was that the A.F.P.F.L (Anti-Fascist People's Freedom League) commanded great influence throughout the country and that if their leaders left the Executive Council the administration of the country would be paralyzed, there would be a police strike, and it would be impossible to maintain Government without the use of force. Indian troops could not be used for this purpose, and British troops could not be made available without serious consequences elsewhere. One brigade could be brought from Malaya. A second brigade could be made available at the cost of weakening our Forces in India or delaying the demobilization scheme. But even so, the administrative troops required to support these brigades would be lacking if, as must be assumed, we were unable to use the Indian administrative troops now in Burma. Finally, even if these could have been provided, it would not be possible with this strength to do more than hold Rangoon and a few other key points; and the countryside generally would be outside our control.[15]

This conclusion clearly reveals the reason for Britain's retreat from Burma. Whether the gentlemanly capitalists were willing or not, colonial rule in Burma could not continue. That colonial rule could no longer be maintained by force was the basic reason for the so-called 'decolonization'.

What does decolonization mean?

Decolonization is a widely used concept both inside and outside academic circles, but its meaning is still ambiguous and controversial. Some commentators use 'decolonization' to mean the process by which empires disintegrate and colonies achieve independence. Scholars in developing countries now often consider decolonization as a process of struggle for ending colonial rule. From this vantage point, decolonization means liberating colonies, whereas in the West it usually means granting independence. I take the view, here and in my other publications, that the substance of decolonization is the actions of the colonial power, including all the strategies, tactics and measures used in the course of a forced imperial retreat, which were taken with the intention of maintaining its own interests.[16] This concept differs from that of Cain and Hopkins.

Colonial powers were never willing to 'decolonize' (give independence to colonies); they only retreated from colonies because they were forced to do so by the national liberation movement and other forces that were opposed to colonialism. The end of the British Empire was not determined by the will of Britain, though Britain did command a certain initiative in the course of the imperial retreat. To some extent, Britain could manage how and to whom power would be transferred. In this respect, British policymakers showed a considerable degree of flexibility and also achieved a great deal of success. Various efforts were made to contain 'radical' nationalists, and power was transferred, wherever possible, to the more 'moderate' nationalists who showed more readiness to co-operate with the colonial power.

Here is one example. In April 1953 Cheddi Jagan's People's Progressive Party won the general election in British Guiana under a new constitution. Jagan became Prime Minister, but because he supported some socialist principles he was considered to be 'radical' by the British Government. In October 1953, a state of emergency was declared and the constitution was suspended. Jagan and many other members of the People's Progressive Party were put into jail. In December 1956, with certain revisions of the constitution, a new election was held. Jagan's People's Progressive Party again won the majority of the elected members. But the suspension of the constitution in 1953 helped to split the nationalists. The split later became a serious problem and led to social conflict. There was another election in August 1961. Once more, the People's Progressive Party won a majority: 20 seats out of 35, with Burnham's People's National Congress getting 11 seats and D'Aguiar's United Force getting 4. But the People's Progressive Party gained only 42.6 per cent of the total vote, while the People's National Congress and the United Force gained 41 per cent and 16.4 per cent respectively. There were sharp differences between the People's Progressive Party and the other two parties. The latter requested that a new election, based on proportional representation, should be held before independence. Burnham and D'Aguiar were considered to be moderate and less radical than Jagan. Thus independence was postponed. In 1964 the British government issued a new Order in Council revising British Guiana's constitution. Proportional representation was adopted and a new election took place in December 1964. The People's Progressive Party won 24 seats out of 53, while the People's National Congress and the United Force got 22 and 7 seats respectively. The People's Progressive Party did not win the majority and the other two parties refused to co-operate with it. Thus Burnham was asked by the Governor to form a government. In the end, the People's Progressive Party was 'out of power' and British Guiana became independent in May 1966 with Burnham as the first Prime Minister of Guyana.[17] This story illustrates vividly that Britain did have an ability to direct the transfer of power in the course of her imperial retreat, and power was transferred preferably to the more moderate nationalists.

The core of decolonization was the transfer of power and the transition of relations. In the course of the imperial retreat, Britain's strategy was to establish new relations with the emergent or newly independent countries which could maintain the old relations as far as possible and thus ensure the continuity of British interests. Part of this strategy was to bring newly independent countries into the Commonwealth. This was a long-term policy of British governments. As the Commonwealth Secretary put it in September 1954:

> However uncomfortable it may be to have some of the emergent territories as full Commonwealth partners, we are quite clear that the wiser course is to admit them to a status of nominal equality, and seek from the start to ensure that, through sharing in that intimate exchange of views and information on foreign policy which marks relations between Members of the Commonwealth, they will

remain within our own sphere of influence...the existence of a Commonwealth composed of like-minded, independent and freely associating Members drawn from every continent, is a source of strength and prestige for the United Kingdom.[18]

In this way, the British government achieved great successes and most newly independent countries became members of the Commonwealth. As a result, British interests were largely secured and established relations largely maintained.

Neocolonialism, which Cain and Hopkins admit, 'can undoubtedly be found in parts of the former empire' did indeed manifest itself in the course of the imperial retreat.[19] Decolonization can be considered as a transitional process from colonialism to neocolonialism. What constitutes neocolonialism is another topic on which my colleagues and I have recently published a book.[20]

For a variety of reasons, the strength of nationalism was not equal in different colonial territories. The upsurge of the national liberation movement thus arrived earlier in one territory than in another. This is why some territories obtained independence before others. Generally speaking, wherever the national liberation movement was strong, the imperial retreat took place earlier than where it was weak. This explains why the major territories of South Asia became independent in the years immediately following the Second World War, whereas most colonies in Africa did not achieve independence until the 1960s.

The colonial empires collapsed in the three decades following the Second World War. The British Empire was no exception. The fundamental reason for this was that, in the postwar period, there was an unprecedented upsurge of nationalism across the colonies and semi-colonies and also a high tide of the international communist movement, which was a strong force against colonialism. These developments led to a great change in the international power balance. All colonial powers, whether or not they had a 'gentlemanly capitalist' element which played a similar role to its British counterpart, had to 'decolonize'. They all faced the same external pressures.

In the last pages of their work, Cain and Hopkins make a brief observation about the implications of their analysis for the study of rival imperialist powers, especially those in Europe. But they do not take the matter further. They admit that they could not 'decide whether the particular configuration of interests we have identified was both present and of equal importance elsewhere, or whether it was specific to the

British case'. 'The reason for the difficulty is simply that the evidence currently available is insufficiently detailed to allow generalizations to be made with confidence.'[21] This kind of elusive statement offers no help in understanding why all colonial empires collapsed so rapidly at the same time. Historians need to be aware that there must be some overwhelming force outside the metropolitan powers that pushed the empires to their end.

Cain and Hopkins made only a partial investigation into 'decolonization'. Many issues concerned with the postwar imperial retreat were not even touched. If we consider all the major issues as a whole, financial problems were only a part, perhaps only a small part, of the British government's concerns. A basic strategy of Britain's imperial retreat was to establish a new relationship with the newly independent countries, which would ensure, as far as possible, a continuation of the old relations. A major aim of this strategy was to keep the newly independent countries within the Commonwealth and within the 'free world' when the Cold War was at its height. To maintain financial relations so as to secure the interests of 'gentlemanly capitalism' was only a part of this strategy.

When we look into the treaties and agreements signed between Britain and the emergent territories or newly independent countries in the course of imperial retreat, we find that most of them were not concerned with financial issues.[22] A great number were related to military or strategic affairs; they were about the maintenance of British military bases and the status of British troops stationed in the territories concerned, or about British military assistance to the newly independent countries, for instance, providing military facilities and helping to train the armed forces of the countries concerned.[23]

The other major group of agreements signed between Britain and the emergent territories at the time of independence concerned public service. Almost all the territories signed such agreements with Britain. The first one was the *British–Ceylon Public Officers Agreement*. This agreement was very short, only a few hundred words, but it contained the basic elements that later agreements also had.[24] These agreements usually had clear definitions about qualifications, conditions of service and retirement, and the preservation, payment and increase of pensions. There were also provisions on the release of public officers for employment elsewhere. These agreements ensured pensions for public officers who had worked in the colonies and who would continue to work in the newly independent countries. They tended to encourage public officers to stay in these countries. The chief purpose of these agreements was to ensure a stable transition of the established relations.

There were indeed agreements of a financial nature. But they were mainly concerned with the sterling balances, signed mainly between Britain and the South Asian territories: India, Pakistan and Ceylon. These agreements set the conditions whereby sterling balances held in London would be gradually released. The first financial agreement of this kind (between India and Britain) came into force on 31 August 1947 and terminated on 31 December 1947. The agreement was extended or replaced by new ones until the 1950s, when the problem of the sterling balances was finally resolved. Afterwards, there were few similar agreements signed between Britain and other emergent territories.

If we look through the conclusions of postwar British Cabinet meetings, which are available in the Public Record Office (CAB 128), we will find that financial issues between Britain and the emergent territories were not often discussed in Cabinet meetings. Apart from the matter of the colonial sterling balances, only a few entries were directly linked with colonial financial issues. The following is one example. On 26 July 1960, in a meeting on overseas civil service:

> there was general agreement in the Cabinet that in present circumstances high priority must be given to the maintenance of an efficient system of administration in Colonies advancing towards independence. In recent experience in Africa and in Asia there was ample evidence that without this, the structure of society in emergent countries could easily collapse. This could imply, not merely a failure of our Colonial Policy, but serious damage to our investment in those countries – which would impose a much more serious strain on our balance of payments.[25]

The British government here showed a great concern with financial issues. Even so, this concern should not be considered to be solely in the interests of 'gentlemanly capitalism'. Rather, it represented the whole of Britain's economic interests.

British governments did take into consideration the interests of British investments in colonies that were approaching independence. Again, however, this was only a part of governmental concerns. It can be seen from British Cabinet discussions of the colonies down to the late 1960s, that there were more entries on constitutional reform, colonial services, and the development of colonial resources and military affairs, such as emergencies and defence. Financial issues regarding the colonies were not frequently discussed in Cabinet meetings. Of course, many financial issues were dealt with at the departmental level, but this means that what was then discussed by the Cabinet was of some importance.

Conclusion

The Cain and Hopkins theme of 'gentlemanly capitalism' has its limitations both in explaining the causes of imperialism and in presenting the whole picture of Britain's imperial experience. Cain and Hopkins also distort imperialism, which is much whitewashed. In reading their work, one may often feel that imperialism was something good, something positive to world progress. The picture of imperialism illustrated by them is a partial one. The numerous problems and evils caused by imperialism are ignored or rarely mentioned. This carries the danger of misleading readers who do not have a command of the real history of modern imperialism.

The concept of 'gentlemanly capitalism' invented by Cain and Hopkins is also misleading because of its ambiguity. Does 'gentlemanly capitalism' only mean the capitalism of gentlemen or also the capitalism that is gentle or gentleman-like? Reviewers have not yet discussed this problem and the work of Cain and Hopkins does not exclude such an interpretation.

History is a form of science and should be based on historical facts – impartial and complete. In order to write a scientific and objective history it is necessary to consult research material as widely as possible. To do so, a historian needs to consult records kept in different languages. On topics relating to international affairs, it is particularly necessary to consult the literature of 'both sides'. Cain and Hopkins failed to consult original materials written in Eastern languages. The chapters on China do not make use of original Chinese materials. It is perhaps unfair to criticize them on this score, for it would be impossible for any historian to consult original documents written in many different languages. In writing generally on a subject like imperialism, one needs to depend largely on secondary sources, as Cain and Hopkins did. However, imperialism concerned not only the colonial powers, but also the colonies and semi-colonies. It is therefore essential to consult materials produced by both sides in order to come to a fairer conclusion. Failing to do so damages the strength of any theme, theory or argument derived from historical inquiry. Only when defects of this kind in the writings of Cain and Hopkins are recognized, does it become clear how fantastic is the idea that Britain's 'one China policy' succeeded in holding China together, as

Cain and Hopkins claim.[26] In historical reality it was a simple fact that Britain was a leading actor in the 'scramble' for China.

The British Empire was the largest of the European colonial empires and was an integral and massive component of modern world history. In the centuries of its existence, it changed the world considerably. The destructive influence of British imperialism brought down established institutions in many societies, and replaced them to a large extent with British institutions during the era of colonial rule. The pressure imposed by British imperialism forced the societies concerned to respond. This, in turn, led to fundamental changes in these societies. Britain's 'gentlemanly capitalism' certainly had a great impact on global history. The Empire ended, but it evolved into the Commonwealth, an international body now consisting of more than fifty countries across the world. Today there is no formal empire in the world, but Cain and Hopkins's 'gentlemanly capitalism' is still there and it will continue to impose its influence upon global history.

Notes

1　Raymond E. Dumett (ed.), *Gentlemanly Capitalism and British Imperialism: the New Debate on Empire*, Longman, 1999.
2　D.K. Fieldhouse, 'Gentlemen, Capitalists, and the British Empire', *The Journal of Imperial and Commonwealth History*, Vol. 22, No. 3 (1994), p. 536.
3　P.J. Cain and A.G. Hopkins, *British Imperialism: Innovation and Expansion 1688–1914*, Longman, 1993, p. 470 (2nd edition, p. 400); P.J. Cain and A.G. Hopkins, *British Imperialism: Crisis and Deconstruction 1914–1990*, Longman, 1993, p. 300 (2nd edition, p. 647).
4　P.J. Cain and A.G. Hopkins, *British Imperialism: Innovation and Expansion 1688–1914*, pp. 42–3 (2nd edition, p. 54).
5　Ibid., p. 34 (2nd edition, p. 47).
6　Here are some English publications on the embassy: Earl H. Pritchard, *The Crucial Years of Early Anglo-Chinese Relations 1750–1800*, Pullman, 1936; Robert A. Bickers (ed.), *Ritual and Diplomacy: the Macartney Mission to China 1792–1794*, Wellsweep, 1993; James L. Hevia, *Cherishing Men from Afar: Qing Guest Ritual and the Macartney Embassy of 1793*, Duke University Press, 1996.
7　*An Embassy to China: Being the Journal Kept by Lord Macartney during his Embassy to the Emperor Ch'ien-lung 1793–1794*, edited with an introduction and notes by J.L. Cranmer-Byng, Longmans, 1962, p. 150.
8　The Macartney embassy brought with it many presents to the Qing Court. Among them there were quadrants, glass lustres, watches, porcelain and broadcloth.
9　Hu Sheng, *Cong Yapian Zhanzheng Dao Wusi Yundong (From the Opium War to the May 4th Movement)* (Red Flag Publishing House, 1982), pp. 317–25.
10　For an example, see Wang Jingyu (ed.), *Zhongguo Jindai Jingji Shi (Modern Economic History of China)* (People's Publishing House, 2000), Vol. 1, ch. 2,

'The Financial Activities of Foreign Countries in China', ch. 3, 'China's Foreign Debts in the Control of the Power Politics of Powers' and ch. 4, 'Foreign Investments in Industry, Mining and Transportation in China'.

11   P.J. Cain and A.G. Hopkins, *British Imperialism: Crisis and Deconstruction 1914–1990*, p. 7 (2nd edition, p. 408).

12   Ibid., p. 290 (2nd edition, p. 639).

13   Ibid., p. 174 (2nd edition, p. 543).

14   CAB 128/8, CM 104 (46) 3, 10 Dec 1946, 'India: Constitutional Position: Cabinet Conclusions', *British Document on the End of Empire*, Series A, Vol. 2: *The Labour Government and the End of Empire 1945–1951* (edited by Ronald Hyam), London: HMSO, 1992, part I, Doc 13.

15   CAB 128/6, CM 107 (46) 2, 19 Dec. 1946, 'Burma: Constitutional Position: Cabinet Conclusions', Ibid., Doc 14.

16   In an article entitled 'On British Decolonization', I first gave an explanation of what 'decolonization' should mean. See *World History* (a journal edited by the Institute of World History, Chinese Academy of Social Sciences), No. 6, 1996.

17   I made an inquiry into this story in the book *Da Ying Diguo De Wajie* (*The Collapse of the British Empire*) (in Chinese by Shunhong Zhang, *et al.*, China Social Science Documentation Publishing House, 1997), see ch. 3 'British Suppression and Separation of Colonial Nationalist Movement' and ch. 5, 'Constitutional Reforms and Transfer of Power'.

18   CCM (54) 8, 21 Sep. 1954, CAB 134/786. Quoted in W. David McIntyre's 'The Admission of Small States to the Commonwealth', *Journal of Imperial and Commonwealth History*, vol. 24, No. 2, May 1996, p. 257.

19   P.J. Cain and A.G. Hopkins, *British Imperialism: Crisis and Deconstruction 1914–1990*, p. 313 (2nd edition, p. 658).

20   Zhang Shunhong, Meng Qinglong and Bi Jiankang, (*Ying Mei Xin Zhiminzhuyi*) (*Anglo-American Neocolonialism*) (in Chinese), China Social Science Documentation Publishing House, 1999.

21   Ibid., pp. 314–15 (2nd edition, p. 659).

22   I have made a general survey of the treaties and agreements in the course of British imperial retreat, see ch. 6, 'Treaties and Agreements: the Transition of Relations' in *The Collapse of the British Empire*, written by Shunhong Zhang, *et al.*, China Social Science Documentation Publishing House, 1997.

23   Here are a couple of examples of such agreements: *United Kingdom–Ceylon Defence Agreement*, see Cmd. 7257 *Proposals for Conferring on Ceylon Fully Responsible Status within the British Commonwealth of Nations*, HMSO, Nov. 1947; DO 118/353 (Public Record Office, London): *Exchange of Letters between the United Kingdom and Kenya concerning the Provision of British Military Personnel to Assist in the Staffing, Administration and Training of Kenya Armed Forces*, 27 Nov. 1964; Cmnd 3110 *Agreement on Mutual Defence and Assistance between the Government of the United Kingdom of Great Britain and Northern Ireland and the Government of Malta* (21 Sep. 1964), HMSO, Oct. 1966.

24   For example, see Cmnd. 2285 *Public Officers' Agreement between Her Majesty's Government in the United Kingdom and the Government of Kenya*, HMSO, Feb. 1964, Cmnd. 3109 *Public Officers Agreement between the Government of the*

United Kingdom of Great Britain and Northern Ireland and the Government of Guyana, HMSO, Oct. 1966.
25 CAB 128/34 CC (60), 'Overseas Civil Service', 26 July 1960.
26 Cain and Hopkins, *British Imperialism: Innovation and Expansion 1688–1914*, Longman, 1993, p. 446 (2nd edition, p. 380).

8
The International Order of Asia in the 1930s

Shigeru Akita and Naoto Kagotani

The purpose of this chapter is to reconsider the nature and the formation of the 'International Order of Asia' in the 1930s in the light of new historiographical revisions in Great Britain as well as in Japan. Recently several Japanese economic historians have offered a new perspective on Asian economic history.[1] They argue that the economic growth of Asian countries was led by the phenomenon of intra-Asian trade which began to grow rapidly around the turn of the 19th–20th centuries. On the other side, the British imperial historians, P.J. Cain and A.G. Hopkins have presented their own provocative interpretation, 'Gentlemanly capitalism and British expansion overseas', in which they emphasize the leading role of the service sector rather than that of British industry in assessing the nature of British expansion overseas.[2] We will attempt here to integrate these new perspectives[3] and to present a fresh interpretation of the international order of Asia in the 1930s. In this chapter, 'Asia' is taken to mean East Asia and Southeast and South Asia. The former includes Japan, the most industrialized country in Asia, the rising sovereign state of China and the then Japanese colony of Taiwan (Formosa). The latter consists mainly of the colonies of the European Powers, including British India and the Dutch East Indies.

This chapter is divided into three sections. At first, we will present broader frameworks and viewpoints of analysis on the international order of Asia in the 1930s, based upon our collaborative work with Japanese and Taiwanese scholars.[4] Secondly, we try to analyze the British perceptions of Japanese economic development in the early 1930s. And thirdly, we will consider Japanese cotton-textile diplomacy in the first half of the 1930s.

I   Viewpoints of analysis on the International Order of Asia in the 1930s

1   The International Order, economic responses and interdependence

In the context of world economic history, the 1930s have been characterized by the long economic depression that followed the Great Depression of 1929, and by the steady erosion of the liberal free trade regime owing to the shift towards bloc economies. It has thus been described as a period in which the relationship of economic interdependence receded to a great extent, thus paving the way to the outbreak of the Second World War. From an Asian perspective, the 1930s have been interpreted as a period of increasing nationalism against the Western Powers. Independence from European colonial rule became a national slogan and economic 'interdependence' was recognized as a vulnerability of each region or state. In general, with the collapse of the international political-economic order in the 1920s, the next decade has been identified as an era of 'crisis' as the imperial powers pursued self-reliance.[5] The cause of and responsibility for the collapse of the international order in the 1930s has been attributed to the nation-states at 'the core' of the Modern World System, and we can say that the interpretation of the 1930s is still dominated by the historiography of the Western Powers. However, we shall try to move away from Eurocentric analysis and to describe the formation of the 'Asian International Order' on the assumption that the inter-regional order of Asia in the 1930s developed unique characteristics.

In the 1930s, the Western countries had many colonies in Southeast and South Asia, whose economic histories have been written in the context of a passivity under the strong influences of the Western Powers. Each area was incorporated into the European spheres of influence and divided separately by the implementation of bloc economies. On the other hand, in the political context, the nationalistic interpretation of history has put much emphasis on the aspects of resistance and self-assertion against colonial rule, and the 1930s have been pictured as a prelude to political independence or decolonization after the Second World War. This defensive aspect or passivity in Asian economic history on the one hand, and the aggressive stance or activity in Asian political history on the other hand, has led to a dichotomy in contemporary Asian history in the 1930s between the 'economic domination' of the Western Powers and the 'political resistance' of the Asian regions. Moreover, it seems that the stronger the economic control or exploitation by the metropolitan powers was, the more intense the national claims for political independence tended to be. This is a strange correlation to find in contemporary Asian history. However, an important aspect of Asian history has disappeared from this historiography. In short, the spontaneous economic responses of Asia to metropolitan control have not been fully explained, despite the strong political reactions to Western colonial rule and the rise of nationalism. There still exists an assumption among Asian scholars that the options for an economic response from the Asian side were very limited owing to the lack of political autonomy under colonial rule. We intend to present the positive aspects in the field of Asian economic history, by referring to recent works by Japanese historians.

We would also like to mention another important viewpoint with regard to the history of international relations. That is the formation of mutual interdependence or interconnectedness between 'the Core' and 'the Periphery' of the Modern World System. This picture cannot be comprehended from an orthodox interpretation of 'domination and opposition' between the ruler and the ruled. For example, in the context of Asian history in the late 1930s, it used to be insisted that the Asian regions claimed sovereignty in political struggles for independence or resistance to the Japanese military invasion. This insistence has led to too much emphasis on the importance of domestic factors for the formation of a 'nation state', and the exclusion of external influences from the interpretation of contemporary Asian history. A Japanese economist, Nawa Touitsu, has argued that the capitalist development of Japan in the late 1930s was highly fragile because of the heavy dependence on external factors, such as the Chinese market for cotton textiles, the import of capital goods and oil from the United States and the supply of raw materials from the British Empire (the Commonwealth).[6] The rise of nationalism in the 1930s thus tended to emphasize the strategy of import-substituting industrialization, and relationships of economic interdependence were regarded as leading to the vulnerability of the 'nation state'. Therefore, it was not imaginable to think seriously about the formation of an international order of Asia through a metropolitan-peripheral relationship. We would, however, like to reconsider the historical meaning of interdependence and complementary relationships in Asia, not only by looking at metropolitan-peripheral relations but also at the formation of inter-regional relations within Asia.

2   Economic nationalism, the 'Imperial division of labour' and 'complementarity'

First, we shall try to reconsider the historical significance of Asian industrialization in the 1930s from a global perspective. It has often been said that the trade frictions in the 1930s represented a scramble for Asian markets between the Lancashire and Japanese cotton industries and that they were regarded as a clash of manufacturing interests. However, the recent works in the field of British Imperial History, especially the arguments of 'Gentlemanly Capitalism' by Cain and Hopkins, suggest that the financial and service sectors had always dominated British economic interests and that manufacturing was secondary. The external economic policies of Great Britain reflected this structure of the British economy. They put much emphasis on the payment of interest and dividends from the colonies, and the defrayal of administrative costs by dependencies. They stress that the maintenance of credibility of sterling was imperative for the British 'official mind'.[7] The same logic can be applied in the case of the Netherlands and her colonial rule over the Dutch East Indies.[8] Following these new interpretations, it is noticeable that some kind of 'coexistence' of economic interests tended to appear in Asia between the British and Dutch financial interests and the Asian manufacturing interest, supported by the rise of nationalism. The industrialized countries of Great Britain and the Netherlands transferred their labour-intensive (cotton) industries to Asian countries and tended to concentrate on the economic activities of the financial and service sectors. It was therefore reasonable for them to ratify the industrialization of Asia through this shift of economic interests. It is one of the prominent features of the international order of Asia in the 1930s.

The rise of economic nationalism in each Asian region was an essential factor for the development of Asian industrialization. To promote industrialization in Asia, it was important to get two institutional frameworks; first, tariff autonomy and, second, an independent currency policy, which are the essential requirements of 'national economies'.[9] Japan recovered the former in 1899 by the revision of the so-called 'unequal treaties' and got the latter in 1897 through the adoption of the gold standard. China recovered the first requirement in 1929 and obtained the second in 1935 in the process of its own currency reform. In the case of British India, the process of attaining tariff autonomy was a gradual step-by-step process. But she could not control her currency policy, especially the exchange rates of Indian rupee to the sterling.[10] Its lack of currency autonomy led to an upsurge of nationalistic feelings and accelerated the acquisition of tariff autonomy in the 1920s.

However, an important element in Asian industrialization was the 'complementarity' between the Western powers and the Asian regions. The industrialization of Asia in the 1930s is not solely explainable by a confrontational schema or rivalry between 'the Core' and 'the Periphery'. In the case of British India, the loss of competitiveness of the Lancashire cotton industry in the Indian market used to be interpreted as an 'economic triumph' for Indian nationalism.[11] However, industrialization in British India was achieved by utilizing the imperialistic order of the British Empire even under colonial administration.[12] In the 1920s the Government of India gradually raised the level of import duties in order to attain more revenues and to balance Indian finances. This increase in the Indian tariffs had the effect of smoothing the payment of administrative costs to Great Britain (the remittance of 'home charges'). In this sense, the British Government implicitly allowed the raising of Indian import duties and confirmed the protective effect of duties for Indian industries, even when they enforced terms of 'Imperial Preference' after the Ottawa Agreement of 1932. British India in the 1930s started its import-substituting industrialization through a complementary economic relationship between British financial interests and herself. From the British financial point of view, Indian industrialization was useful for the collection of Indian debts, if British India could produce a trade surplus from Britain by reducing her imports and establishing a favourable balance of payments. The Indian nationalists recognized this logic through the political negotiations for acquiring tariff autonomy. In the third section of this chapter, we will analyze more details on this subject.

We can also identify the same kind of complementary relationship between China and the United Kingdom in the 1930s, especially in the case of Chinese currency reform in 1935. The Nationalist Government of China suffered financially from a heavy outflow of silver in 1933–35, caused by fluctuations in silver prices in the American market. They received some advice from American financial advisers such as the Kemmeller Commission and A.N. Young about possible remedial action. However, in the end, Chinese ministers of finance, T.V. Soong (1928–33) and H.H. Kung (1933–47) almost completed the planning of monetary reform by themselves and carried it out resolutely in November 1935 in opposition to Japanese obstruction. The British Leith–Ross Mission visited Japan and China on the eve of the currency reform to persuade the Japanese government to agree to a joint-loan to China. The Chinese

Nationalist Government tacitly took advantage of this opportunity, and successfully obtained support from the representative of British financial interests in China, the Hongkong and Shanghai Bank. On the other hand, just after the announcement of reform, they were able to sell huge amounts of nationalized silver bullion to the United States in accordance with the Chinese–American Silver Agreement which was signed with the US Department of the Treasury on 2 November 1935.[13] Through these actions the market value of the new Chinese dollar stabilized without it being linked to either sterling or the US dollar. The success of monetary reform led to the acceleration of import-substituting industrialization and the increase of Chinese exports. This masterly implementation of Chinese currency reform was based on a shrewd political calculation of the balance of power and the exploitation of Anglo-American rivalry in order to increase the economic influence of the Chinese Government. As a natural course of events, the Nationalist Government of China took the initiative in currency reform and achieved a great success in the late 1930s.[14]

These two examples of British India and China reflect the unique features of the industrialization of Asia in the 1930s, and a similar economic relationship has been discerned between Japan and the United Kingdom at the turn of the 19th–20th centuries.[15] They demonstrate the need to reconsider Asian economic links from the new angle of complementary relationships with, rather than antagonism against, the Western powers. Asian industrialization made steady progress by taking full advantage of the imperialistic international order of the world in the 1930s.

3   The 'openness' of the Imperialistic International Order and Asia

It has been argued that the European Powers and Japan in the 1930s divided Asia into their spheres of influence through exclusive 'bloc' economies and that their rivalry was a contributory factor to the Asia-Pacific War (the Second World War). However, we would like to insist that European policies toward Asia in the 1930s were not so exclusive as is so often argued and that the Ottawa Trade Agreement and the sterling area of Great Britain possessed a degree of 'openness' as a bloc economy. We agree with the new interpretation of Cain and Hopkins on the following point: the Ottawa Agreement was intended primarily to promote the financial and service interests of the City of London rather than British manufacturing interests, by smoothing the

payment of interest and dividends from the colonies to the metropolis.[16]

In order to achieve this smooth payment of interest, it was imperative to increase and maintain the trade surpluses of the colonies.
Therefore, the metropolis, especially Great Britain, had to be the largest
purchaser of primary products from the colonies. As a result, the
Ottawa Trade Agreement gave priority to the expansion of colonial
exports of primary products rather than the export of manufactures
from the United Kingdom. A contemporary publication by the Royal
Institute of International Affairs clearly points out the logic behind this
and the results of the sterling area in the late 1930s.[17] However, it was
difficult to maintain a large trade surplus for the colonies by relying
only on the sterling area. It had to be complemented by the growth of
exports to other advanced industrial nations, such as the United States
and Japan, from the British Empire and Commonwealth. It is worth
noting here that B.R. Tomlinson has pointed out the following points:
the Ottawa Agreement and Imperial Preference rarely functioned to
strengthen the economic links within the British Empire, and the
application of Imperial Preference to British India was completely
irrelevant.[18] As we have already mentioned, British India in the 1930s
industrialized by taking full advantage of the protection of Imperial
Preference. The main concern of the United Kingdom was not to
implement tariff policies for the protection of British domestic industries, but to maintain the international value of sterling along with the
'financial and service interests' of the City. The British Empire and
Commonwealth in the 1930s was not a 'closed' bloc protected by
Preferential Tariff. It was open and responsive to the external world in
order to promote British 'financial and service interests'. In the third
section of this chapter, we will reveal the Japanese response to this
'openness' of the sterling area, by analyzing the economic diplomacy
of the 1930s, especially the Indo-Japanese trade negotiations in
1933–34, and the Dutch–Japanese trade negotiations in 1934. Kaoru
Sugihara also points out the unofficial linkage between the Japanese
Yen, the Chinese dollar and the sterling area, which constituted a
de facto 'devaluation zone' in the middle of the 1930s. The emergence of
this 'devaluation zone' contributed, to a great extent, to the industrialization of Asian regions.[19] Britain depended heavily on a relatively
'free-trade' regime, balanced budgets and low military expenditure in
the 1930s. A 'closed' empire usually increases the cost of maintaining
an empire,[20] and the British Empire provides a good example of how to
reduce costs through the 'openness' of an empire.

II   British perceptions of Japanese economic development in the early 1930s

In this section, we attempt to analyze the British perceptions of Japanese economic development in the 1930s, to back up our arguments, especially, those of 'complementarity'. The traditional view has been that Britain and other Great Powers generally discouraged industrialization in the non-European world and that Japan achieved industrialization by reacting against the Western encroachment or the Western impact. We shall argue rather that there was a recognized sense of complementarity between British and Japanese economic and political interests, which encouraged Japanese industrialization, and that the interest of the City of London played an important role in setting out the economic and political framework under which it took place. We will explore several kinds of complementary relationships between the UK and Japanese industrialization.

1   Commercial Counsellor, Sir George Sansom

The main source of our study is the *Report on the Commercial, Industrial, and Financial Situation of Japan*, published annually by the Department of Overseas Trade. In addition, we refer to other contemporary printed materials, such as the *Board of Trade Journals*, *The Economist* and *The Banker's Magazine*.

These documents are only tiny fragments of a large amount of commercial information collected by the British in those days. However, one prominent diplomat had played an important and significant role in writing the *British Commercial Reports of Japan* for the Department of Overseas Trade. His name was Sir George B. Sansom. He was the Commercial Counsellor at His Majesty's Embassy in Tokyo. In the explanation on the front page of every *British Commercial Report*, we can see the status of British Commercial Diplomatic Services in foreign countries as follows:

> There are 38 Commercial Diplomatic posts in all the more important foreign markets of the world. The members of the commercial Diplomatic Service are styled 'Commercial Counsellors' in the highest grade, and 'Commercial Secretaries' in the three lower grades. They are members of the staff of the British Embassy or Legation in which they serve. The Commercial Diplomatic Officer has general supervision over the commercial work of the consular officers in his area and, with the cooperation of these two services, a complete

network of Government commercial representatives is thrown over foreign countries.[21]

Sir George Sansom had three different careers in his life.[22] First, he was well known among Japanese academics as a prominent scholar of Japanese studies in the United States. He published three books on Japanese history: *Japan: a Short Cultural History* (1931), *The Western World and Japan: a study in the interaction of European and Asiatic cultures* (1950) and *A History of Japan*, 3 volumes (1958–63). He became the first Director of the Institute of East Asian Studies, University of Columbia. However, he had originally entered consular service and first came to Japan in 1904. He continued to be stationed in Tokyo for 35 years, becoming a veteran diplomat and the best informed foreign specialist on Japanese affairs. From 1923, he was engaged as the Commercial Counsellor and played a leading role in this field. He also attended the Indo-Japanese trade negotiations in 1933–34 as one of the British delegates.[23] Thirdly, after returning to England before the outbreak of the Second World War, he reappeared on the public stage as the British Minister to the United States in 1943 and was responsible for negotiations with American military officials about the postwar reconstruction scheme of Japan.[24]

We refer to the first stage of the multitalented activities of Sir George Sansom as a Commercial Counsellor. Owing to his high reputation in the British Foreign Office as well as his surpassing knowledge and acquaintance with Japan, the *British Commercial Reports* in the interwar years seemed to reflect a dominant and influential opinion or perception on Japanese economic affairs in those days.

2   Sansom's analyses of Japanese economic development

The changing perspective of 'complementarity'

In an article, one of the authors has emphasized the existence of a complementary relationship between the United Kingdom and Japanese industrialization at the turn of the last century.[25] During the interwar years, this complementarity tended to diminish, especially in the case of British exports of machinery. Just after the First World War, 'American competition is being keenly felt and threatens to become a permanent danger'. 'The pre-war positions of Great Britain and America have been reversed and a recapture of the market will be a matter of the greatest difficulty,' and 'a great advance was made in local [Japanese] manufacture'.[26] This situation continued and the rapid growth of the Japanese manufacturing industry was accelerated in the 1920s and the early 1930s 'under the stimulus of a vigorous campaign for the encouragement of home products',[27] especially in electrical machinery. This reflects 'the increasing ability of Japan to supply her own machinery requirements',[28] and Japan started to export her machinery and machine tools to Manchuria in the 1930s (1934). Therefore, the competitiveness of British machinery was lost in the Japanese import market and led to the weakening of a recognized sense of complementarity, keeping pace with the higher development of Japanese industrialization.

On the other hand, British financial interests also witnessed a diminishing share in Japan. Japan reopened her foreign-bond issues in 1923, especially for the reconstruction projects following the Great Earthquake. She raised $536,000,000 (£57,000,000) from foreign capital markets up to 1931, when she was forced to readopt an embargo on sales of gold following the abolition of the gold standard by the British government. This period in the 1920s was referred to as the second introductory period of foreign capital. However, the proportion of British capital was reduced owing to the heavy inflow of American money in the 1920s. In these processes, the financial presence and influence of the City of London also declined to a great extent. Moreover, the Japanese government adopted new monetary and financial policies from 1932.

Changes in the character of the Japanese import trade

On the eve of the Great Depression of 1929, Japanese economic development was described as 'remarkable and well-sustained'[29] even despite the Financial Crisis of 1927. Over half of her imports were raw materials, and it was noted that 'Japan's position is not unlike that of Great Britain.... She must purchase abroad the raw materials of industry, and with her profits buy such finished goods as she requires'.[30] This changing character in Japan's import trade gradually increased the value of imports from India [raw cotton and pig-iron], Malaya [iron-ore and rubber], Australia [wool] and the Dutch East Indies [sugar].

> As her manufacturing capacity advances, she buys more raw materials and less finished products, to the advantage of those countries which supply such commodities as raw cotton, wool, wheat, iron, oil and timber.[31]

The importance of the British Empire, especially that of British India, increased greatly, whereas the imports of manufactured goods from the United Kingdom to Japan dropped drastically at that time.

Sansom observed that 'this appears to be an inevitable tendency in world trade...the scale of vast quantities of raw materials by these regions increases in the long run their purchasing power and their consumption of manufactured goods'.[32] He also pointed out that:

> disturbed conditions, or any other causes which reduce purchasing power in China or British India, affect seriously the total volume of her [Japanese] exports and, indirectly, her purchasing power in foreign markets in general...The defeat of a customer in one market may mean the loss of a customer in another.[33]

His remarks revealed the so-called 'final demand linkage effect', which comes from the consumer goods demand of producers of primary products for export, according to the definition of Kaoru Sugihara.[34] Through the process of rapid recovery from the Great Depression, Japan became an 'important buyer in the world's markets for raw materials'[35] and 'one of the most important consumers of raw materials'.[36] Therefore, Japanese demands and imports of raw materials contributed, to a great extent, to the economies of the primary-producing countries. In this sense, Japanese economic development had a vital link with and influence upon the recovery of the world economy in the early 1930s.

The strong competitiveness of Japanese exports

As mentioned before, achieving rapid economic development in 1928, 'Japan has already...developed from an importer, through an intermediate stage of production for domestic needs, into an exporter'. She was 'not only...an importer of manufactured products but also...a potential competitor in other markets'.[37] This trend continued in spite of the Great Depression, and in 1932

> Japan offers less and less prospect as a market for the manufactured goods of other countries....She is now established as one of the most serious competitors of those countries, and is at the same time one of the most important consumers of raw materials.[38]

The Japanese export market changed drastically in the early 1930s. On 11 January 1930, the Japanese government lifted the gold-embargo under deflationary policies and her economy fell into unusual difficulties. Sansom pointed out at the time that 'her main economic interests are in two regions, the USA and Asia...which must have an important bearing upon her foreign policy'.[39] However, owing to the financial depression in the USA and political unrest in China, combined with the development of the Chinese manufacturing industry, by 1934 Sansom was forced to observe that 'the two leading markets have lost their relative importance' and that 'it is somewhat surprising to find 1934 exports to British India valued at 238 million yen, whereas exports to what is described as China in the Japanese trade returns were only 117 million yen'.[40] British India became the largest trading partner of Japan in 1933 and this development led to the trade dispute with India. Sansom had already insisted in 1930 that:

> Japan must turn more and more to the production of finished goods to supply not only her present markets but also to attempt to push far afield into Africa, Near Eastern, and South American areas hitherto supplied mainly by Lancashire.[41]

The Economist also pointed out that:

> under pressure of boycott in China and restrictions in India, Japan has been forced to seek new markets for her goods, and has been successful in opening new connections in Central and South America, Africa and Eastern Europe.[42]

In the early 1930s, many Japanese commercial missions were dispatched to these latter regions in order to open new export markets, which took about one-quarter of total Japanese exports in 1934. Through the rapid recovery from the Great Depression, the export trade of Japan diversified. New exports such as rayon (artificial silk), woollen tissues and steel ingots increased, and 'tinned and bottled foodstuffs, chemicals, instruments and machinery, lamps, iron manufactures and glass ware'[43] were added. Sansom observed that this trend 'has reduced Japan's dependence upon the sale of a single preponderant commodity [silk]' and 'important progress in heavy industry, hitherto perhaps the weakest point in Japan's industrial economy is in a fair way of becoming a major industry'.[44] The qualities of Japanese exports greatly improved and the competition for better quality of goods started, especially in the case of cotton textiles. Sansom highly valued these kinds of transformation.

The positive estimate for Japanese economic nationalism

Sansom put much emphasis and high value upon the Japanese economic and financial policies introduced from 1932 by the Finance

Minister, Korekiyo Takahashi. His economic policy was characterized as 'a policy of State expenditure financed by State borrowing', reflation and liberal spending. 'The loan-financed expenditure of the Government has set in motion economic factors which were awaiting release and has thus produced those favorable conditions.' 'It is at least true that a country which is rapidly increasing its production can more safely depart from financial orthodoxy than one where production is stationary.' 'It may be regarded as an experiment in recovery from depression by an un-orthodox programme of public works financed by public loans.'[45] The Japanese government issued domestic bonds of £200,000,000 [about 3 billion Yen]. According to Sansom's judgement, these bonds were 'not an excessive price to pay'. Takahashi's financial policies might be called Keynesian, even in the first half of the 1930s. Of course, Sansom also mentioned that the loan-financed expenditure was mainly poured into military spending, leading to the poverty of Japanese farmers, and that 'the capital resources of Japan do not suffice for the economic development of Manchuria at the pace which it has hitherto maintained'. 'A Japan–Manchuria economic bloc has not yet been constituted.'[46]

However, the depreciation of the Yen and a fall in the exchange rate gave a great advantage to Japanese exports. 'Most exporting industries benefited' and a 'spectacular revival in foreign trade'[47] was achieved within a short period. Sansom also tried to analyze other secrets of Japanese competitiveness. He referred to the 'rationalization' of industries, the bid for increased efficiency and the beneficial role of government assistance, especially subsidies for shipping. These kinds of economic policies of the Japanese government and the positive roles played by the state were highly appreciated as they were in sharp contrast with the poor performance of the British government.

III Japanese cotton-textile diplomacy in the first half of the 1930s

Next, as the case studies of our arguments, we would like to analyze Japanese cotton-textile diplomacy with British India and the Dutch East Indies.

1 Was Japan isolated from the world economy?

In the first half of the 1930s, Japan was able to take advantage of its proximity to the markets in South and Southeast Asia to compete successfully with European goods. The main factors behind the increase in exports of

Japanese cotton textiles were their low prices that had come about through the rationalization of the cotton industry since the 1920s and the devaluation of the Japanese yen, particularly in the second half of 1932.[48] The Japanese yen fell very rapidly in value relative to the Dutch guilder and Indian rupee.[49] This accelerated the increase in exports of Japanese cotton textiles to British India and the Dutch East Indies. The increase in exports of Japanese textiles became a central conflict in Anglo-Japanese and Dutch–Japanese commercial relations, and it prompted Japan to hold trade negotiations with Britain and the Government of India in 1933, and with the Dutch colonial government in 1934.[50]

Until now in Japanese historiography, most scholars see these trade negotiations as part of the process of adjusting the differences in industrial interests between the European and Japanese cotton industries.[51] Thus, they emphasize that each country's diplomatic policies toward the trade negotiations were formulated to serve the interests of each country's cotton textile industry; that is, to secure its markets abroad. Some have even suggested that the culmination of the Pacific War was brought about partly by the tendency of the Japanese cotton industries to expand rapidly into Asian markets, most of which were under European control in the 1930s.[52] They claim that the increase in exports of Japanese cotton textiles to the European colonies in Asia forced the European powers to intensify their protectionist policies, thus isolating Japan from the world economy. The common understanding is that these trends intensified after the Dutch–Japanese trade negotiations, which were suspended in December 1934. The historiography in Japan has further supposed that the negotiations were 'broken off',[53] and that Japan abandoned its co-operation with industrial Europe. Thus, they concluded that Japan's diplomatic policy toward Europe in the 1930s was formulated to serve the interests of its cotton textile industry, and did not maintain the status quo.

However, if we look at the figures from the cotton statistics yearbooks of that time period, edited by the Japan Cotton Spinners' Association, this argument does not hold up. That is, the trade statistics do not correspond with the notion that Japan was forced into isolation from the world economy. The amount of exports of Japanese cotton textiles to British India was 478 million yards in 1936, compared with 357 million yards in 1928. In the case of the Dutch East Indies, Japanese cotton textile exports amounted to 350 million yards in 1936 compared with 172 million yards in 1928.[54] This fact proves that Japanese cotton exports were maintained at the same level, even after the two rounds of trade negotiations.

The idea of gentlemanly capitalism offers an alternative interpretation regarding the motivation behind British policy in Asia.[55] Not only were the colonies expected to serve as markets for European goods, but they also had to pay the interest on government loans, dividends on investments, and the political costs of the home government such as home charges in the case of British India, and pension payments in the case of the Dutch East Indies.

Figure 8.1 shows that two kinds of economic policies were needed for the home country to enable the colonies to pay such interest, dividends, and political costs on a regular basis. One was to maintain an export surplus from the colonies, which was necessary for payment of their debts to Europe. So, the colonies were encouraged to promote exports of primary products, such as raw cotton, tin, rubber, sugar and timber, to industrial countries.[56] This is why Britain was prepared to open its home market to the dominions in the 1930s. The Ottawa Preferential Arrangements led to a far more rapid rise in colonial imports to Britain than British exports to the colonies.[57] Without securing a significant slice of the British market, many colonies and dominions, including India, could not have paid their debts to Britain. It is thought that these relationships also existed between Holland and its colonies in Southeast Asia. The Dutch colonies, however, were encouraged to increase exports of primary products to industrial countries, especially to the United States and Japan. Japan was a particularly attractive market because its recovery from the Great Depression was very rapid after 1932.[58]

The second policy was to force the colonies in Asia to set their exchange rates relatively high.[59] The tendency in East Asia was to devalue the currency, such as in Japan after 1932 and China after 1935, while South and Southeast Asia increased or set their exchange rates relatively high. In the latter case, the exchange rate was often more or less fixed, because exchange rate fluctuations were not desirable from the point of view of regular debt payments. Japan's re-embargo of gold exports in December 1931, and the subsequent depreciation of the Japanese yen, facilitated a rapid increase in Japanese exports, especially to British India and the Dutch East Indies. Japanese exports were promoted by the fact that the exchange rate of the European colonies was set relatively high.[60]

At the same time these relatively high exchange rates aggravated deflation in the colonies in the 1930s.[61] Western colonies needed Japanese exports, which consisted mostly of cheap consumer goods, because the purchasing power of consumers in the colonies was

158

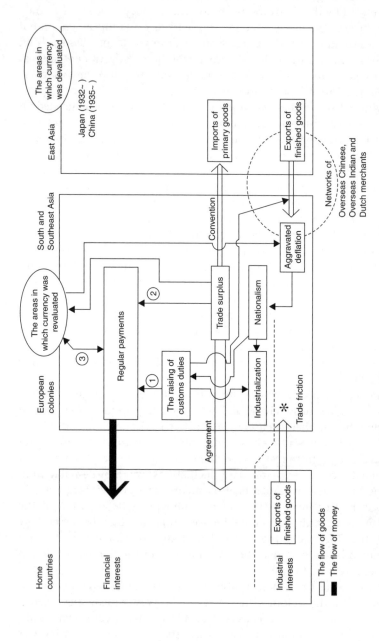

Figure 8.1 The Emerging 'Devaluation Sphere' in East Asia and the International Order of Asia in the 1930s

weakened in the 1930s. This was a kind of social policy for colonial consumers.

2 The nature of the cotton trade negotiations from 1933 to 1934

The Government of India and the Dutch East Indies government tried to co-operate with third-country foreign markets, especially Japan, in order to export food and raw materials and to secure smooth payments to the home country. Thus, the following two subjects became the focus of each round of trade negotiations from 1933 to 1934;[62]

1) What amount of primary products, such as raw cotton and sugar, was Japan willing to buy from the European colonies, to enable the colonies to secure an export surplus?
2) What amount of Japanese cotton textile goods would Japan be permitted to export? In the case of the Dutch East Indies, especially, what proportion of Japanese cotton textile goods would Japan grant to Dutch merchant importers, to profit them in dealing with Japanese goods so that they could pay dividends to Holland regularly?

The idea that the increase in Japanese competition in British India and the Dutch East Indies was a threat to European manufacturers was not the focus of each round of cotton trade negotiations. Thus the Japanese formal delegations in the Indo-Japanese and the Dutch–Japanese trade negotiations did not include a member of the cotton textile industry. The documents of the Japan Cotton Spinners' Association, one of the most powerful industrial bodies, show that the representatives of this Association voluntarily went to British India and the Dutch East Indies to report back to the Association in Osaka.[63] This means that the interests of the private manufacturing sector, especially the Japanese cotton industry, were not reflected in these negotiations and that there was a discrepancy in the interests of the representative of the Japanese government and private representatives.

In the case of the Indo-Japanese trade negotiations in 1933–34, Japan boycotted the import of Indian raw cotton from August to December 1933. But this aggressive act was led by the Japan Cotton Spinners' Association, and was not actually orchestrated by the Japanese government. The representatives of the Japanese government was prepared to purchase raw cotton regularly, but they used the boycott movement as a lever to improve the conditions of the Indo-Japanese cotton treaty for Japan's benefit. As Keizo Kurata, who was a leader of this boycott and an executive of Dai Nihon Boseki Kaisha (one of the big five cotton spinning companies in the prewar period), pointed out, the boycott was not actually in effect in December 1933, because European and Indian merchants bought Indian raw cotton in the inner district even while the Japanese trading companies maintained a policy of not purchasing raw cotton.[64] When the representatives of the Japanese government realized that the boycott led by a private body was no longer in effect, they immediately concluded a trade agreement, conceding to the British Indian government. The Indo-Japanese negotiations were completed in early January 1934. The agreement was on a barter basis: Japan was allowed to export 400 million yards of cotton textiles to India, provided that it imported 1.5 million bales of Indian cotton in return. This implied that the Japanese market was also necessary in order for British India to secure an export surplus from the point of view of maintaining London's financial position and the stability of the empire in the 1930s. The focus of the Indo-Japanese cotton trade negotiations was to maintain the level of exports of Indian raw cotton.[65]

In the case of the Dutch–Japanese trade negotiations in 1934, most studies emphasize that they were not completely successful, because negotiations were suspended until June 1936.[66] But during negotiations, both sides tried to make a compromise in the following two agendas:

1) Japanese trading firms in the Dutch East Indies were to handle a quarter of the total imports on the basis of the 1933 figures.
2) The Japanese government 'advised' the business circles concerned to give a preference to the Dutch East Indies in its raw sugar purchases.

The first agenda indicated that Japan's Foreign Ministry conceded to the government of the Dutch East Indies, because Japanese firms handled 38 per cent of total imports in 1933. This meant that the handling of 13 per cent of total imports on the basis of the 1933 figures were conceded to Dutch importers, such as N.V. Internationale Crediet-en Handels-Vereeniging 'Rotterdam', Borneo-Sumatra Maatschappij, Jacobson & van den Berg, and Geo. Wehry & Co.[67] The Japanese government proposed this first agenda without asking the Japan Cotton Spinners' Association or the Japanese trading companies dealing with Japanese cotton textile goods. The Japanese government negotiated on the basis of wanting to co-operate with Holland and the Dutch East Indies, not taking into account the interests of Japanese cotton industries.[68] Seizaburo Nakayama, an employee of Mitsui Bussan dealing with Javanese sugar, was the only private representative in the formal delegation. Japan's Foreign Ministry needed him as an expert. If Japan were to give preference to the Dutch East Indies in its raw sugar purchases, then Japan's Foreign Ministry would need to deal with a conflict of interests that would erupt between the Javanese and Taiwanese sugar industries.[69]

However, the negotiations were suspended due to antagonisms on the Japanese side. The increase in imports of Javanese sugar aroused the keen competition of Taiwanese sugar in East Asia. Japan's Foreign Ministry decided not to make a formal agreement with the Dutch East Indies government, because the Governor-General of Taiwan opposed a preference to the Dutch East Indies. Thus, the negotiations could only result in a 'gentlemen's agreement'; that is, the Japanese government would vaguely recommend to the business circles concerned that they show preference to the Dutch East Indies in its raw sugar purchases. It might be argued that these negotiations were formally broken off and Japan began to abandon co-operation with industrial Europe.

But the interdependence between Japan and the Dutch East Indies was in fact maintained. Japan increased its imports of Javanese sugar. Japan took 10 per cent of the total exports of Javanese sugar in 1930–33 and 17 per cent in 1934–36, increasing in line with the fall in Javanese exports to British India. Additionally, the Dutch merchants' share of imports of Japanese cotton textile goods increased. They took 18.4 per cent in 1932 and 44.3 per cent in 1935. Toyo Menka, which handled about 10 per cent of Japan's total exports of cotton textiles in the 1930s, reinforced its connection with the Dutch merchants. When a provisional commercial treaty, known as the Ishizawa–Hart Agreement, was signed in April 1937, Japanese merchants in the Dutch East Indies were to handle a quarter of the total imports on the basis of the 1933 figures, and Japan promised to give preference to the Dutch East Indies in its raw sugar purchases. These provisions were made in confirmation of accomplished facts.[70]

Conclusion

Finally, we will try to summarize our arguments on the international order of Asia in the 1930s. First, during the interwar years, especially in the first half of the 1930s, the arguments of *British Commercial Reports on Japan* tended to shift their focus from the British home economy to the markets of the British Empire. The importance of British India greatly increased for the Japanese export economy in the early 1930s, as an expanding market for the Japanese cotton industry and as a vital source of raw cotton. British Malaya and Australia also played important roles in the rapid recovery and further expansion of Japanese exports. In return, Japan's huge import of primary products from the British Empire was an essential factor in helping the colonies to continue to pay their debts to Great Britain. Therefore, a kind of complementarity of economic interests emerged between the British Empire and Japan rather than between Great Britain and Japan.

Second, Sir George Sansom joined the Indo-Japanese trade negotiations in 1933–34 as a member of the British delegation.[71] After returning to Japan, he commented on bilateral (trade) agreements as follows: 'a new Indo-Japanese Convention and Protocol...may be said to have solved for the time being the question of Japanese competition in India in the cotton trade'. However, 'a policy of balancing trade as between pairs of countries would very greatly reduce international trade'. 'Though palliative measures have been applied, no fundamental solution has yet been found for the problems raised by Japanese competition.'[72] In this sense, Sansom worried about the emergence of economic blocs and strongly supported the maintenance of a free-trade regime on the global scale and the economic co-operation of the major powers. Based on these arguments, he assessed the rapid development of the Japanese industrial economy quite positively.

From the recent works in Asian and Japanese economic histories, we can reach the same kind of conclusions. The standard understanding has been that Western reactions to the export of Japanese goods to their colonies helped strengthen the case for building the yen bloc. Japan then began to abandon co-operation with industrial Europe after the Indo-Japanese and the Dutch–Japanese negotiations. Until 1937, however, Japan did not give up its intention of maintaining a certain level of interdependence with British India and the Dutch East Indies. Japan's diplomatic policy toward Europe in the 1930s was formulated primarily by considering the financial interests of Europe, not by taking into account the interests of the cotton textile industry.

The Japanese share of imports in the Dutch East Indies and British India increased rather than decreased after 1932. Through this trade, overseas Chinese[73] and Indian merchants[74] were the ones who strongly promoted exports of Japanese goods. They continued to deal with Japanese cotton textiles, although British and Dutch attempts to block Japanese goods gave preference to the goods produced within the Empire. There was clearly a complementary sense between European financial interests and Japanese exports to the Asian markets by stimulating the networks of Chinese and Indian merchants. This also means that the interests of the Western manufacturing sector were sacrificed by stimulating the Asian merchants' activities in the difference of the currency policy between Japan and the Western colonies in Asia.

The earlier drafts of this chapter were presented to the British Imperial Seminar, chaired by Prof. Andrew Porter, at the Institute of Historical Research, University of London, on 28 March 2000. We appreciate the valuable comments and suggestions on our draft from the participants. And we especially thank Dr Antony Best of the London School of Economics for his critical review of our paper. Section II was written by Shigeru Akita and Section III by Naoto Kagotani.

Notes

1 Kaoru Sugihara, *Ajiakan Boeki no Keisei to Kozo* [*The Formation and Structure of Intra-Asian Trade*] (Kyoto,1996); Naoto Kagotani, *Ajia Kokusai-Tsusho Chitsujo to Kindai Nihon* [*The Asian International Trading Order and Modern Japan*] (Nagoya, 2000); Shigeru Akita, *Igirisu Teikoku to Ajia Kokusai-Chitsujo* [*The British Empire and International Order of Asia*] (Nagoya, 2002).
2 P.J. Cain and A.G. Hopkins, *British Imperialism, 1688–2000* (2nd edition, London and New York, 2001).
3 As for the debate on Gentlemanly Capitalism and East Asia, see ibid., 'Forward: the Continuing Debate on Empire', pp. 16–17; Shigeru Akita, 'British Informal Empire in East Asia, 1880–1939: a Japanese perspective', in Raymond E. Dumett (ed.), *Gentlemanly Capitalism and British Imperialism: the New Debate on Empire* (London and New York, 1999), ch. 6.
4 Shigeru Akita and Naoto Kagotani (eds), *1930-nendai Ajia Kokusai Chitujo* [*International Order of Asia in the 1930s*] (Hiroshima, 2000) [Thereafter, *1930-nendai Ajia*].
5 Yoichi Kibata, 'Kiki to Senso no Nijyu-nen' [The Twenty Years during the Crises and Wars], in *Iwanami Koza Sekai-Rekishi* [*Iwanami Series of World History*] 24: *Kaiho no Hikari to Kage* [*The Light and Shadow of the Liberalization*] (Tokyo, 1998).
6 Nawa Touitsu, *Nihon Bouseki-gyo to Genmen-mondai Kenkyu* [*A Study of the Japanese Cotton Spinning Industry and the Problem of Raw Cotton*] (Osaka, 1937).
7 Cain and Hopkins, *British Imperialism, 1688–2000*, chs 17, 23 and 25.
8 Naoto Kagotani, 'Japanese Cotton-textile Diplomacy in the First Half of the 1930s: the case of the Dutch–Japanese trade negotiation in 1934', *Bulletin of Asia-Pacific Studies*, Vol. VII (1997).
9 Yuzo Yamamoto, *Nihon Shokuminchi Keizaishi Kenkyu* [*A Study of the History of Japanese Colonial Economies*] (Nagoya, 1992), ch. 2.
10 B.R. Tomlinson, *The Political Economy of the Raj 1914–1947: the Economics of Decolonization in India* (London, 1979); do., *The New Cambridge History of India*, III-3, *The Economy of Modern India 1860–1970* (Cambridge, 1993).
11 Basudev Chatterji, *Trade, Tariffs and Empire: Lancashire and British Policy in India 1919–1939* (Delhi, 1992).

12 Nobuko Nagasaki, 'Hi-bouryoku to Jiritsu no Indo [India under the Non-violence and Independence],' in Naoki Hazama and Nobuko Nagasaki (eds), *Sekai no Rekishi [Series of World History]* 27: *Jiritsu ni mukau Ajia [Asian Movements towards Independence]* (Tokyo, 1999).

13 On the Chinese currency reform in 1935, see Arther N. Young, *China's Nation-Building Effort, 1927–1937: the Financial and Political Record* (Stanford, 1971), chs. 7 and 8; Yutaka Nozawa (ed.), *Chugoku no Heisei-Kaikaku to Kokusai-Kankei [Currency Reform in China (1935) and China's Relations with Japan, Britain and America]* (Tokyo, 1981); P.J. Cain, 'British Economic Imperialism in China in the 1930s: the Leith–Ross Mission', *Bulletin of Asia-Pacific Studies*, Vol. VII (1997).

14 Toru Kubo, *Senkan-ki Chugoku Jiritsu eno Mosaku: Kanzei-Tsuka Seisaku to Keizai-hatten [China's Quest for Sovereignty in the Inter-war Period: Tariff Policy and Economic Development]* (Tokyo, 1999), ch. 8.

15 Shigeru Akita, *Igirisu Teikoku to Ajia Kokusai-Chitsujo [The British Empire and International Order of Asia]* (2002), chs 5 and 6.

16 Cain and Hopkins, *British Imperialism, 1688–2000*, ch. 20.

17 The Royal Institute of International Affairs, *The Problem of International Investment* (London, 1937).

18 B.R. Tomlinson, 'Imperial Power and Foreign Trade: Britain and India (1900–1970)', in P. Mathias and J.A. Davis (eds), *The Nature of Industrialization*, Vol. 5, *International Trade and British Economic Growth from the Eighteenth Century to the Present Day* (Oxford, 1996).

19 Kaoru Sugihara, 'The Emergence of an Industrialization-promoting Monetary Regime in East Asia: the Sterling Area versus the East Asian Devaluation', in Akita and Kagotani (eds), *1930-nendai Ajia*, ch. 2.

20 Patrick K. O'Brien with Leandro Prados de la Escosura, 'The Costs and Benefits of European Imperialism from the Conquest of Ceuta, 1415 to the Treaty of Lusaka 1974', *Revista de Historia Economica*, Ano XVI, invierno 1998, no.1; Avner Offer, 'The British Empire, 1870–1914: a waste of money?', *The Economic History Review*, 2nd ser., 46 (1993).

21 Department of Overseas Trade, *Report on Economic and Commercial Conditions in Japan*, June 1936, ii.

22 Gordon Daniels, 'Sir George Sansom (1883–1965): Historian and Diplomat', in Sir Hugh Cortazzi and Gordon Daniels (eds), *Britain and Japan 1859–1991: Themes and Personalities* (London, 1991); Ian Nish, 'George Bailey Sansom, Diplomat and Historian' (unpublished lecture paper, London, 1999).

23 *Typescript: Reminiscences of Sir George Sansom* (Oral History Research Office, Columbia University, 1957), in *Sir George Sansom Papers* at St Antony's College, Oxford, box 9.

24 Chihiro Hosoya, *Nihon Gaikou no Zahyou [The Frameworks of Japanese Diplomacy]* (Tokyo, 1979), pp. 140–66; Sir George B. Sansom, *Postwar Relations with Japan: Tenth Conference of the Institute of Pacific Relations*, Sep. 1947, (The Royal Institute of International Affairs, 1947).

25 Shigeru Akita, '"Gentlemanly Capitalism", intra-Asian Trade and Japanese Industrialization at the Turn of the Last Century,' *Japan Forum*, 8(1) (1996), pp. 51–65.

26 Department of Overseas Trade, *Report on Economic and Commercial Conditions in Japan*, 1919, p. 39.

27 Ibid., no. 541, 1932, p. 68.
28 Ibid.
29 Ibid., 1929, p. 1.
30 Ibid., 1929 – Foreign Trade.
31 Ibid., 1930, p. 18.
32 Ibid., 1927, p. 64.
33 Ibid., 1929, p. 18.
34 Kaoru Sugihara, 'Japan as an Engine of the Asian International Economy, c. 1880–1936', *Japan Forum*, 2(1), (1990).
35 Department of Overseas Trade, *Report on Economic and Commercial Conditions in Japan*, 1928 – Foreign Trade, general.
36 Ibid., no. 541, 1932, p. 39.
37 Ibid., 1928, p. 34.
38 Ibid., no. 541, 1932, p. 39.
39 Ibid., 1930, p. 16.
40 Ibid., 1933–34, p. 103.
41 Ibid., 1930, p. 27. Cf. *The Economist* (2 March 1935), 'Japan – Workshop of the Orient'.
42 *The Economist* (3 June 1933), 'Japanese Export Competition'; *The Economist* (16 Feb. 1935), 'Prosperity – Japanese Style'.
43 Department of Overseas Trade, *Report on Economic and Commercial Conditions in Japan*, 1933–34, p. 93. Cf. Osamu Ishi, *Sekai-Kyoukou to Nihon no 'Keizai-Gaikou' – 1930–1936 [The Great Depression and Japanese Economic Diplomacy, 1930–1936]* (Tokyo, 1995).
44 Department of Overseas Trade, *Report on Economic and Commercial Conditions in Japan*, 1933–34, Major Industries and p. 68.
45 Ibid., 1933–34, pp. 14–15. Cf. *The Economist* (28 Sep. 1935), 'Loan Expenditure in Japan'.
46 Ibid., 1933–34, p. 16.
47 Ibid., 1932, no. 541, pp. 12, 17.
48 Kaoru Sugihara, 'Japan's Industrial Recovery 1931–1936', in Ian Brown(ed.), *The Economies of Africa and Asia during the Inter-war Depression* (London, 1989); Alex J. Robertson 'Lancashire and the Rise of Japan', in Mary B. Rose (ed.), *International Competition and Strategic Response in the Textile Industries since 1890* (London, 1991).
49 Kaoru Sugihara, 'Intra-Asian Trade and East Asia's Industrialization, 1919–1939', in Gareth Austin(ed.), *Industrial Growth in the Third World, c. 1870–c. 1990: Depressions, Intra-regional Trade, and Ethnic Networks*, LSE Working Papers in Economic History, 44/98, London School of Economic and Political Science, London, 1998.
50 Osamu Ishii, 'Rivalries over Cotton Goods Markets, 1930–36', in Ian Nish and Yoichi Kibata (eds), *The Political-Diplomatic Dimension, 1931–2000, the History of Anglo-Japanese Relations, 1600–2000*, Vol. 2 (London, 2000).
51 Oasamu Ishii, *Cotton-textile Diplomacy: Japan, Great Britain and the United States, 1930–1936* (Michigan, 1977).
52 Antony Best, 'Keizai teki Yuuwa seisaku ka, Keizai teki Nashonarizumu ka' ['Economic Appeasement or Economic Nationalism?'], *Jinbun Gakuho [The Journal of the Institute of Research in Humanities, Kyoto University]*, no. 85 (Kyoto, 2001).

53   Ishii, *Cotton-textile Diplomacy*; Shinya Sugiyama, 'The Expansion of Japan's Cotton Textile Exports into South-East Asia', in Sugiyama and Ian Brown (eds), *International Rivalry in South-East Asia in the Interwar Period* (Itcha, 1995).

54   The Japan Cotton Spinners' Association (ed.), *The Statistics of the Cotton Trade, 1919–1936*. These Statistics are kept in the Library of the Japan Cotton Spinners' Association (Osaka).

55   P.J. Cain and A.G. Hopkins, *British Imperialism, 1688–2000*, chs. 20, 23 and 25.

56   Naoto Kagotani, *Ajia Kokusai Tsusho Chitujyo to Kindai Nihon* [*The Asian International Trading Order and Modern Japan*], ch. 5.

57   Ragnar Nurkse, *International Currency Experience: Lessons of the Inter-War Period* (Geneva, 1944), ch. 3.

58   Jyuro Hashimoto, *Dai kyoko ka no Nihon Shihonn-shugi* [*Japanese Capitalism under the Great Depression*] (Tokyo, 1984), ch. 3.

59   B.R. Tomlinson, *The Political Economy of the Raj 1914–1947*, ch. 3; Ann Booth, 'The Evolution of Fiscal Policy and the Role of Government in the Colonial Economy', in Ann Booth, W.J. O'Malley and Ann Weidemann (eds), *Indonesian Economic History in the Dutch Colonial Era* (Itcha, 1990); Ian Brown, *Economic Change in South-East Asia, c. 1830–1980* (Oxford, 1997), ch. 13.

60   Kaoru Sugihara, *Ajiakan Boeki no Keisei to Kozo* [*The Formation and Structure of Intra-Asian Trade*], ch. 4.

61   Basudev Chatterji, *Trade, Tariff and Empire*, chs. 7 and 8.

62   Hiroshi Shimizu, 'A Study of Japan's Commercial Expansion into the Netherlands Indies from 1914 to 1941', *Nagoya Shoka Daigaku Ronshu* [*The Journal of Nagoya Commercial University*], vol. 34, no. 2, 1990.

63   Keizo Kurata, *Nichi-In Kaisho ni Kansuru Denpo Ofuku Hikae* [*The File of all Telegrams for Indo-Japanese Cotton Trade Negotiations*] (The Japan Cotton Spinners Association, April 1934); Yasuo Tawa, *Nichi-Ran Kaisho no Keika* [*The Process of Dutch–Japanese Cotton Trade Negotiations, 1934*] (The Japan Cotton Spinners Association, March 1935). These documents are kept in the Library of the Japan Cotton Spinners' Association (Osaka).

64   Keizo Kurata, 30 December 1933, from Kurata to Osaka, *Nichi-In Kaisho ni Kansuru Denpo Ofuku Hikae*; Kagotani, *Ajia Kokusai Tsusho Chitujyo to Kindai Nihon*, ch. 4.

65   Kagotani, *Ajia Kokusai Tsusho Chitujyo to Kindai Nihon*, chs. 6 and 7.

66   Ishii, *Cotton-textile Diplomacy*; Shimizu, 'A Study of Japan's Commercial Expansion into the Netherlands Indies from 1914 to 1941'; Sugiyama, 'The Expansion of Japan's Cotton Textile Exports into South-East Asia'.

67   Kagotani, *Ajia Kokusai Tsusho Chitujyo to Kindai Nihon*, ch. 8; G.C. Allen and Audrey G. Donnithorne, *Western Enterprise in Indonesia and Malaya* (London, 1957), ch. 14.

68   Tawa, *Nichi-Ran Kaisho no Keika*, p. 126.

69   Kagotani, *Ajia Kokusai Tsusho Chitujyo to Kindai Nihon*, ch. 8.

70   Ibid.

71   *Typescript: Reminiscences of Sir George Sansom*, pp. 30–4.

72   Department of Overseas Trade, *Report on Economic and Commercial Conditions in Japan*, 1933–34, pp. 97, 100.

73   Peter Post, 'Chinese Business Networks and Japanese Capital in South-East Asia, 1880–1940', in Rajeswary Ampalavanar Brown (ed.), *Chinese Business*

Enterprise in Asia (London, 1995); Horoshi Shimizu and Hitoshi Hirakawa, *Japan and Singapore in the World Economy: Japan's Economic Advance into Singapore 1870–1965* (London, 1999), p. 87.

74 Rajeswary Ampalavanar Brown, *Capital and Entrepreneurship in South-East Asia* (London, 1994), ch. 10; Claude Markovits, *The Global World of Indian Merchants, 1750–1947: Trader of Sind from Bukhara to Panama* (Cambridge, 2000), ch. 4.

9
Reasserting Imperial Power? Britain and East Asia in the 1930s

Yoichi Kibata

One of the characteristics of *British Imperialism 1688–2000* written by P.J. Cain and A.G. Hopkins is the emphasis put on China as an area in which the working of British imperial policy propelled by gentlemanly capitalism was clearly discerned.[1] Given the important place of China in the imperialist world order, this is a rewarding exercise, and the function of British financial interests in China is convincingly borne out in their work. In the case of the 1930s, which is the period discussed in this chapter, they stress the continuity of British policy towards China: 'The main issues, as in the 1920s, were financial, and centred on securing payments on existing debts and creating the conditions for new investment.'[2] And they point out that 'the most ambitious reform was the attempt to draw China into the emerging Sterling Area after Britain left the gold standard in 1931'.[3]

Accepting the validity of this assertion, the present author thinks that the analysis of British policy towards China in the 1930s in *British Imperialism 1688–2000* is not sufficiently supported by the argument about the wider international setting in east Asia, particularly British relations with Japan. It is true that Cain and Hopkins are well aware of the importance of examining British policy towards China in the context of British foreign policy in general, but their treatment of various factors surrounding Anglo-Chinese relations is, albeit inevitable in such a gigantic undertaking, rather sketchy. Though in his response to Shigeru Akita's criticism Peter Cain touches upon British appeasement policy towards Japan and develops some interesting points, he does not go into details.[4] Given the fact that international relations in east Asia underwent great changes after the start of the Japanese invasion of north-eastern China (Manchuria) in 1931, the analysis of the British

169

position in and policy towards China should be supplemented by that of British policy towards Japan. The aim of this chapter is to outline the British stance in east Asia from 1931 to 1937, when the Sino-Japanese war broke out, with the emphasis on its relations with Japan.[5]

1   1931 – a year of change in the British Empire?

Before looking at the British policy towards Japan after the Manchurian Incident, which started on 18 September 1931, brief mention should be made about three events which took place in Britain in the same month. At first sight these events had little to do with the topic of this chapter, but in fact they symbolized the changing nature of the British Empire at this juncture and had close bearing on the British policy in east Asia.

First, from 7 September the Round Table Conference about India was convened in London and Mahatma Gandhi attended it from the 14th. Secondly, on the 15th a large-scale naval mutiny broke out at the naval port of Cromarty Firth in Scotland ('the Invergordon Mutiny'). And thirdly, on the 21st, the British government decided to abandon the gold standard.

The Indian Round Table Conference followed the first conference that took place in the autumn of 1930, and the representatives from the Indian National Congress, who were absent from the first one, took part in the second one. Though the demand of the National Congress for the complete independence of India received a cool reception at the conference, the sight of Gandhi, who epitomized the forces opposing British imperial rule, joining the conference barefooted, was shocking enough to those who cherished the notion of the British title to prolonged rule over India. As will be seen in this chapter, British policy in east Asia could not be separated from its consideration of the security of British rule in India, which was likely to be disrupted by the upsurge of the power of the nationalists.

The holding of the Round Table Conference showed that Britain was ready to concede, to some extent, to demands from various parts of the Empire. Just like the setting up of the British Commonwealth of Nations by the Westminster Statute of December 1931, which in form recognized equal status among its members but in substance retained the central and dominating position of Britain, the Round Table Conference was a ploy to maintain the British grip on India by making a gesture towards negotiating with the Indian nationalist leaders.[6]

If the convening of this conference indicated the weakening of the ruling power of Britain over nationalist movements, the Invergordon Mutiny was a symptom of the new inscrutability of the strength of the British navy, which was the most important military foundation of British imperial power. It was a historical irony that the battleship *Repulse* which occupied the key position in this mutiny was to be sunk by the Japanese air force off Singapore together with another battleship *Prince of Wales* in December 1941 immediately after the outbreak of the Asia-Pacific War. This mutiny soon came to an end after the severe pay-cuts, which were the cause of the revolt, were modified, but the shock-wave sent out from this revolt was considerable.[7] According to Paul Haggie, it was 'not until January 1933, when Admiral Field was succeeded as First Sea Lord by Sir Ernle Chatfield, that the echoes of Invergordon were effectively stilled'.[8] As is discussed below, the British attitude towards events in east Asia was much influenced by its consideration of viable naval power which could be deployed in the Asia-Pacific, and the state of affairs which came to the fore in this mutiny was certainly detrimental to the British assertion of naval power.

Finally, the decision to leave the gold standard was also a significant event in the history of the British Empire. Cain and Hopkins describe its meaning and the subsequent development of British imperial economic policy as follows:

> The abandonment of the gold standard in September 1931 was a defeat for the City, for gentlemanly capitalism and for cosmopolitanism. But the impact of the depression was even greater in the United States, and her international economic sphere shrank markedly in the 1930s. As the United States retreated into economic isolationism, leaving wreckage strewn across the world, the British were left with the freedom to strike out on their own and to try to regain, within the confines of the empire and the Sterling Area, the power they had exercised before 1914 but which had eluded them in the 1920s.[9]

After abandoning the gold standard, Britain increased its drive to construct an international financial system centred on sterling, and in this attempt east Asia occupied an important part. Japan chose to link the value of yen to sterling in line with the formation of the sterling area,[10] and Britain tried to incorporate China into the orbit of the power of sterling. This formed the background of British policy in east Asia after the Manchurian Incident.

2   Britain and the Japanese invasion of Manchuria

On 18 September 1931, in the middle of these three events, the Japanese army started to invade Manchuria. In the course of the Manchurian Incident, which was nothing but a war between China and Japan and lasted until the Tangku Truce in May 1933, Britain continued to show magnanimity towards Japan. It is true that Britain adopted a relatively firm stance to rein in Japanese activities during the Shanghai Incident in early 1932, but it was only a temporary reaction, and, once Japan's threat to Shanghai, where British economic interests were heavily concentrated, receded, Britain went back to its accommodating attitude towards Japan.

Such an attitude was based on the perception of British policymakers who thought that Japan's actions did not pose a serious threat to British imperial interests and that the Manchurian Incident could be contained as a local conflict. Japanese domination over Manchuria would rather create a situation in which Britain and Japan could coexist and co-operate in China as imperialist allies sharing common interests in keeping down Chinese nationalism.

What was important for Britain was to maintain its economic interests in those parts in China over which it had exercised its influence as an 'informal empire'. In fact around this period there was a widespread perception about the increasing economic importance of China with its vast territory and huge population. For example, the British government established a committee to survey the future of the Chinese market under the Economic Advisory Council, an organ which was the brainchild of the Labour Prime Minister, Ramsay MacDonald, and put emphasis on the importance of trade with China. The report of this committee argued that 'the revival and development of the trade of China would be a factor of first importance in reviving British trade'.[11] A similar sort of expectation was raised by *The Times* a little later: 'as greater security is established and the peaceful organization of the country progresses the Chinese market is seen to be almost illimitable'.[12]

In addition to such an economic consideration, the British attitude towards China and the Japanese action in China was much determined by the fact that maintaining a British position in China could be a good barometer of its worldwide prestige as a great imperial power. In January 1927, immediately after the December Memorandum about China, which is mentioned below, was issued, Austen Chamberlain, the Foreign Secretary, wrote to Lloyd Geoge: 'You will understand all that would be involved for our position throughout the Far East, in India,

Afganistan, Persia and even Turkey by a disaster at Shanghai.'[13] Chamberlain may have been exaggerating the repercussions which a British retreat in Shanghai would entail, but from this observation one can detect the political significance of the British informal empire in China.

The crucial problem for Britain was that its grip on this informal empire was increasingly threatened by the rise of Chinese nationalism. The December Memorandum in 1926 was a British reaction to this changing political climate in China. The Memorandum recognized the political changes in China, and admitted that existing treaties were in many respects out of date. It further argued:

> The political disintegration in China has...been accompanied by the growth of a powerful Nationalist movement,... and any failure to meet this movement with sympathy and understanding would not respond to the real intentions of the Powers towards China.[14]

This policy orientation is in line with the overall trend of British imperial policy epitomized in the Indian Round Table Conference, which was dealt with in the previous section.

The British attitude towards Japan after 1931 should be considered against this background. British policymakers thought that, as long as Japanese activities did not directly infringe upon British interests in China, Japanese power could be utilized as a factor restraining Chinese nationalism. Even during the period of the Shanghai Incident in 1932, when Britain adopted a somewhat harder stance *vis-à-vis* Japan, Sir John Simon, the Foreign Secretary, stated in a Cabinet meeting: 'From the point of view of the security of the Settlement it appeared better that the Japanese should succeed than the Chinese'.[15] It may be argued that the basic stance of Britain under the Anglo-Japanese alliance still died hard. But it should also be remembered that such sympathy with Japan was often accompanied by a feeling of racial and national superiority. A Foreign Office memorandum drafted around the time of the abrogation of the Anglo-Japanese Alliance in the early 1920s stated that, however powerful Japan might eventually become, the white races would never admit its equality.[16] At the same time it could be reasoned that the Japanese could be entrusted with the role of curbing the nationalism of the Chinese, with whom they were, after all, racially close. In 1933 Admiral Sir Frederic Dreyer, the Commander-in-Chief of the China Station of the British Navy, wrote:

We should admit that they [the Japanese], as a great Eastern people, have every right to a line of commercial expansion in the direction of China. We should offer to cooperate with them in the Yangtse Valley and Shantung, at the same time trying to keep them from going south on the Yangtse Valley. We should realise that they are Orientals and know how to deal with the Chinese far better than we do. We are not so competent to instruct the Chinese Government how to restore order out of chaos amongst 400 million Chinese.[17]

From such a standpoint the worst scenario was the possible combination between the forces threatening imperial rule from within and Japanese activities which could disrupt the empire from without. The tendency, especially among some Indian nationalists to look to Japan as their protector was a cause for concern among some colonial administrators and the behaviour of Indian nationalists residing in Japan such as Behari Bose was constantly kept under surveillance.[18]

As long as Japan refrained from overtly supporting Asian nationalist movements, this kind of anxiety remained latent, but from time to time the fear about Japan's possible role in leading pan-Asiatic movements surfaced. In 1933 before leaving for India to attend the trade negotiations between India and Japan, Sir George Sansom, Commercial Counsellor at the British Embassy in Japan, wrote to Sir Edward Crowe of the Department of Overseas Trade:

If we seriously hamper Japan's trade expansion in other parts of the world then she will obviously try to make good her losses by action nearer home...I can imagine a very unpleasant sequence of events in the next decade, if we play into the hands of the wild men. Thus: strong action in China; loss of our position and possibly our investments in Shanghai; trouble, to put it euphemistically, at Hong Kong; Japanese penetration in the Netherlands East Indies; and in general a pan-Asiatic movement which, though it might not work out ultimately to Japan's advantage, would do great damage to British rule in Malaya and in India.[19]

It is noteworthy that such a remark about Japan's relations with Asian nationalism was made by Sansom, who was a Japanese specialist well-versed in Japan's history and culture as well as in the Japanese economy and, generally speaking, took a critical stance towards overt attempts at appeasing Japan.

Britain's accommodating attitude towards Japan after 1931 was further buttressed by its doubt about the actual physical power which it could exercise in confronting Japan. Here the naval factor mattered. In the global strategy of Britain at that time the defence of the Far East was a priority and it was planned that in the event of a war with Japan the main fleet would be dispatched to the East.[20] However, the strengthening of the Singapore naval base, which was to be the linchpin of this naval strategy, was much delayed.[21] Under such circumstances, the British military and naval leaders and decision-makers could not help but adopt a pessimistic posture about a possible conflict with Japan. One can also add that the shadow of the Invergordon Mutiny might have been hanging over the Far Eastern scene.

It should be noted that this kind of military calculation was not the primary factor that determined British policy in east Asia during the Manchurian Incident. As has been argued above, the most crucial motive behind British magnanimity towards Japan was its desire to accommodate Japan as a partner in the project of prolonging the imperialist world order which was increasingly threatened by colonial nationalism. And this orientation became more evident in the mid-1930s after the end of the Manchurian Incident.

3　British attempts to appease Japan

In the wake of the Manchurian Incident, which came to an end in 1933, several attempts to achieve rapprochement with Japan were made by the British policymakers. In 1934 Neville Chamberlain, the powerful Chancellor of the Exchequer, tried to conclude a non-aggression pact with Japan, and in the same year the Barnby Mission sent by the Federation of British Industries visited Japan and 'Manchukuo' with the intention of promoting British trade with 'Manchukuo', to which Britain had not given diplomatic recognition. In 1935 Sir Frederick Leith-Ross, who was a currency expert at the Treasury and was sent to China to help currency reform there, proposed to Japan an Anglo-Japanese joint credit to 'Manchukuo', so that it could then be handed to China as compensation for the loss of 'Manchukuo'.

Having dealt with these moves in detail elsewhere,[22] the author would like to place these attempts in the context of British imperialism discussed in the previous section. But before doing so, one point should be made about the relations between these and the theory of gentlemanly capitalism. Both in *British Imperialism 1688–2000* and Peter Cain's article, 'British Economic Imperialism in China in the 1930s',[23] the meaning of the Leith-Ross Mission was much stressed as a case which supports the theory of gentlemanly capitalism. Sharing the reservation expressed by Shigeru Akita – that is, that the part played by the Leith-Ross Mission was relatively less important in the process of Chinese currency reform than was suggested by Cain and Hopkins and that the roles of China itself and of the United States should be taken into account more fully,[24] the author accepts that this mission was a good example of gentlemanly capitalism at work. But at the same time the significance of the Barnby Mission should not be underestimated. The Mission's economic aim was to probe into the chance of expanding British exports to 'Manchukuo', especially the export of capital goods. Though this aim was never fulfilled, such an activity on the part of industrial capitalists in east Asia should be properly placed in the discussion of British imperialism.

What should be noted about this mission was that, just like the Leith-Ross Mission, it had a strong political character. The common feature of the overtures made by the British side in 1934 and 1935 was the inclination to maintain its influence in China on the basis of imperialistic co-operation with Japan through the *de facto*, if not *de jure*, recognition of 'Manchukuo', a puppet state created by Japan as the result of the Manchurian Incident. The abortive plan about the Anglo-Japanese non-aggression pact pointed to the acceptance of the status quo after the establishment of 'Manchukuo', and both the Barnby Mission and the Leith-Ross Mission embodied a more candid posture by giving *de facto* recognition to 'Manchukuo'. When Sir Charles Seligman, a member of the Mission, met Sir Montagu Norman, the Governor of the Bank of England, before the departure of the Mission, Norman told him frankly that the Barnby Mission was political though dressed as industrial.[25] The Japanese government was well aware of this, and during the Mission's stay in Japan it tried to create the atmosphere that the Mission had the political task of promoting Anglo-Japanese rapprochement and symbolized a friendly stance on the part of Britain towards the outcome of the Manchurian Incident.[26]

In this way, those in Britain who pursued appeasement towards Japan aimed at promoting friendly relations with Japan by removing the diplomatic thorn of 'Manchukuo' and at securing or even expanding British interests in China. In a letter to his sister Hilda, Neville Chamberlain, who was the central and most active advocate of Anglo-Japanese co-operation, wrote in the spring of 1935 after a meeting with leading British industrialists in China:

I have been astonished to find what confidence they all have in the future of the China market. They are also unanimous in thinking that while Japan will certainly take her place as China's mentor if she thinks we don't care, we have only to assert ourselves a little and she will be quite ready to work alongside of us *since there is room for both.* China too would be delighted if we would show that we meant to retain our interests in her country and a good deal of discussion has already taken place between Chinese and British as to the advantages of joint action in the development of railways which has only failed to materialise because of the doubts about British policy...I told the men of business that I could not say what would be done for them but they might rely on it that some decision would be taken.[27] (emphasis by the author)

The view that the further participation in the development of railways would be beneficial to British interests in China was, of course, not unique to Chamberlain, but it is noteworthy that he put much emphasis on this point and that he believed in the possibility of coexistence with Japan in China.

Two crucial preconditions for such an expectation were, first, that Japanese aggression in China would not further increase to the point of threatening British interests and, secondly, that Chinese nationalism would be contained within limits that were also safe for British interests. The latter condition was realized in the wake of the currency reform. Though Britain could not fully integrate China into the sterling area,[28] the new currency, which Britain helped to create, worked towards economic recovery and the unification of China and as a consequence prevented Chinese nationalism from increasing anti-British momentum. On the other hand, the Japanese military was angered by the British gesture of helping China, and intensified its activities in north China. But this did not make British policymakers like Neville Chamberlain abandon their appeasement policy towards Japan. In fact, various factors affecting the Empire-Commonwealth system of Britain in the mid-1930s assisted the continuation of this attitude.

4   The road to the Sino-Japanese war

The Empire-Commonwealth was increasingly threatened by the aggressive stance of fascist Italy and nazi Germany in the mid-1930s. Italy launched the invasion into Ethiopia in 1935 and succeeded in conquering it, and Germany started to remilitarize in 1935 and advanced into the Rhineland in 1936, thus making clearer its determination to bury the Versailles system. If these two countries and Japan had acted at the same time with the purpose of undermining the British Empire, Britain would have faced a truly dangerous situation, as Sir Maurice Hankey, the powerful Secretary of the Committee of Imperial Defence, stated in June 1936:

> For the British Empire at the present time the main issue is with Germany. There are serious subsidiary issues with Japan and Italy – both arising out of our commitments under the Covenant of the League of Nations. All three countries are, by their systems of Government and by economic need, potential aggressors... We must at all costs avoid the simultaneous antagonism of Germany, Japan and Italy, bearing ever in mind that the moment we become engaged with any of the three, the other two are liable to see the opportunity to realise their ambitions. So long as we keep the peace we hold the balance of power – in our present weakness a precarious balance, but as we grow stronger it may become decisive.[29]

British foreign policy in the mid-1930s was much influenced by such a consideration, and various attempts were made to avoid confrontation with those so-called 'have-not powers'. The Hoare–Laval plan during the Ethiopian war was the most blatant example of the British appeasement policy towards Italy, and it should also be noted that after 1936 serious discussion was started about the return of the African colonies to Germany as a means to satisfy its desire for territorial expansion.[30] British policy in east Asia should be placed in this international context.

In addition to this desire to lessen the simultaneous threat to the British empire from without, the British policy of accommodation with Japan was buttressed, if not overtly, by the impending fear about the crisis within the empire. The disturbances in the West Indies, especially in Jamaica between 1935 and 1938 and the Arab revolt which began in 1936 were the most notable examples. Not that these events directly affected British policymaking on east Asia, but the critical atmosphere in the empire provided a background against which various policies, including those in east Asia, were formulated.

Nearer to the area under discussion, India was also unstable from the British viewpoint. Even if the new India Act of 1935, which was a consequence of the Round Table conference mentioned at the beginning of this chapter, was, as is pointed out by Cain and Hopkins, the result of a plan 'for salvaging British finance on a raft of constitutional reform',[31] it nonetheless contributed very little to assuaging British anxiety about the future of Indian nationalism. One example of the supposed linkage between British policy towards Japan and the situation in India can be seen in a memorandum prepared by the British military (the Joint Planning Sub-Committee) in May 1937:

> It appears that the most dangerous economic consequence of the war [with Japan] is likely to be the dislocation of the Indian trade... The total effect of the war – losses, interference with supplies, trade and financial dislocation, unemployment, and increase in prices, is not likely to be such as would seriously affect the war endurance of a White Dominion, but its effect on a very poor population, liable to be exposed to subversive agitation, may be really serious in its polit-ical reactions, and is likely to be turned to full account by agitators.[32]

In order to prevent the empire from being weakened both from without and from within, the British government searched for the means of rapprochement with Japan. The choice for these means, however, was limited.

Given the important position of China in the wide imperial system of Britain, it was inconceivable that Britain would renounce or reduce its interests in China to satisfy Japan. On the contrary, the British eco-nomic interest in China seems to have increased after the success of Chinese currency reform. Especially after the autumn of 1936 those in the British government who had stakes in east Asia started to have a more sanguine view about the future of British interests in China. Frank Ashton-Gwatkin, an economic expert at the Foreign Office remarked: 'owing to hatred of Japan, Canton is 'pro-British' for the first time in a hundred years'.[33] Cherishing such an optimistic assumption, British policymakers came to adopt a more favourable attitude to Chinese demands for a new railway loan, to which Britain had until then reacted negatively. And Sir Charles Addis of the Hongkong and Shanghai Bank, who had long been involved in British economic and financial relations with China, thought that the realization of the new loan made China effectively 'a member of the sterling area'.[34]

Under these circumstances, the British appeasement policy towards Japan in the mid-1930s was still being pursued. What the author regards as important at this stage is what can be called 'economic appeasement'. It centred on the proposed abolition of the import quota system in the British empire, which had been laid down in 1934 to counter competi-tion from Japanese goods, especially cotton products. Ashton-Gwatkin, for one, expected that the abolition of the quota system would lead to an improvement in the political relationship between Britain and Japan.[35] Such a policy was actually recommended in the report of the Interdepartmental Committee on Trade Policy at the beginning of June 1937, in which it was agreed that: 'the government should inform the Lancashire industry that they desire to see an arrangement made by which the Colonial textile quotas are replaced by a voluntary restriction of Japanese exports'.[36]

When this quota system was introduced owing to strong pressure from the textile industries, severe criticism was voiced in some colonies, where the poorest classes would be badly hit by the exclusion of cheap Japanese goods.[37] Neville Chamberlain himself showed a negative attitude towards this policy.[38] Since it was not too popular from the outset and resulted in an increase in Japanese textile exports in the markets outside the British colonies, this quota system was easily singled out as a factor, the removal of which would soothe the Japanese discontent and bring 'moderate' pro-British elements in Japan to a more friendly position towards Britain.[39]

As a matter of fact, in the first half of 1937 there appeared in Japan a tendency that seemed to justify such optimism on the British side. The diplomacy pursued by Naotake Sato, Foreign Minister in the cabinet headed by Senjuro Hayashi, has been evaluated by some historians as the one which had the greatest prospect of changing the course of events leading to the Asia-Pacific war, especially as it corresponded with a new and conciliatory attitude towards China on the part of the Japanese military.[40] Facing the increasing tendency towards domestic unity in China after the Sian Incident of December 1936, the Japanese army and navy started to modify their China policies. The basic policy document, 'Policies to be executed towards China', adopted in April 1937, reflected this new policy orientation. Whereas the earlier version of this policy document in the previous year stressed the creation of a Japanese sphere of influence in north China, this new version stated clearly that 'no political attempt should be made which aims at the creation of a separate sphere in north China'.[41] And another policy document which was adopted at the same time gave importance to economic developments in north China and to co-operation in this field with Britain and the United States.[42]

It seemed that such a change in Japanese attitude, if realized in actual policies, would have opened a way towards Anglo-Japanese co-operation in the manner which British policymakers like Chamberlain desired: a state in which Britain would maintain and even, if conditions permitted, expand its interests in China while securing a friendly relationship with Japan. But the 'Sato diplomacy' had too short a life to be actually tested, and the outbreak of the Sino-Japanese War on 7 July 1937 deprived such a scenario of the prospect of implementation.

On 5 July 1937, the Japanese Ambassador in China, Shigeru Kawagoe, sent a despatch, arguing that, in view of the strong possibility of a new British loan to China, Japan should co-operate with Britain in financial assistance to China. If Japan stood aside and allowed Britain to go ahead alone, 'not only Chinese finance but the whole of China itself would come under British (or international) control', and at the same time, given the international situation, it would be difficult to use force in China to prevent the realization of the loan. Kawagoe thus recommended that Japan should join Britain in providing China with a loan and that this should be made a turning point for 'bringing about a great change in Japan's China policy'.[43] It is remarkable that this proposal was made only two days before the outbreak of the Sino-Japanese War. Though it is a very big 'if', *if* Japan had had enough leeway to think seriously about such a proposal, Anglo-Japanese relations and international relations in east Asia might have followed a different course. But voices like Kawagoe's were soon drowned out in the battle cry, and a prolonged war in China, which ultimately led to the Asia-Pacific War, came to dominate the east Asian international scene.

5 The eclipse of the British Empire

Though the British desire to reconstruct the Empire-Commonwealth system in east Asia did not dissipate after the Sino-Japanese War started, the room for British initiative in this part of the world did diminish greatly. It became increasingly clear during the course of the Sino-Japanese War that Britain had to follow the lead of the United States, which was emerging as the successor to Britain as the hegemonic power in Asia.

To put the subsequent development briefly, British interests in China, which British leaders such as Chamberlain wanted to preserve through imperialistic co-operation with Japan, were infringed by the Sino-Japanese War, and the prestige of Britain as the greatest imperial power was shattered by the swift defeat of its forces in Malaya and Singapore in the initial phase of the Asia-Pacific War. And, notwithstanding the true intention of the Japanese,[44] the nationalist movements in the British empire gained momentum as the result of the Asia-Pacific War, paving the roads to independence in various parts in Asia.

It is true that, as Cain and Hopkins maintain in *British Imperialism 1688–2000*, 'the outbreak of World War II did not mark the end of Britain's long history of imperial expansion'.[45] But, when the world plunged into the Second World War, the future of the empire was clearly doomed, and, from this perspective, the period from 1931 to 1937 can be regarded as the last one during which Britain could manoeuvre to reorganize the imperialist international order in east Asia, where Britain had long played the central role.

Notes

1 P.J. Cain and A.G. Hopkins, *British Imperialism 1688–2000* (Harlow and New York, 2001), chs 13, 25.

2 Cain and Hopkins, *British Imperialism 1688–2000*, p. 607.

3 Ibid., p. 608.

4 See Peter Cain, 'British Economic Imperialism in China in the 1930s: the Leith-Ross Mission', *Bulletin of Asia-Pacific Studies* (Osaka University of Foreign Studies), Vol. 7 (1999).

5 I have already presented my analysis of Anglo-Japanese relations from 1931 to 1941. See Yoichi Kibata, 'Anglo-Japanese Relations from the Manchurian Incident to Pearl Harbor: Missed Opportunities?' in: Ian Nish and Yoichi Kibata (eds), *The History of Anglo-Japanese Relations, 1600–2000*, Vol. 2, *The Political-Diplomatic Dimension, 1930–2000* (Basingstoke and London, 2000). This chapter contains some parts which overlap with my former article.

6 See John Darwin, 'Imperialism in Decline? Tendencies in British Imperial Policy between the Wars', *Historical Journal*, 23–3 (1980).

7 Alan Ereira, *The Invergordon Mutiny* (London, 1981).

8 Paul Haggie, *Britannia at Bay. The Defence of the British Empire against Japan 1931–1941* (Oxford, 1981), p. 21.

9 Cain and Hopkins, *British Imperialism 1688–2000*, p. 463.

10 Kaoru Sugihara, 'Higashi ajia ni okeru kogyoka-gata tsuka chitsujo no seiritsu' (The Formation of a Financial System of the Industrializing Type in East Asia), in: Shigeru Akita and Naoto Kagotani (eds), *1930 nendai no Ajia kokusai chitsujo* (Asian International Order in the 1930s) (Kyoto, 2001).

11 S. Howson and D. Winch, *The Economic Advisory Council 1930–1939* (Cambridge, 1977), p. 75.

12 *The Times*, 1 May 1934.

13 Sir Austen Chamberlain to Lloyd George, 19 Jan. 1927, Lloyd George Papers, G/4/3/3, House of Lords Record Office.

14 A.J. Toynbee (ed.), *Survey of International Affairs 1926* (London, 1928), p. 489. As a recent assessment of the December Memorandum, see Harumi Goto-Shibata, *Japan and Britain in Shanghai 1925–31* (Basingstoke and London, 1995), pp. 38–9.

15 Christopher Thorne, *The Limits of Foreign Policy. The West, the League and the Far Eastern Crisis of 1931–1933* (London, 1972), p. 262.

16 Memo by Ashton-Gwatkin, 10 Oct. 1921, quoted in: Frank Furedi, *The Silent War. Imperialism and the Changing Perception of Race* (London, 1998), p. 30.

17 China General Letter No. 8, 3 Nov. 1933, ADM 116/2973, Public Record Office [PRO].

18 For example, see Clive to Simon, 8 Nov. 1934, FO 371/18185, PRO. This is a detailed report about Indian activities in Yokohama, Tokyo, Osaka and Kobe. See also T.R. Sareen, *Indian Revolutionaries, Japan and British Imperialism* (New Delhi, 1993), ch.1.

19 Sansom to Crowe, 17 Aug. 1933, BT 11/219, PRO.

20 Haggie, *Britannia at Bay*, chs 1, 2.

21 W. David McIntyre, *The Rise and Fall of the Singapore Naval Base, 1919–1942* (Basingstoke and London, 1979), p. 1.

22 Kibata, 'Anglo-Japanese Relations from the Manchurian Incident to Pearl Harbor', pp. 6–11.

23 See n. 4 above.

24 Shigeru Akita, 'British Informal Empire in East Asia, 1880–1939: a Japanese Perspective', in: Raymond E. Dumett (ed.), *Gentlemanly Capitalism and British Imperialism. The New Debate on Empire* (London and New York, 1999), pp. 147–52. See also Yutaka Nozawa (ed.), *Chugoku no heisei kaikaku to kokusai kankei* (Currency Reform in China (1935) and China's Relations with Japan, Britain and America) (Tokyo, 1981).

25 Robert A. Dayer, *Finance and Empire. Sir Charles Addis 1861–1945* (Basingstoke and London, 1988), pp. 289–90.

26 Prof. Inoue Toshikazu puts forward an interesting interpretation about the meaning of the Barnby Mission. According to him, the Mission could have offered Japan the opportunity to construct a new regional order with economic co-operation between Japan, Britain and 'Manchukuo', which China could have been invited to join. He ascribes the reason for the failure of the Mission not to Japan's military ambition in China, but rather to Britain's inability to provide 'Manchukuo' with the long-term investment necessary for its economic development. This argument, which discusses the problem in terms of financial capacity, has some bearings on the thesis of gentlemanly capitalism, but Inoue does not grapple with the British side. Toshikazu Inoue, *Kiki no naka no kyocho gaiko* (Co-operative Diplomacy at the Time of Crisis) (Tokyo, 1994), pp. 232–7. The Japanese diplomatic records reveal that there was a difference in attitude towards the Mission between the East Asian Department and the Commercial Department of the Japanese Foreign Ministry. While the former was rather critical of the British move, the latter was prepared to co-operate with Britain in 'Manchukuo'. *Nihon gaiko bunsho* (Documents on Japanese Foreign Policy), Showa Period, II-2–3 (Tokyo, 1999), no. 201.

27 Neville Chamberlain to Hilda Chamberlain, 6 April 1935, Neville Chamberlain Papers (Birmingham University), NC18/1/912.

28 As Shigeru Akita points out, the new Chinese dollar was officially linked to neither the US dollar nor the pound sterling. It seems that Cain and Hopkins tend to overstate the degree of actual linking of the new Chinese currency with sterling. Akita, 'British Informal Empire in East Asia, 1880–1939', p. 152.

29 Haggie, *Britannia at Bay*, p. 101.

30 See Andrew J. Crozier, *Appeasement and Germany's Last Bid for Colonies* (Basingstoke and London, 1988).

31 Cain and Hopkins, *British Imperialism 1688–2000*, p. 558.

32   Far Eastern Appreciation, 1937, 7 May 1937, CAB 53/31, PRO.
33   Dayer, *Finance and Empire*, p. 300.
34   Cain and Hopkins, *British Imperialism 1688–2000*, p. 609, quoting Dayer, *Finance and Empire*, p. 301.
35   Memo by Ashton-Gwatkin, March 1937, FO 371/21215, PRO.
36   Report of the Interdepartmental Committee on Trade Policy, 7 June 1937, FO371/21247, PRO.
37   For example, see 'Japanese Competition – Imposition of Textile Quotas in Ceylon', CAB 24/249, PRO.
38   JTC (34) 1st Meeting, 27 March 1934, CAB 27/568, PRO.
39   Memo by Beale, 6 April 1937, FO 371/20965, PRO.
40   See Katsumi Usui, 'Sato gaiko to Nitchu kankei' (Sato Diplomacy and Sino-Japanese Relations), in: Akira Iriye and Tadashi Aruga (eds), *Senkanki no nihon gaiko* (Japanese Diplomacy in the Interwar Years) (Tokyo, 1984).
41   Ibid., pp. 250–1.
42   *Nihon gaiko nenpyo narabi ni shuyo bunsho* (Chronology of Japanese Diplomacy and Major Documents), Vol. 2 (Tokyo, 1966), p. 362.
43   Kawagoe to Hirota, 5 July 1937, Japanese Diplomatic Records, A.2.1.0.C6, Diplomatic Record Office, Tokyo.
44   In spite of Japan's official proclamation about its intention of liberating Asian people from the European imperialist rule, the gist of the Japanese policy towards nationalist movements in territories occupied by Japan was to 'avoid the quick encouragement of the movements for national independence'. *Nihon gaiko nenpyo narabi ni shuyo bunsho*, Vol. 2, p. 562.
45   Cain and Hopkins, *British Imperialism 1688–2000*, p. 408.

10
British Imperialism, the City of London and Global Industrialization[1]

Kaoru Sugihara

1 Introduction

The concept of 'gentlemanly capitalism', a term that was coined by P.J. Cain and A.G. Hopkins to characterize the nature of British capitalism, has been at the centre of scholarly debate for some time. In *British Imperialism*, first published in two volumes in 1993 (the second edition was published in a single volume in 2001, with foreword and afterword), the authors have attempted to provide a comprehensive analysis of the history of British imperialism. It is based on the reading of a vast amount of secondary literature, covering three centuries and key British colonies and spheres of influence, and deals with a number of major issues on modern British history. Naturally, many empirical and methodological points have been taken up and debated by British and imperial historians since its publication. However, the themes and issues involved are so wide-ranging that there is room for further discussion on possible thematic links with various literatures which neither authors nor critics have so far considered.

This chapter outlines how the gentlemanly capitalism debate has blended with recent Japanese-language literature on modern Asian international economic history. The latter is over twenty years old,[2] and part of it is now available in English.[3] This literature tries to account for the growth of intra-Asian trade and Japanese industrialization since the late nineteenth century, and asks how and why they became possible under the international order dominated by the Western powers, particularly Britain, while similar developments did not occur in the rest of the non-European world. It is concerned with the identification of

Asian merchants and manufacturers, as well as the independent governments that backed them, who carried out the modernization of Asian economies. It discusses the historical links of East Asia's industrialization both with Japanese aggression in the 1930s and early 1940s, and with postwar East Asian economic growth. The contention of this chapter is that these two streams of literature could be fruitfully tied together, to help formulate a broader vision of the history of the development of the capitalist world economy. Put another way, the chapter attempts to locate both the role of British imperialism and the City of London in the wider context of the development of the capitalist world economy, from which East Asia eventually emerged as its vital component.

Going back to Cain and Hopkins, there are two main arguments running through their narrative. The first concerns the motivations behind British expansion. In contrast to the emphasis of mainstream political historians on the role of local conflicts in the periphery, the authors argue that the driving force behind the expansion came from the economic interests in the metropole, particularly of the landlord elites in the earlier period, and of the financial and service interests centring around the City of London after 1850.

The second argument relates to a critique of the literature, which emphasizes British decline since the late nineteenth century. The authors argue that most literature on British history assumes that, as British manufacturing competitiveness declined, so did British hegemony in the international economic and political order. In fact, Britain's power actually increased well into the twentieth century, first absolutely, and after the First World War relative to other powers, because of her financial and service sector supremacy. The target of this critique is primarily Marxist literature, but it also includes any writings which tend to directly associate industrial strength with political hegemony.

The authors substantiate these historical arguments both by showing landed elites' (and later financial and service sector interests') dominance in the political and economic decision-making process in the southern counties in Britain, and by demonstrating their significance in accounting for British expansion abroad. The close connections between Whitehall and the City, their maintenance of the culture of 'gentlemanly capitalism', and the role of public school networks in sustaining this culture are emphasized, while the British government's willingness to give up the protection of Lancashire and other manufacturing interests whenever these came into conflict with the interests of the City is highlighted.

Thus, as far as the period after 1850 is concerned,[4] this study is essentially a history of British imperialism from the perspective of the City. Its strength is that the authors make their case through academic arguments and the use of historical evidence, rather than by identifying themselves with the value standard of gentlemanly capitalism. In fact their stance often comes close to that of J.A. Hobson, one of the most profound critics of British imperialism. They bring out both positive and negative attributes associated with service sector orientation. There is no doubt that the two central ideas are important arguments, and are likely to make a lasting impact on literature.

The weakness of their approach lies in the fact that its *scope* of analysis is largely limited to the perspective of the City. As a result, in spite of its vast coverage of the history of the non-European world, it does not explicitly address the question of how to locate the achievements and failures of City-centred British capitalism in the wider context of the development of the capitalist world economy. It seems to me that, the authors' interest in linking their thesis to industrial development notwithstanding, the fundamental significance of global industrialization for the long-term survival and vitality of the City is insufficiently developed in their narrative. This, in turn, affects their interpretation of the relative strength of British imperialism. In what follows, I shall try to explore these points from the perspective of modern Asian international economic history, and suggest ways in which to assess British contributions to global history.

2   The role of the financial and service sectors in global industrialization

As stated above, one of the main targets of the authors' attack is the straightforward association frequently made between the rise and relative decline of industrial capitalism, and economic and political strength. I would like to begin by confirming that this association has also been largely accepted in the works on modern Asian economic history (roughly from 1850 to 1945), at least until very recently. Firstly, Britain was seen to be the superpower which colonized many South and Southeast Asian countries, forced the East Asian doors open in the nineteenth century, and introduced an entirely new set of technologies and organizations to the region.[5] Secondly, Britain has been regarded as a model which countries like Japan attempted to emulate, or a target against which anti-Western nationalist sentiments were aimed. In many writings, the British experience was assumed to be a typical example of capitalist development, and this perception played an important role in the understanding of the nature of capitalist development in East Asia.[6]

If such a 'British model' was inaccurately conceived, and the British case was in fact best described as 'gentlemanly capitalism' rather than all-powerful industrial capitalism, then it helps us to understand that there could be a strong element of complementarity between the British service sector interests and Japanese industrial ambitions. In Japanese historiography, emphasis had been traditionally placed on the significance of imports of British textiles to Japan for the fate of Japanese hand-spinners and hand-weavers, or, for the later period, of Japanese competition for the fate of British textile manufacturers. In other words, the two countries had been seen to be competing with each other. Essentially the same observation can be made with regard to the historiography of other Asian countries such as China and India. Britain's stake in financial and service sector activities in East Asia was not fully considered, although, with regard to India, a large stake in British investment was directly associated with colonial rule. However, British consular reports viewed Japan's industrial development as something which Britain should welcome, because it would enable her to export capital, textile and other machinery to Japan.[7] Moreover, as Cain and Hopkins suggest, British interests in China during the nineteenth century were heavily oriented towards financial and service activities. Such British attitudes, in turn, provided an environment in which Japan was able to pursue her industrial ambitions and export promotions. During the early twentieth century, the balance of power between British interests and Asian economic forces gradually shifted in favour of the latter, and the former became increasingly dependent on the growth of intra-Asian trade which was largely generated by the industrial growth of Japan and other Asian countries, and the networks of Chinese and Indian merchants.[8] Since Cain and Hopkins's picture of British imperialism places a new emphasis on Britain's service sector interests and its persistence throughout the period in question, it fits better than the old model in accounting for Asian economic development under the British-dominated international order between the 1880s and the 1930s. Their approach enables Asian economic historians to better appreciate the crucial role that Britain played. The British presence was a declining but positive force behind modern Asian economic development.

However, Cain and Hopkins concentrate on accounting for the motivations behind the British presence in Asia, and do not go beyond discussing direct gains and losses from that presence. While the British presence was instrumental in stimulating industrialization in East Asia, the process of industrialization was actually carried out by East Asians themselves, without accepting full British supremacy. The reason why the City's political influence continued was that East Asia emulated industrial technology rather more quickly than it was able to upgrade its capacity to conduct a large flow of international capital. It was easier for East Asia to imitate the former because it was easier to separate industrial technology from European culture, while, as Cain and Hopkins demonstrate, London's global financial supremacy was based on the accumulation of knowledge and experience which was much more culture-specific. We shall return to this point later, but it is important to recognize here that this particular kind of 'division of labour' was found to be acceptable to both sides.[9]

Why did East Asia fail to establish an alternative financial centre for the growth of intra-Asian trade between 1850 and 1945? In fact a number of such plans were contemplated, especially during the First World War and also in the 1930s.[10] Moreover, Hong Kong and Singapore had functioned as sub-centres of international financial transactions to some extent, for most of the period under review. Nevertheless, unlike Britain, Japan as Asia's first industrial nation did not opt for service sector specialization. She did not try to imitate this aspect of the 'British model', for gentlemanly capitalism did not ideologically embrace a comprehensive set of capitalist development options, and did not suit Japan's national purpose, which was to become an internationally competitive industrial power. This Japanese choice had an important implication for the fate of the City, insofar as it represented a more general trend in which late-developers could exploit other developmental options. The City survived by adapting and finding a new role in the world economy, and, as the authors emphasized, even strengthened its relative position *vis-à-vis* other financial centres. Paradoxically, it did so by increasingly exposing the partial nature of its interests in global industrialization, and the City increasingly came to depend on the global diffusion of industrialization.

By the 1930s, it became apparent that it was Japan, not the City, that was putting Lancashire into trouble. It was the strength of East Asian industrialization, not the strength of the City, that sustained the tacit alliance between them. The nature of local British politics (which occupy a central place in the discussion of the strength of the City in the Cain and Hopkins narrative), such as the disproportionate influence of the southern counties, cannot fully explain the strength of the City. It was the complementarity between the City and the manufacturing interests in other industrializing countries that enabled the City to dominate British politics. In other words, international relations shifted the balance of British domestic politics in a significant way.

It seems to me that essentially the same point could be made with regard to the history of the relationships between the City, and the industrial economies of Continental Europe and the United States.[11] Once these late-developer countries had acquired international manufacturing competitiveness, there emerged the possibility of an international division of labour where Britain specialized in financial and service sectors, while industrial Europe and the United States specialized in manufacturing. It is important to view this shifting balance of power between the City, and Continental Europe and the United States during the first half of this century, not just as a process generated by the rising industrial powers, but as a result of the pursuit of financial and service sector supremacy by Britain. She was to remain the centre of the multilateral patterns of world trade and international capital flows, as well as the centre of the system of the international gold standard. The expectation was that international adjustments between major powers could occur smoothly for mutual gain. This can be contrasted with the conclusion of Lenin who, while recognizing the importance of coalitions between major powers, regarded imperialist power struggles and war as inevitable. A general point is that, while the authors examine the City's economic strengths, together with Britain's political strengths, from the perspective of national and imperial history, it is in the last analysis impossible to accurately assess these strengths without locating them in the development of the capitalist world economy.

3   The City, colonialism and East Asia's industrialization

In the period under consideration there was no international political organization to regulate the diffusion of industrialization, so what necessitated the rest of the world to co-operate with the City? The City offered an institutional mechanism through which all the countries, dominions and colonies of the world were rated in terms of risk premiums and the degree of conformity to the liberal regime of free trade and free movement of capital. To qualify for such a role, openness and fluidity had to be combined with trustworthy institutions and respectable values. Gentlemanly capitalism was as much a product of this requirement as a force which shaped it. The capitalist world economy needed something like this, to ensure that the process of industrialization – which was dictated by different ecological, cultural and other factor endowments – was diffused smoothly through international competition. It was important that the City, and by implication Britain to some extent, acted as if they were outside this industrial competition. The City was in a position to benefit from the growth of world output and trade no matter who the winners were, so it should have been impartial to the competition. On the one hand, this accounts for the uniqueness and irreproducibility of gentlemanly capitalism. The core attributes of this function cannot and should not be copied, although smaller centres (such as Hong Kong) could and should serve as sub-centres of the London-centred international networks. At the same time, this understanding of the role of the City of London explains why a purely national perspective does not work in assessing its strength.

Thus, from the perspective of the City, any action that violated this liberal regime, such as the protection of home industry, was to be effectively resisted, if necessary, with the use of threats or force. Naturally, some industries felt that they were being victimized, and the victims included British industries, sometimes even important ones such as the Lancashire cotton textile industry. J.A. Hobson's internationalism was consistent with such a view. At the same time, Hobson was also an interventionist, whenever a fair rule or an institutional framework was missing or under threat. This made him not only a leading liberal social reformer at home, but a profound critic of British imperialism abroad. His picture of Western imperialism in Asia highlights the limitations of Western officials' understanding of local languages, cultures and institutions, hence how difficult it is to argue the success of colonial rule in the first place.

By contrast, Cain and Hopkins offer a more rigorous narrative on how strongly the interests of the City were represented in British policy in India and China. That they were more strongly represented than the interests of Lancashire from the very early stages of the nineteenth century, and that this service sector orientation persisted right down to the late 1930s are both important insights. But the authors do not appear to consider the changes in the global effects of this orientation upon the strength of the British empire as fundamental to their study. Once again, they only make links between British colonial policy and the City within the perspective of national and imperial history.

If their argument holds, however, it seems to me that this orientation must have increasingly weakened both British rule in India, and British influence in Asia generally, as a result of global industrialization. During most of the nineteenth century, the complementarity between British policy and Asia's industrialization worked well for Britain and there was little or no contradiction between service sector orientation and colonial rule. However, in 1893 the rupee was linked to gold via sterling, primarily to secure the value of British investment and the personal income of British officials in India. This artificial raising of the value of the rupee severely damaged India's position in Asian trade and the Asian monetary system which was based on silver. Japan was the chief beneficiary of this, rapidly capturing the vital part of the Chinese cotton yarn market that was previously dominated by Indian yarn. The large amount of British investment worked against colonial development in this respect.[12] During the interwar period Britain continued to discourage India's industrialization by keeping the value of the rupee consistently high. In the 1930s, the drastic devaluation of the yen was a vital element in Japan's industrial recovery,[13] while Britain retained the policy of protecting investors' interests and allowed Japanese industrial goods to penetrate into imperial markets.[14] In this respect, Japan's industrialization and British service sector orientation in the colonies reinforced each other. Together, they weakened Britain's political and economic grip on the empire, by causing abandonment of the effort to implement an overall developmental strategy. This indirectly helped the nationalist cause in Asia, albeit unintentionally. In the 1930s, faced with the Great Depression and the collapse of world trade, gentlemanly capitalism became increasingly reliant on the protected environment of the British empire. It was precisely at that point that the identification of the interests of the City with the empire had to be seriously qualified,[15] and by the early 1940s it had to be abandoned, partly because of the changes in Asian international politics and partly due to the pressure for decolonization from the United States.[16] While Cain and Hopkins are right in arguing that British hegemony in the international order did not decline as fast as Britain's manufacturing competitiveness, it did decline against the growth of initiatives of industrial economies. Service sector interests came to be exposed to political negotiations with industrial economies, without the backing of the empire.

In fact Cain and Hopkins have also noted that 'the City assisted the growth of manufacturing within and beyond the empire in ways that in the long run contributed to the process of decolonization', and emphasized 'the importance of the 1930s as a turning point in this regard'.[17] They rightly remind us of their contribution to our understanding of these links, especially with regard to the dominions. I am making a further point here that the City's contribution to the growth of manufacturing, when considered from the point of view of the growth of the Asian regional economy, tended to be greater outside the empire than inside it, and that this paradoxical tendency at the regional level made the association of the interests of the City with the protection of the empire much more difficult than otherwise.

On the other hand, Britain succeeded in maintaining her international position, by making sterling the key currency after she abandoned the gold standard in 1931. Admittedly, this was made possible by various imperial devices, such as replacing the gold reserves of colonies and dominions by sterling and keeping them in London. But its effect was worldwide, going well beyond the confines of the formal and informal empire, as sterling became the first currency that was accepted by many independent countries of the world, without the guarantee of it being exchanged for gold. The 'sterling area', by which I mean an area in which the value of the local currency was linked to sterling,[18] extended well beyond the tariff protection set out under the Ottawa agreement of 1932. It was not just Scandinavia and many other smaller countries that linked the value of their currencies to sterling. After 1933, the United States agreed to link the value of the dollar as well, as a result of which the two currencies effectively replaced gold by acting as the standard of value against which the value of a number of other currencies was measured.

East Asia was no exception. After abandoning the gold standard in 1931 and sharply devaluing the yen, Japan decided to link its currency to sterling in 1932, in the hope of stabilizing its value. Although she continued her effort to expand the 'yen bloc' in the continent, the majority of Japanese trade was conducted with countries outside the bloc. So, the stabilization of the currency was vital to the procurement of raw material and fuel from abroad, needed for rapid industrialization, territorial expansion and the preparation of war. To the extent that the international confidence of the yen now depended on its linkage to sterling, not to gold, the entire yen bloc can be said to have belonged to the 'sterling area'.[19] Thus the more the yen bloc expanded, the greater became the influence of sterling and the sterling-linked international monetary system on East Asia. Meanwhile, the Chinese currency also came to be linked to sterling in 1935, as a result of the currency reform implemented by the nationalist government with the co-operation of Britain. Since the Chinese currency was originally linked to silver and had been heavily devalued against gold before 1931, this linkage also meant that the Chinese government opted for devaluation, to carry out import-substitution industrialization. Thus during the brief period from 1935 to 1938, nearly all of the East Asian economies were linked to sterling at a heavily devalued rate. As a result, the exchange rate between yen and yuan was more or less completely stabilized.

On the one hand, this suited East Asia whose priority was industrial-ization and the need to restrict imports of industrial goods from the West and export their own to other developing countries. At the same time, it enabled both Japan and China to issue a large amount of yen- or yuan-denominated notes at home and in the colonies, the sphere of influence and disputed areas, not backed by gold or silver but linked to sterling via the central government. This was a much more acceptable solution for Britain than either the French-led gold bloc or the German-led mark bloc, as it helped avoid the worsening of the liquidity trap felt worldwide since 1929, while simultaneously maintaining the trade between East Asia and the rest of the world at a reasonable level. Devaluation was tolerated, as the Western stake in investment in East Asia was not as important as in their colonies in South and Southeast Asia. In spite of the 'currency war' and the effects of the Sino-Japanese War itself, which began in 1937, the value of the Chinese currency did not collapse before the second quarter of 1938. The final blow to the sterling-linked East Asian monetary regime came when the Second World War began in Europe in 1939 and the value of sterling collapsed, after which the yen bloc was rapidly transformed into a regional autarky, rather similar to the mark bloc in Europe.[20]

An important result of the region's linkage with sterling for much of the 1930s, was that intra-Asian trade became progressively concentrated on East Asia, while the share of colonies of the Western powers in South and Southeast Asia diminished. Thus, as far as Asia is concerned, the vitality of the City became more and more dependent on the industri-alization of East Asia, rather than on the resources of the British empire. Yet by this time Britain's military and political muscle was no longer strong enough to contain Japan. Faced with a fight for survival as the world's major financial centre, that is, the need to find a 'new role' in global development, the City by the late 1930s had no choice but to support the British government's appeasement policy towards Japan, in spite of its moral and political sympathy with China. In British Malaya, overseas Chinese remittances to mainland China, which were sent in order to support national resistance against Japan, were discouraged by the colonial government which disliked the flow of monetary resources from the empire. The British service sector orientation effectively ended up supporting Japanese aggression.[21] It was surely an act against the principle of Hobson's internationalism.

Looking at the changes in the structure of the capitalist world econ-omy in the interwar period as a whole, however, the presence of an international regime of free trade and capital flows centred around

London was crucial in promoting East Asia's industrialization by making the Western technology available to the region. It was the City, not those manufacturers who carried out national industrial advance in the West, that made this technology transfer internationally acceptable and politically possible. It was gentlemanly capitalism, not national economic interests, that helped the global diffusion of industrialization.

4   Decolonization, the Cold War regime and postwar East Asian growth

After the Second World War, Britain tried to regain her position as imperialist power, and the City of London attempted to restore the sterling area and maintain the status of sterling as an international currency. By the late 1950s, however, with decolonization and Britain's relative economic decline, the restoration of the prewar order clearly became unrealistic. The City was to find a new role in the global development now led by the United States. In fact this hegemonic shift occurred in close interaction with another major development – the emergence of the Cold War regime.

In East Asia, the communist revolution in China and the outbreak of the Korean War reinforced the American 'reverse course' policy towards Japan, that is, to rehabilitate, rather than destroy, Japanese industrial power and use it to counter the penetration of socialist forces in the region. Thus during the 1950s and 1960s Japan successfully negotiated to become a full member of GATT, in order to benefit from the emerging liberal regime of international trade backed by the United States. In spite of political difficulties arising from the self-inflicted consequences of the Asia-Pacific War, Japan was able to import raw materials and fuel from all over the world, and export labour-intensive industrial goods, especially to the United States and other Asian countries, so that she could carry out economic modernizations at home. A new international division of labour gradually emerged where the United States specialized in capital- and resource-intensive industries and Japan (and later other East Asian countries) specialized in labour-intensive and resource-saving industries. The former industries were often military-related, for example, military, space, aircraft and petrochemical industries, while the latter concentrated on the production of non-military, mass consumer goods. As far as the trade between the West and the rest of the world is concerned, this is a fundamentally different kind of division of labour from the one which operated since the industrial revolution in the early nineteenth century. Under the imperialist order dominated by Britain, the rest of the world was to provide primary products to the Western metropole. Now the nature of complementarity became more interindustrial and much less hierarchical.

As stated above, it was East Asia's industrialization between the wars, especially during the 1930s, that prepared this shift in the patterns of world production and trade. It was at that point that East Asia as a region began to industrialize, with the full use of Western technology. For the first time, a regional and substantially autonomous industrialization, involving hundreds of millions of people, occurred outside Europe. After the war, labour-intensive industrial goods began to be exported from East Asia back to the West, first in the form of textiles and sundries, then in consumer electrical goods, bikes and small cars. It is worth noting that from the early postwar period both competition and co-operation among Asian countries played a vital role in the growth of reverse industrial exports. By the 1960s and 1970s there was fierce competition among East and Southeast Asian exporters in the Western market of cheap mass consumer goods. Thus, if the exports of Japanese textiles were subjected to voluntary restrictions in the American market, it tended to give Hong Kong's textile exporters, rather than the domestic manufacturers, a chance to capture a slice of that market. There was also co-operation. For example, an 'East Asian textile complex', made up of Japanese man-made cloth manufacturers, Taiwanese weavers, Hong Kong apparel manufacturers and Japanese trading companies, combined Japanese technology, Taiwanese cheap labour, Hong Kong's designer skills and Japanese capital and organizational abilities, and emerged as a formidable competitor in the international market. As the Cold War turned to 'long peace' and the demand for mass consumer goods grew much faster than military-related needs, the rate of economic growth of East Asian countries became higher than that of the West. By the 1980s, the quality of Japanese manufactured goods matched that of its American counterparts, and the Pacific became the focus of international competition in high-technology goods. The high-growth segments of the mass consumer market, including some top quality range, also shifted from the United States to East Asia around this time. By then the majority of world trade was being conducted across the Pacific Ocean, and the centuries-old pre-eminence of the Atlantic in world trade, on which the centrality of the City of London depended, had been lost.[22]

The growth of competitive financial and service sectors was crucial for this rise of the Asia-Pacific economy. For much of the postwar period, both Hong Kong and Singapore played an important role in facilitating the recovery and growth of intra-Asian, as well as Pacific, trade and flows of capital. Hong Kong in particular acted as an international centre of trade, finance and services by fully committing itself to the principle of free trade, while remaining a British colony till 1997. Under the international environment of surging nationalism and the Cold War divide, Hong Kong was a crucial counter-force, which neither retaliated strongly against any protectionist actions by its trading partners nor was completely closed to communist China. By offering its neighbouring countries entrepôt facilities and human networks, Hong Kong undoubtedly helped unite Asia's national economies and connect them with the United States through trade, capital, and information and technology flows. East Asian growth economies thus enjoyed both a committed industrial policy at home and an easy access to fast-growing regional and American markets. In this way, Hong Kong contributed to the dynamic growth of the Asia-Pacific economy. It should be possible to acknowledge this largely unintended consequence of global significance, without entering into the debate on the political assessment of British rule there. While its entrepreneurial strength largely came from Chinese merchants and manufacturers (many Shanghai capitalists migrated south to blend with overseas Chinese in Southeast Asia with traditional commercial skills), its institutional setting was unmistakably British, heavily modelled on gentlemanly capitalism. The peculiar relationship between manufacturing, and finance and services was thus transferred to East Asia, to form the heart of its economic success.

Furthermore, there must have been many other international centres of finance and services, which encouraged the growth of manufacturing in the Asia-Pacific region. We need to identify these shifting sets of international apparatus, including indeed part of the activities of the City of London, at each stage of its development. In the most recent past, that is, after the collapse of the Cold War regime, it became clear that the United States came to specialize further in the financial sector, thus creating a new sense of complementarity with East Asian manufacturing interests. In some respects, the 'Wall Street–Treasury Complex' replaced the old 'Military–Industrial Complex'.[23] Thus the nature of complementarity between the United States and East Asia somewhat shifted, from the division of labour between capital-intensive and labour-intensive industries, to the one similar to the relationship between the City and late-developer industrial economies. The peculiar relationship, identified here as the Cain and Hopkins perspective, has arguably survived the hegemonic shift, and has remained a central device for the development of the capitalist world economy to this day.

5   Implications for global history

One of the main issues on global history in recent years has been the assessment of the 'East Asian miracle' and its historical roots. Many writers, including myself, have argued that there was in fact an East Asian pattern of economic development, which has its own roots going back at least to the sixteenth century.[24] While some writers were inclined to play down the significance of the Western impact during the nineteenth century altogether,[25] others such as Gunder Frank suggested that Western dominance was a divergence from the general pattern of East Asia-centred global history for the last six thousand years, for a 'brief' period of a few centuries.[26]

I have instead argued for the significance of the industrial revolution in Britain for the modernization of the Asian economies, though in a different way from that expressed by the more Eurocentric writers. Japan's industrialization since the late nineteenth century occurred, not through a straightforward application of Western technology, but as a result of its extensive adaptation to an environment where land was extremely scarce and labour abundant. This adaptation helped develop the international competitiveness of some Japanese industries, the technological and institutional path of which assumed strong labour-intensive and resource-saving bias. It is inappropriate to view this process simply in terms of 'catching up' with the West, as it was simultan-eously an effort to find a new pattern of complementarity in the growth of the capitalist world economy.

On the European history front, *The Great Divergence* by Kenneth Pomeranz has recently put forward a perspective, which corresponds to mine in a number of respects.[27] Pomeranz acknowledges the significance of the industrial revolution, but argues that it occurred, not as a natural outgrowth of earlier technological and institutional developments in Western Europe, but as a result of two highly contingent factors that were available to England and some other regions of Western Europe, namely the availability of cheap, good quality coal in or near proto-industrial regions, and an access to vast natural resources in the new continents, especially North America. An implication of this argument is that the more general pattern of economic development based on the growth of the market, commer-cialization of agriculture and proto-industrialization, was in fact present not just in Western Europe but in several parts of the world before 1800, and that the growth of the Atlantic economy, with the heavy use of fossil fuel and other natural resources, was a 'great divergence' from this general trend. It is certainly the case that until recently, industrialization was associated with the development of capital- and resource-intensive technology, the use of which was highly contingent upon their availability. The intrinsic value of labour-intensive and resource-saving technology for the steadier and wider diffusion of industrialization has not been the focus of study.

Yet the majority of the world population in manufacturing has clearly been engaged in those industries which belong to the latter category over the last one hundred and fifty years. The East Asian experience amply demonstrates this; so much so that it is impossible to understand why Japan, and later other Asian countries, industrialized at all, without appreciating the region's strong focus on labour-intensive, and more recently human capital-intensive, technology. The region was generally land-scarce and labour-abundant, so the direction of technological development tended towards more labour-intensive and less resource-using, before the Second World War (with or without the Japanese influence). East Asia was 'allowed' to industrialize under the dominance of the Western powers because it found a Ricardian justification *vis-à-vis* the West, to carry out industrialization. After the war, on the basis of the differences in factor endowments between the resource-rich West (which was released from the constraints of land and other natural resources by the growth of the Atlantic economy) and the resource-poor East Asia, the new international division of labour sketched above emerged as a main pattern of global development.[28]

After the 1960s high economic growth gradually pushed up the Asian wage level, first in Japan and then in the NIEs, encouraging labour-intensive industry based on low-wage labour to move further to ASEAN, China and other developing countries. An important result of this 'flying geese pattern of economic development' was a massive absorption of low-wage labour in China (and India and elsewhere) into the industrial sector directly connected to the world market. The textile industries of China and India today are by far the single largest providers of industrial employment in the world. The global diffusion of industrialization has finally reached the world's largest reservoirs of 'unlimited supplies of labour'.

It seems to me that there is room for enriching this ongoing story of the growth of the Asia-Pacific economy by incorporating the Cain and Hopkins perspective into it. One of the less explicit agendas behind their work has been the historical reassessment of the industrial revolution in Britain in the light of the dominance of landed elites and the vital role of financial and service sectors in the first half of the nineteenth century. Their argument calls for a revision of our understanding of industrialization, because they imply that the first industrial revolution was already dependent on the political forces linked to the economic interests outside manufacturing, which created a framework of 'imperialism of free trade' and promoted the growth of the international division of labour.[29] More generally, the Cain and Hopkins perspective encourages us to focus on a link between manufacturing, and finance and services as a central element of the development of capitalism. If Pomeranz tried to isolate the Atlantic bias from our understanding of industrialization in order to grasp the more general pattern of economic development, Cain and Hopkins have extracted the role of financial and service sectors for the global diffusion of industrialization. They effectively identified the necessity of these sectors for economic development in general.

Since the late nineteenth century, therefore, there emerged an additional international division of labour between manufacturing as a whole, and finance and services, which ensured complementarity between the City of London and industrial economies such as Germany and Japan. Looking at it from the perspective of the non-European world, the essence of 'Western impact' was not just the introduction of manufacturing technology, but a combination of that and the availability of international financial capital and services. In other words, the City of London acted as a vital facilitator of technological transfer from the West to East Asia (and eventually to the rest of the world), enabling the global diffusion of industrialization to take place. Insofar as the City's financiers globalized faster and in many ways negotiated with politics more closely than the manufacturers themselves, they were at the frontier of globalization. Gentlemanly capitalism, with emphasis on openness and respectability, pushed this trend forward. In the last analysis, however, it was the global diffusion of industrialization that penetrated into different civilizations and changed the shape of the modern world. From the perspective of global history, the deepest impact of the City of London lay in demonstrating its facilitator role in that great transformation, more clearly than had ever been imagined.

Notes

1 This chapter is a revised and substantially enlarged version of my review article of Cain and Hopkins, *British Imperialism*, published in *Keizai Kenkyu* (Economic Review), 49–3, July 1998, pp. 277–81. I am grateful to Professors

Cain and Hopkins for their comments on the original version, as well as on the draft of this paper.

2   Some main Japanese-language publications in the more recent period include: Takeshi Hamashita, *Kindai Chugoku no Kokusaiteki Keiki: Choko Boeki Shisutemu to Kindai Ajia* (International Factors Affecting Modern China: Tributary Trade System and Modern Asia) (Tokyo Daigaku Shuppankai, Tokyo, 1990); Heita Kawakatsu, *Nihon Bunmei to Kindai Seiyo: 'Sakoku' Saiko* (Japanese Civilization and the Modern West: 'Seclusion' Reconsidered) (Nihon Hoso Shuppan Kyokai, Tokyo, 1991); Takeshi Hamashita and Heita Kawakatsu (eds), *Ajia Koekiken to Nihon Kogyoka: 1500–1900* (Asian Trading Networks and Japan's Industrialization) (new edition, Fujiwara Shoten, Tokyo, 2001); Kaoru Sugihara, *Ajia-kan Boeki no Keisei to Kozo* (Patterns and Development of Intra-Asian Trade) (Mineruva Shobo, Kyoto, 1996); Takeshi Hamashita, *Choko Shisutemu to Kindai Ajia* (Tributary Trade System and Modern Asia) (Iwanami Shoten, Tokyo, 1997); Shinya Sugiyama and Linda Grove (eds), *Kinndai Ajia no Ryutsu Nettowaku* (Distribution Networks in Modern Asia) (Sobunsha, Tokyo, 1999); Naoto Kagotani, *Ajia Kokusai Tsusho Chitsujo to Kindai Nihon* (The Asian International Trading Order and Modern Japan) (Nagoya Daigaku Shuppankai, Nagoya, 2000); Kazuko Furuta, *Shanhai Nettowaku to Kindai Higashi Ajia* (Shanghai Networks and Modern East Asia) (Tokyo Daigaku Shuppankai, Tokyo, 2000); Shigeru Akita and Naoto Kagotani (eds), *1930-nendai no Ajia Kokusai Chitsujo* (The Asian International Order in the 1930s) (Keisuisha, Hiroshima, 2001).

3   Main English-language publications other than those cited in the following footnotes include: Heita Kawakatsu, 'International Competition in Cotton Goods in the Late Nineteenth Century: Britain versus India and East Asia', in Wolfram Fischer *et al.* (eds), The Emergence of a World Economy, 1500–1914, *Beitrage zur Wirtschafts- und Sozialgeschichte*, Band 33, 2 (Franz Steiner, Wiesbaden, 1986); Takeshi Hamashita, 'The Tribute Trade System and Modern Asia', *Memoirs of the Research Department of the Toyo Bunko*, 46, 1988, pp. 7–25; A.J.H. Latham and Heita Kawakatsu (eds), *Japanese Industrialization and the Asian Economy* (Routledge, London, 1994); Satoshi Ikeda, 'The History of the Capitalist World-System vs. the History of East-Southeast Asia', *Review*, 19–1, winter 1996, pp. 49–77; Kaoru Sugihara (ed.), *The Growth of the Asian International Economy: the Chinese Dimension* (forthcoming).

4   Parts of Vol. 1 are devoted to the period from 1688 to 1850, and the continuity between the mercantilist era and the first half of the nineteenth century is an important point of their thesis. However, the bulk of their work, particularly on the history of the Empire, relates to the period after 1850.

5   Kenzo Mori, *Jiyu Boeki Teikokushugi* (Imperialism of Free Trade) (Tokyo Daigaku Shuppankai, Tokyo, 1978).

6   See Kaoru Sugihara, 'The Japanese Capitalism Debate, 1927–1937', in Peter Robb (ed.), *Agrarian Structure and Economic Development*, Occasional Papers in Third-World Economic History 4, SOAS, London, 1992, pp. 24–33.

7   Shigeru Akita, '"Gentlemanly Capitalism", Intra-Asian Trade and Japanese Industrialization at the Turn of the Last Century', *Japan Forum*, 8–1, March 1996, pp. 51–65.

8   Kaoru Sugihara, 'Patterns of Asia's Integration into the World Economy, 1880–1913', in Wolfram Fischer *et al.* (eds) The Emergence of a World

Economy, 1500–1914, *Beitrage zur Wirtschafts- und Sozialgeschichte*, Band 33, 2 (Franz Steiner, Wiesbaden, 1986) (reprinted in C.K. Harley (ed.), *The Integration of the World Economy, 1800–1914*, Vol. 2 (Edward Elgar, Cheltenham, 1996); Kaoru Sugihara, 'Intra-Asian Trade and East Asia's Industrialization, 1919–1939', in Gareth Austin (ed.), *Industrial Growth in the Third World, c. 1870–c. 1990: Depressions, Intra-regional Trade, and Ethnic Networks*, LSE Working Papers in Economic History, 44/98, London School of Economics and Political Science, London, 1998, pp. 25–57.

9 In fact there was also competition between Britain and Asia in some areas, for example between British and Japanese shipping lines, as they both sought market shares in Asian waters. On the whole, however, adjustments were made by creating the more finely tuned 'division of labour' where, for example, certain local and regional routes were taken by the Japanese lines which used Japanese ships and either Japanese trading companies or Chinese merchant networks, while long-distance routes were secured by the British lines which often worked with Western merchants, bankers and insurance companies.

10 For a brief list of references, see Kaoru Sugihara, 'Japan as an Engine of the Asian International Economy, c. 1880–1936', *Japan Forum*, 2–1, April 1990, pp. 141–2.

11 As far as the authors' treatment of the relative strengths of the United States and Britain is concerned, they acknowledge general changes in the balance of power, and bring them into the narrative in an effective way. However, their understanding of the relative strengths of American and British influence in East Asia may be questioned to some degree, along the line of the argument here. See Shigeru Akita, 'British Informal Empire in East Asia, 1880–1939: a Japanese Perspective', in Raymond E. Dumett (ed.), *Gentlemanly Capitalism and British Imperialism: the New Debate on Empire*, Longman, London, 1999.

12 For a more general discussion on the effects on colonial development, see Kaoru Sugihara, 'Trade Statistics of British India, 1834–1947', Discussion Papers in Economics and Business, Graduate School of Economics, Osaka University (2002).

13 Kaoru Sugihara, 'Japan's Industrial Recovery, 1931–1936', in Ian Brown (ed.), *The Economies of Africa and Asia during the Interwar Depression*, Routledge, London, 1989.

14 Much has been discussed about the tariff protection in British India against Japanese textiles since the late 1920s, and the import tariff did go up, at one time to as much as 75 per cent for certain categories of cloth. Nevertheless, after the trade negotiations of 1933 and 1934, the Japanese share in Indian imports did not decline, largely because the effects of the tariff were more than offset by the devaluation of the yen against the rupee. See Sugihara, 'Intra-Asian Trade and East Asia's Industrialization'. A similar point is made with regard to Dutch colonial rule in Kagotani, *Ajia Kokusai Tsusho Chitsujo to Kindai Nihon*, ch. 5.

15 For a comparative assessment of the effects of imperial preference, individual tariff and quota restrictions, and the exchange rates, see Sugihara, 'Intra-Asian Trade and East Asia's Industrialization'.

16 For the role of Japan in this process, see Nobuko Nagasaki, *Indo Dokuritsu: Gyakko no naka no Chandora Bosu* (India's Independence: a Perspective

from the Study of Subhas Chandra Bose) (Asahi Shinbunsha, Tokyo, 1989).

17 Foreword to the second edition of *British Imperialism*, p. 17.

18 The term 'link' is used hereafter to indicate that, although the value of the local currency was not completely 'pegged' to sterling, its exchange rate was consciously kept stable, allowing for minor fluctuations only.

19 Most authors, including Cain and Hopkins, have not regarded East Asia as part of the 'sterling area', but the usage here is consistent with the spirit of those who tried to understand the depth of its global influence. See, for instance, Ragnar Nurkse, *International Currency Experience: Lessons of the Inter-War Period*, Geneva, 1944, ch. 3.

20 Kaoru Sugihara, 'Higashi Ajia ni okeru Kogyokagata Tsuka Chitsujo no Seiritsu' (The Emergence of an Industrialization-promoting Monetary Regime in East Asia), in Akita and Kagotani (eds), *1930-nendai no Ajia Kokusai Chitsujo*.

21 Kaoru Sugihara, 'The Economic Motivations behind Japanese Aggression in the late 1930s: the Perspectives of Freda Utley and Nawa Toichi', *Journal of Contemporary History*, 32–2, April 1997, pp. 259–80.

22 Kaoru Sugihara, *Ajia-Taiheiyo Keizai-ken no Koryu* (The Rise of the Asia-Pacific Economy) (Osaka Daigaku Shuppankai, Osaka 2002).

23 Jagdish Bhagwati, 'The Capital Myth: the Difference between Trade in Widgets and Dollars', *Foreign Affairs*, 77–3, May–June 1998, pp. 7–12.

24 Kaoru Sugihara, 'The East Asian Path of Economic Development: a Long-term Perspective', Discussion Papers in Economics and Business, 00–17, Graduate School of Economics, Osaka University, Oct. 2000.

25 I have argued that Hamashita's work has this tendency, although we are in complete agreement in our determination to correct the Eurocentric bias in our historiography. See Kaoru Sugihara, 'Kindai Ajia Keizaishi ni okeru Renzoku to Danzetsu: Kawakatsu Heita, Hamashita Takeshi-shi no Shosetsu o megutte' (Continuity and Discontinuity in Modern Asian Economic History: a Critique of the Works of Heita Kawakatsu and Takeshi Hamashita), *Shakai Keizai Shigaku*, 62–3, Aug.–Sep. 1996, pp. 80–102.

26 Andre Gunder Frank, *Re-Orient: Global Economy in the Asian Age* (University of California Press, Berkeley, 1998).

27 Kenneth Pomeranz, *The Great Divergence: China, Europe, and the Making of the Modern World Economy*, Princeton University Press, Princeton, 2000. For an exchange of views, see pp. 12–13 in his comments on my work and my response in Sugihara, 'The East Asian Pattern of Economic Development'.

28 See Sugihara, 'Patterns of Asia's Integration into the World Economy' and 'The East Asian Path of Economic Development'.

29 In the Japanese case too, industrialization crucially depended on the support of economic interests outside manufacturing. For example, following the Sino-Japanese War victory of 1894–95, the Ministry of Agriculture and Commerce staged a series of supra-ministerial conferences, meeting three times between 1896 and 1898, and approving a number of important industrial policy proposals. As most export industries were small-scale at that time, the main supporters that helped the implementation of this policy were export-related business interests led by shipping, banking, insurance and

storehouse sectors as well as by large trading companies. This was the case, in spite of the fact that the Japanese strategy was firmly on the promotion of industrial exports rather than of internationally competitive financial and service sectors. Kaoru Sugihara, 'Keiei Hatten no Kiban Seibi' (The Development of an Institutional Infrastructure for Modern Business), Matao Miyamoto and Takeshi Abe (eds), *Nihon Keieishi 2: Keiei Kakushin to Kogyoka* (Iwanami Shoten, Tokyo, 1995), p. 57.

Part III
Response

11
The Peculiarities of British Capitalism: Imperialism and World Development[1]

Peter Cain and A.G. Hopkins

The response to *British Imperialism* since it was first published in two volumes in 1993 has greatly exceeded our expectations. The books were widely reviewed at the time, and the interpretation they put forward, based on the concept of gentlemanly capitalism, has been extensively discussed subsequently, not only in Britain but also elsewhere in Europe, in the United States and in Asia. We have responded to many of these comments and criticisms in the Foreword of the new, one-volume edition of *British Imperialism*.[2] The publication of the present book, which is the second collection of essays devoted to our work on gentlemanly capitalism and British imperialism, shows that this interest remains strong.[3] We are immensely grateful to the ten authors represented here for giving their time and energy to the project. One of them, Shigeru Akita, deserves a special mention. He was the chief organizer of the conference in Osaka from which this book springs, and he has edited the essays with great skill and boundless energy.

Two of the chapters examine the idea of gentlemanly capitalism itself. Bowen finds not only that it flourished in eighteenth-century Britain but also that it developed simultaneously in the American colonies before the Revolution. Krozewski accepts that gentlemanly capitalism was highly influential in the nineteenth century, but questions the validity of the concept for the period after the Second World War. Darwin bridges both these chapters by placing our interpretation of Britain's expansion overseas in the context of even broader international developments between 1830 and 1960. Phimister reappraises our interpretation of the classic case of imperialist rivalries within this period by focusing on the 'scramble' for Africa. Five of the nine chapters are concerned with (and originate in) East Asia. Shunhong's paper offers a wide-ranging critique of our arguments from a Chinese Marxist standpoint. Petersson's contribution complements Phimister's by placing Britain's role in the Edwardian 'scramble' for China in the context of rivalries among the great powers at the turn of the twentieth century. The remaining three essays concentrate on Britain's policy and presence in China and on her relationships with Japan. Sugihara looks at the effects of gentlemanly capitalist economic policies on industrialization in Asia; Akita and Kagotani pursue the same theme with reference to the 1930s and the evolution of the sterling area; Kibata supplements their analysis by linking Britain's policy in China to her relations with Japan in the same period.

Between them, these nine essays provide fresh insight into the modern age of European imperialism, whether by offering new evidence or by extending current thinking. Each contribution merits careful attention in its own right. But the larger picture has also to be kept in mind; we shall offer some reflections on where the subject now stands at the end of the commentary that follows.

I

The chapters by Huw Bowen and Gerold Krozewski are the two most distant from each other in terms of chronology, but they have in common the fact that they both deal with periods that we were obliged to present in a highly compressed fashion. What we hoped to do, in both cases, was to show how our interpretation might be applied, while recognizing that we lacked sufficient space to unpack the argument and to engage with the detailed literature. We are therefore especially grateful to these contributors for pursuing our line of enquiry further than we did ourselves and for considering whether it stands the test of the detailed research that is now available.

Bowen's essay bears out our view that a gentlemanly capitalist elite emerged in the course of the eighteenth century. The definition of gentility shifted as the social composition of the elite changed, and there was a fierce debate (as there was in the nineteenth century too) between those who were eager to open the door to social mobility and those who were keen to keep it shut. Consequently, it was not always easy to know who was a gentleman and who was not. But this problem does not weaken the value of the term; it is rather an accurate reflection of the fluid realities of the time.[4] Bowen's main interest, however, is less with domestic history than with showing how the gentlemanly order extended its international reach as the century advanced and created what might be termed 'peripheral gentlemanly capitalism'. Our own treatment of this theme, as Bowen points out, was truncated, and studies by other historians tend to be confined to particular regions. While Bowen takes most of his illustrations from the mainland colonies, he also draws attention to the rise of a gentlemanly elite in India, and his story could readily be expanded to include the West Indies too. His analysis traces the ways in which the shared values and life-styles associated with gentlemanly conduct at home took root abroad and led eventually to the creation of new cosmopolitan elites. The colonial gentry of America and India were never merely 'carbon copies' of the originals, and indeed were coloured in various shades by their local environment.[5] Nevertheless, they resisted the 'call of the wild' and they never lost the key to the codes of conduct that derived from their metropolitan origins.

The extension of the gentlemanly elite overseas, as Bowen points out, helped to shape the concept of empire and ultimately provided it with a strong thread of unity. Ideas of empire that were diverse and shifting in the early eighteenth century[6] were consolidated and pinned down during the era of war and revolution that ran from 1756 to 1815.[7] The role of the state has long been considered to be central to these developments. Eighteenth-century governments inherited and augmented a battery of legislation to regulate external trade and shipping, and they put in place a patronage system that was sufficiently large, visible and objectionable to arouse vociferous opposition in the 1770s and 1780s. However, the familiar and now rather dated picture of the mercantilist state has been redrawn in recent years to emphasize its more positive features.[8] The military-fiscal state, as it is now seen, was an efficient tax-gathering machine that funded the public investment needed to weld the nation and promote overseas expansion. Taking the century as a whole, 'government and defence' was probably the fastest growing sector of the economy as well as being very considerable in absolute terms.[9] By 1815, Britain's overseas trade, boosted by government investment in naval power and by strategic acquisitions, had shifted decisively from Europe to the wider world. It is in this context that British governments made determined efforts to increase their hold on the mainland colonies after 1763, when the threat from France was (temporarily) removed, on India in the 1760s and 1770s, when the East India Company fell into financial difficulties, and on Australasia at the close of the century, when opportunities for creating a dependent neo-Europe arose.

Without denying the significance of this revisionist view of the state, Bowen's analysis suggests that emphasis should also be placed on the role of informal influences and the unofficial mind of imperialism in the twin processes of nation-building at home and imperial expansion abroad. Eighteenth-century governments were less able than their successors in the nineteenth and twentieth centuries to translate intentions into results, especially where their writ had to be carried to distant lands overseas. Consequently, there was considerable scope for the 'unofficial mind' of imperialism to influence events during this period. The eighteenth-century state was also more permeable than its successors: public and private interests joined hands through patronage and found expression in the emerging empire, most notably in the East India Company. The state was the executive arm, not of the bourgeoisie, but of the gentlemanly elite, which straddled public and private spheres with an ease born of long practice. Determining the relative importance of state and private influences is therefore not just a matter of establishing an appropriate balance: it involves recognizing that the boundaries between social and self were far less distinct than they were to become in the nineteenth century, when New Probity finally replaced Old Corruption.

In making a case for the importance of private influences in creating an empire that was both imagined and highly material, Bowen directs our attention to questions that he himself was unable to pursue, though there is space to speculate on only two of these here. The first concerns the relationship between private interests and informal empire. Robinson and Gallagher used the term informal empire to draw attention to impulses towards imperialism that lay outside the formal, constitutional empire. Given this definition, there is no reason why, in principle, the phrase could not be applied to the eighteenth century. Contemporaries were undoubtedly aware of the possibility. In the late eighteenth century, Josiah Tucker anticipated the notion of 'free-trade imperialism' by arguing that it would be more cost-effective to control the thirteen colonies through trade and investment than through direct rule.[10] In practice, however, historians of the eighteenth century have not followed this lead: the debate on informal empire, though voluminous, has been confined almost entirely to the nineteenth century. Aside from historiographical convention – a force not to be underestimated – it has been assumed that the conditions that made an informal empire possible were not present until Britain had passed through the industrial revolution and had achieved technological supremacy. At that point, her interests overseas could be promoted effectively through informal means by both governments and private interests: the formal empire, in Robinson and Gallagher's celebrated phrase, was merely the tip of the iceberg.[11]

Assuming for the moment that eighteenth-century governments used mainly formal rather than informal means (though this claim is open to challenge), Bowen's argument raises the issue of whether there is scope for linking private interests with the expansion of informal influence and, possibly, the creation of informal empire. India would appear to be the most favourable case, for it was there that private traders arose not only to challenge the East India Company but also to establish new frontiers inland. However, the mainland colonies should not be discounted, even though they were held within the formal empire. There, too, the frontier was moved and staked by unofficial as well as by official interests, while government itself, being of slender means, relied heavily on the co-operation of private interests, to which it was in varying degrees beholden. Formal rule was filled out by an informal presence; colonial management depended on what would later be called indirect rule through white, gentlemanly 'chiefs' whose collaboration (as Gallagher and Robinson would have put it), was essential to the continuation of the formal, constitutional empire. At the same time, the informal or unofficial presence could also be transformed into a sub-imperialism that reduced rather than enhanced the power of the centre. The growth of settlement in the 13 colonies, for example, promoted a type of sub-imperial expansion that pushed the frontier westwards, weakened the grip of the authorities, and eventually helped to precipitate revolution.

Even if these speculations turn out to be fanciful, they have the residual merit of directing attention to a second question: the long-standing divide between the study of the eighteenth and the nineteenth centuries, and the appeal to 'long' centuries to fit an argument or to cover an uncertainty. The long eighteenth century typically begins in 1688 and terminates in 1815, but can be extended to the 1830s; the long nineteenth century always ends in 1914 but may have a starting point as early as the 1760s. Bowen's colonial gentlemen survived the upheavals of the late eighteenth century and prospered after 1815. If a break in continuity is to be found, it is probably in changes to the wider social formation of which they were a part, specifically the shift to free trade, the dismantling of Old Corruption, and the demise of the military-fiscal state. This process began in the 1820s, was hurried on in the 1830s and 40s, and was substantially achieved (even though it was still incomplete) by 1850. By this time, too, the concept of empire, which Bowen refers to, had undergone a parallel change. The English empire had become British, and any residual universalism that survived the French Wars had been harnessed to the cause of the nation state.[12] These developments reflected, in part, the creation from the late eighteenth century onwards of a truly British gentlemanly elite[13] some of whose new wealth derived directly from the vigorous imperial expansion that accompanied the contest between Britain and France to become Europe's first superpower.

II

John Darwin's wide-ranging essay begins at this moment of transition, which he dates from the 1830s. We would amend his starting point by suggesting, as we have in commenting on Bowen's essay, that the whole period 1815–50 was one of protracted and painful transition between the Old Colonial System and the new era of free-trade imperialism.[14] The transition was made possible eventually by railways, steamships, discoveries of gold, and spurts in both capital exports and emigration, as new possibilities for global economic growth were opened up. What Darwin appositely calls Britain's 'cocktail of social energies' gave her the means of benefiting from these developments to a greater extent than any other modernizing power in the nineteenth century. A potent ingredient in the cocktail was a transformed and revived gentlemanly capitalism. This initial comment is not intended to disturb Darwin's central argument, which does not depend on dating its starting point precisely. His main purpose is the much broader one of placing the British experience in the context of global history. Here, he offers a bold and valuable corrective to our 'island story', and one that the argument advanced in *British Imperialism* – if fully extended – undoubtedly requires.

We took the view that an understanding of Britain's overseas policy and presence called for a reappraisal of their domestic roots.[15] International developments and their intersection with forces propelled by the nation state were of course important, but we could not see how, in the first instance at least, we could devise an argument that derived the latter from the former. This is not to deny that Britain was influenced by external developments that, at various times and in various places, were beyond her control. However, the difficulty with this viewpoint (as Darwin recognizes) is that it can easily make human agency dependent on outside forces that seem to have no concrete, observable origin. It can also appear to make the tail wag the dog.[16]

Critics can then complain that the interpretation is both determinist and improbable. The reality was that Britain was not a micro-state, but the world's superpower. As such, she played a formative role in shaping the global system that ran from the nineteenth century to the 1950s. It is certainly the case that the structure and balance of the international order began to change, visibly from the 1930s and rapidly after 1945, as it grew in scale and gathered more constituents. Nevertheless, it would be misleading to conclude, even at this late point in the history of empire, that Britain had ceased to contribute significantly to managing the system she had done so much to create. Even the end of empire, unwelcome though it was in some quarters, was partly a reflection of shifting interests in Britain herself, and was accompanied by a conscious reorientation of trade and politics towards the highly developed regions of the world – a trend that eventually led to the form of globalization we know today.

This reaffirmation of the position taken in *British Imperialism* is consistent in principle with Darwin's emphasis on the forces that constrained Britain's ambitions. One of our acknowledged difficulties lay in writing a history of and from the centre without appearing to ignore important new research on the colonized world. Since we were interested in causes rather than in consequences, we were able to limit the scope of our enquiries. Even so, we should have said much more about interactions between British and indigenous forces, as well as between Britain and her continental rivals, and we would have done so had we been able to face the task of writing an additional volume (or two). Darwin deftly indicates a number of areas where additional thought accompanied by matching space would at the very least have amplified our argument. One good example is the extent to which resistance among indigenous peoples restrained the extension of informal as well as formal empire in the nineteenth century. Another is the need to reintroduce France and Germany into the story of British expansion in the late nineteenth century, though in Darwin's view not as causes or symptoms of Britain's decline.

In making these observations, Darwin also notes some similarities between our own approach and that of Robinson and Gallagher, especially in agreeing that imperialism had informal as well as formal dimensions. In the end, however, Darwin's version of Britain's imperial trajectory is much closer to our own than it is to that of Robinson and Gallagher. He confirms our judgement that Britain's informal empire was expanding, not declining, in the period 1870–1914, and that when Britain emerged from the First World War she was still the greatest of the imperial powers and the only one whose economic reach was truly global. Darwin's interpretation of the period after 1914 is also broadly in line with our own. His reminder that Britain's position relative to other European great powers was enhanced as a result of the First World War chimes with the emphasis we placed on this point in *British Imperialism*.[17] Like him, we too stress the fact that Britain's imperial fortunes enjoyed an Indian summer in the 1940s and 1950s.

On the other hand, our assessment of the interwar period differs from his in at least two important respects. We agree that the 1930s were a turning point in that they disrupted the open economy that had been so important to Britain's prosperity and discredited the liberal ideology that accompanied it. Fragile economies made stable polities weak and already weak polities unstable. Nonetheless, we would underline the importance of the period not only for rupturing free trade but for creating the beginnings of structural economic change in overseas countries that were either within or dependent on the imperial system. These changes, including the coming of imperial preference and protection, were part of a subtle shift in the intricate financial and trading relations that linked Britain, the imperial periphery and some of her industrial rivals. They represent a vigorous and partly successful adaptation to the crisis of the times; their significance will become apparent in our discussion of the chapters by Sugihara and by Akita and Kagatoni.

We also have a different perspective on Britain's economic relations with the United States.[18] Darwin's reference to an Anglo-American alliance in the 1920s draws attention to one aspiring line of thinking but understates the degree of alarm and potential antagonism that also motivated contemporary commentators and policy-makers. Britain regarded the USA as being a serious threat to her dominance of international services. The interwar period saw intense rivalry between the two powers across the world, from Latin America to China, for control of airways and airwaves as well as of trade and investment opportunities. Moreover, there was a growing conviction among policy-makers in the United States that the British had to be pushed aside in the struggle for global economic supremacy.[19] To speak of a 'collapse' of this alliance in the 1930s is therefore misleading. The picture Darwin paints of Britain's international position in the 1930s is a shade too gloomy. He forgets that the economic depression hit the United States much harder than Britain, whose rapid adaptation to the crisis raised the prospect of reclaiming ground lost to the USA between 1914 and 1929. It was only after 1936, when faced with a resurgent Germany, Italy and Japan, that despair began to set in and dependence on the United States soon became a reality.[20] Even so, as Darwin notes, the business of empire, like the empire of business, survived the war. The imperial mandate was relaunched; a 'second colonial occupation' was undertaken. Britain was obliged to respond to international developments, but was not yet being driven before them.

III

Bowen and Darwin are at one in holding that imperialism was a systematic and to that extent a coherent phenomenon. The contingent, the unforeseen and the accidental were all present but they do not explain a global process. Phimister's analysis of the partition of Africa takes the same view, though he also argues, as we did too in *British Imperialism*,[21] that different explanations are required for different parts of the continent. Since our remarks on this chapter are rather more extensive than on others, we should make it clear that our intention is not to give priority to Phimister's contribution, valuable though it is, but to take the opportunity to enlarge on aspects of our treatment of the African case, which has attracted comments from other scholars too.[22]

Phimister begins his assessment in Egypt, which was Gallagher and Robinson's starting point as well in *Africa and the Victorians*. The weight of research, in his judgement, favours the interpretation put forward in *British Imperialism*, though he mentions the dissenting opinion of Andrew Porter. It is perhaps worth noting that Porter's brief reference to Egypt was made in 1990 and referred not to *British Imperialism*, which was still being written, but to an article published in 1986. While the treatment of the Egyptian case in *British Imperialism* followed the interpretation advanced in our earlier work, we took the opportunity to strengthen the argument by drawing on new material – some published since 1986 and some already available but unjustly neglected.[23] The most recent assessments encourage us to believe that the account given in *British Imperialism* is well founded.[24] In particular, Samir Saul's authoritative study of the French sources, has confirmed the overwhelming significance of financial considerations in drawing Britain and France into Egypt.[25]

Phimister is less satisfied with our treatment of tropical Africa. Nevertheless, his account of West Africa is fully in accord with our interpretation, which has been elaborated over many years and, broadly speaking, is in line with conclusions reached independently by other scholars.[26] The last quarter of the nineteenth century witnessed a crisis of legitimate commerce: mercantile interests were deeply troubled by the squeeze on profits and by the rise, simultaneously, of new competitors, and there were growing fears that French expansionism would draw the region into a protectionist regime. In these circumstances, provincial merchant pressure groups, which had connections with both service and manufacturing sectors, were important in stimulating government action. The argument advanced at this point was intended to carry forward, but also to be consistent with, the case put in our earlier work, where we drew attention to the difficulties experienced by Britain's manufactured exports at crucial points in the nineteenth century.[27] It is much harder to fathom the motives behind the partition of East Africa. The regional literature is more fragmentary than in the case of West Africa, and the lack of a comprehensive, modern study of the scramble for this part of the continent ensures that all approaches to the subject face formidable difficulties. Phimister suggests that British interests in the region were limited, but that private entrepreneurs (including Leopold II) were attracted by new opportunities that opened up in the 1870s. This development, he claims, stands in contrast to the situation on the West Coast, where large and long-established trading firms were running into serious problems stemming from the Great Depression (1873–96).

There is certainly a case for arguing, as we did in *British Imperialism*,[28] that speculative interest in East Africa grew following the opening of the Suez Canal in 1869, the decision to appoint a Consul-General in Zanzibar in 1873, and the abolition of the external slave trade in the same year. However, it is not clear that these developments stand in contrast with those in West Africa, as Phimister claims. East Africa had its own problems in making the transition to legitimate commerce.[29] It is true that the prices of the two major exports, cloves and ivory, held up (broadly speaking) during the period of partition.[30] However, clove prices remained strong in the 1870s partly because the hurricane of 1872 devastated plantations on Zanzibar and cut output dramatically. Although export volumes picked up in the 1880s, it is by no means certain that profitability revived too. Export values peaked in 1880 and did not recover till the 1890s; slave labour was no longer available as readily or as cheaply as it had been before 1873; many planters were heavily in debt. The price of ivory, the more important of the two leading exports, remained high, but the volume of exports dropped as the ivory frontier was hunted out. It is likely that profits were cut, too: the cost of collecting ivory mounted as the resource became scarce; protection costs rose as competition among ivory traders in the interior grew; transport costs increased as the distance between sources of supply and ports of shipment lengthened. Moreover, once the source of the River Congo was traced (in 1877), it became cheaper to transport ivory from central Africa to the west coast rather than by land to Zanzibar. It is no coincidence that King Leopold shifted his interest from the East Coast to the Congo at this time.

The new, speculative interest in East Africa noted by Phimister, and by ourselves,[31] has therefore to be set against a background of transition on the mainland that may well be closer to the situation in West Africa than he allows. As economic difficulties translated into political action in West Africa, so the economic basis of the Sultan's position was being eroded even as Kirk, Britain's Consul-General in Zanzibar, was trying to build it up.[32] Britain's informal empire on the East Coast was no more substantial than it was on the West Coast.[33] Other powers, principally France and Germany, were able to steal a march on the British and annex impressive stretches of territory. All the same, the value of their gains should not be exaggerated. The British held on to some of the most desirable parts of West Africa (notably the regions that became Nigeria and the Gold Coast) and took control of Kenya. French territory, on the other hand, contained a high proportion of the sahel and the Sahara, while Germany acquired the equally unpromising terrain that eventually became Tanzania.

Phimister's broader concern is that the interpretation of the partition of tropical Africa advanced in *British Imperialism*,[34] sits uncomfortably with our 'insistence...on the proactive part played even here by gentlemanly capitalism'. We think that this is a misreading of our argument. We nowhere claim or imply that gentlemanly capitalism was 'proactive' in this region, which the City found deeply unappealing. The only direct reference we make in the case of West Africa is to the exceptional example of the United African Company's 'complement of aristocrats and reputable financiers'.[35] In summarizing our findings on tropical Africa as a whole, we concluded that the Royal Niger Company and the Imperial British East Africa Company 'represented gentlemanly capitalist interests in a dilute form'.[36] This is surely an uncontroversial claim and is consistent with what is known of the very limited part played by the City and finance generally in influencing British policy in the region. This is not to deny the possibility that small doses of capital administered by chartered companies could have significant effects when applied to poor, 'new-start' territories.[37] Nevertheless, had we tried to force tropical Africa into the framework of gentlemanly capitalism we would have been accused of perpetrating a sizeable exaggeration. At the same time, we judged that we should

guard against the alternative criticism, namely that tropical Africa dis-
proves our thesis, by drawing attention to its low ranking on the scale
of Britain's world-wide priorities and by underlining the overwhelming
importance of Egypt and South Africa, where British interests were
upheld and expanded. In assessing the outcome of the scramble,
specialists on Africa, especially tropical Africa, need to keep the wider
picture in view. Britain's substantial ties with the large, developing
economies of the white empire, Latin America and India made it less
necessary and indeed often counter-productive for her to compete
unreservedly for risky areas, such as China, the Ottoman Empire and
tropical Africa, where high costs were guaranteed, where the returns
were problematic, and where destabilizing wars could easily break out.
Our argument was never that gentlemanly capitalism provides the key
to all doors, but that it offers considerable leverage in explaining the
main trends of imperial expansion over the long term and in the most
important cases.

Phimister takes a different tack with regard to South Africa, accusing
us in this case of sounding too much like Robinson and Gallagher. He
also makes the interesting claim that we sell the concept of gentlemanly
capitalism short by failing to recognize an implicit contradiction
between the South Africa that was developing as a result of economic
change and that desired by the politicians. His central point is that
Selborne's famous memorandum of 1896, which formed the main plank
of British policy after the failure of the notorious Jameson Raid in the
previous year, did not forecast that South Africa would fall under
Afrikaner dominance if the Transvaal remained independent, as we and
Robinson and Gallagher suggested. Rather, the memorandum was concerned with the emergence of a regime in the Transvaal dominated by
white settlers who had been attracted to the gold fields and who,
Selborne predicted, would shortly become ascendant in South Africa as
a whole. Other scholars have seen this point,[38] but Phimister is the first
to pursue it. He interprets this emerging settler capitalism as being a
good example of informal imperialism driven by the City – an offshoot,
that is to say, of gentlemanly capitalism. However, it was also a development that cut across the aims of British statesmen – another arm of
gentlemanly capitalism – who wanted to unite South Africa under the
British flag, as they had done in Canada, and feared that the settlers
would steer a more independent course. Phimister's conclusion, therefore, is that politics and economics were at war with each other in South
Africa and that the former had to bring the latter to heel in the Anglo-
Boer war of 1899–1902.

We accept Phimister's suggestive interpretation of the content of Selborne's memorandum, and we recognize, too, that capital and politics could sometimes march in different directions in South Africa. Rothschild's loan to the Transvaal regime in 1892, for example, was intended to bring it under closer financial control. In practice, however, the loan allowed Kruger to finish the construction of a railway line that gave the Transvaal an outlet to the sea in Portuguese Mozambique and enhanced the republic's independence from Britain.[39] Phimister's argument could also be bolstered by noting that a rising proportion of the white settlers in the Transvaal came from Germany, Scandinavia and Ireland, and were not natural allies in schemes hatched in London for uniting South Africa under the British flag and the Colonial Office.[40] The Colonial Office viewed this development as increasing the threat posed by German imperialism in South Africa;[41] the Boers themselves came to be regarded as 'outriders of German expansionism'.[42]

Even when these allowances have been made, however, it does not necessarily follow that what was unfolding in South Africa implied a fundamental antagonism between two arms of gentlemanly capitalism. Some senior figures in Britain wanted to see British settlers in control of the Transvaal. Others, however, were willing to accept the emergence in the Republic of either a mixed settler regime or a liberalized Afrikaner one. They assumed that this state would be the forerunner of a united South Africa that would be tied to Britain in the same loose but effective way as the other fledgling Dominions, such as Canada and Australia. It is important to keep in mind the fact that the continued dependence of the Dominions on the City of London ensured that they remained part of Britain's financial empire long after the devolution of formal political control, and that their independence was heavily constrained as a result. Most Liberal statesmen and some prominent Conservatives (including Balfour)[43] thought that South Africa would follow this model; had they been in control of policy after 1895, it is possible that war might have been avoided.

The advent of Joseph Chamberlain as Colonial Secretary in 1895 and of Milner, the High Commissioner from 1897, moved policy in a different direction. Their overarching aim was to bring about a united white empire, if necessary under tariff protection. In their view, Britain would have to become 'Greater Britain' if it were to be strong enough to meet the challenge of the United States and Germany in the twentieth century.[44] The loosely jointed South African federation favoured by the Liberals would not have served this cause and might well have undermined it altogether. As Chamberlain put it in 1895: 'an entirely independent Republic, governed by or for the capitalists of the Rand, would be very much worse for British interests in the Transvaal itself and for British influence in South Africa'.[45] More assertive policies were needed if the imperial superstate was to be realized, and it was these that eventually ended in war in 1899.[46] Thus it can be argued that there was a built-in antagonism between Chamberlain's strategy and the finance-led policy of informal empire that preceded it in South Africa and that it was generally much more representative of British attitudes to areas of white settlement. The South African statesman, Jan Christian Smuts, later held that British policy between 1895 and 1905 was an aberration, and in many ways he was right.[47] Chamberlain's agenda *was* unusual: it was driven by concerns about the future of British industry rather than guided by the usual gentlemanly norms. Indeed, it is even tempting to suggest that the South African war may be that rare event in British history, an example of 'industrial imperialism'.[48]

However, if South Africa is placed in the context of Chamberlain's overall policy as Colonial Secretary after 1895, this judgement can be seen to be too extreme. Chamberlain wanted to use the apparatus of the state to develop the economic resources of the empire by means of 'constructive imperialism'.[49] To achieve this aim he had to bring together a new coalition of interests, giving industry a more prominent place, but with the City and gentlemanly institutions like the Treasury and the Crown Agents incorporated within it.[50] Given Chamberlain's background, it could be argued that such a coalition, had it materialized, would have been an expression of industrial imperialism: his famous speech to the City in 1904 certainly argued that the prosperity of finance depended upon the health of industry rather than the reverse.[51] Alternatively, Chamberlain's strategy can be thought of as an attempt to forge a new partnership between the City, industry and the state, one that would reshape and re-energize, rather than replace, gentlemanly capitalist forces.

In whatever way Chamberlain's initiatives are interpreted, his policy was short-lived: his crusade for empire unity, like his proposals for imperial development, died in the election of 1906. The South African Union of 1910 was built on fairly traditional lines, with strong local self-government constrained by the invisible, but powerful, reins of financial dependence. This outcome was closer to Selborne's vision than to Chamberlain's.[52] Selborne's ideas are particularly interesting in this connection given the emphasis Phimister places on his thinking and the fact that, as High Commissioner in South Africa between 1906 and 1910, he was the key figure in bringing about the Union. As Under-

Secretary at the Colonial Office in the late 1890s, Selborne went along with Chamberlain's views on colonial development, including supporting tariff reform and imperial federation. However, Selborne had a more flexible attitude to South African union than either Chamberlain or Milner. The defeat of tariff reform in 1906 did not deflect him from pursuing the goal of a unified South Africa within a federated empire. To this end he was much more inclined to co-operate with the Afrikaners, whereas Chamberlain and Milner were obsessed with making South Africa ethnically British. Selborne also showed greater willingness to encourage local political autonomy. Moreover, his concern with creating a South African Union was directly related to the problem of establishing a credit-worthy political unit. Union under the British Crown would enable South Africa to raise funds in the City of London to build the infrastructure that, Selborne believed, was crucial to bringing Afrikaner, British and foreign communities together and to forging a strong state on the basis of successful economic development.

It seems to us, therefore, that Phimister's analysis of the content of Selborne's memorandum can support a conclusion that differs from the one he drew. Selborne recognized that there was work to be done in associating South Africa's settlers with the empire, but he did not believe that there was a fundamental incompatibility between the two. Above all, Selborne was far friendlier to the City than Chamberlain was, and he had a firm belief in its ability to spread capitalist development on a global scale. Since he was both 'a gentleman and a capitalist',[53] his conviction on this matter should cause no surprise. Moreover, Selborne's beliefs outlived Chamberlain's. Not for the first time, gentlemanly capitalism proved its staying power.

IV

Exactly when the gentlemanly capitalist elite ran out of stamina is the central concern of Krozewski's chapter, which carries the story forward to the concluding stages of empire. Krozewski is in sympathy with our emphasis on the centrality of financial considerations, and has himself made a major contribution to our understanding of this theme in relation to decolonization.[54] However, he is dissatisfied with other aspects of what he terms our 'continuity thesis' because he feels that we have projected a set of nineteenth-century relationships forward to the mid-twentieth century, when the structure of society and governments had changed markedly, without demonstrating that the gentlemanly capitalist elite (assuming that it existed after 1945) remained in charge of policy. By extension, he claims that we failed to offer an analysis of the British state in the period after the Second World War and that we underestimated the changing international context, which acted as an increasing constraint on policy-makers, whether gentlemen or not. This leads him to offer a further qualification of our 'continuity thesis' by arguing that after 1960 policy-makers had no interest in revitalizing 'the old empire in an informal way'.

We willingly accept that our argument for the period after 1945 was schematic; its purpose, as we explicitly stated, was 'less to prove a thesis than to show how it might be constructed'.[55] Krozewski's thoughts on how the period might be opened up by a more detailed analysis that improves on our own are therefore to be welcomed. However, it does not seem to us that this desirable enlargement of our thinking requires the abandonment either of our continuity thesis or of the notion of gentlemanly capitalism. Our main concern in carrying our interpretation into the twentieth century was to escape from the traditional historical divide which treated the period before 1914 as being one of imperial expansion and the period after 1918 as being one of decline. In our view, long-established priorities of international and imperial policy, held in place by a gentlemanly elite, survived the war, were applied to the changing conditions of the world slump, the Second World War, and the needs of postwar reconstruction, and achieved greater success during this period than historians have usually allowed.

Rubinstein's recent research provides systematic evidence to show that the gentlemanly elite was not eliminated after 1914, despite the ravages of war, and that it remained in robust health throughout the interwar period.[56] Gentlemanly values underwent a form of 'moral rearmament' in the 1920s in response to the twin threats of Bolshevism from abroad and heightened radicalism (symbolized by the General Strike of 1926) at home.[57] Indeed, the General Strike marked the end of the social solidarity induced by the wartime emergency: 'officers and gentlemen' were prominent among the volunteer strike-breakers who helped to defend property and privilege against the radical challenge. Prewar policy priorities were reaffirmed in the celebratory 'bonfire of controls' that followed the peace settlement, in the return to the gold standard, and in the hope that 'normal service' would shortly be resumed on a world-wide scale.

Unfortunately, Rubinstein's work, or its equivalent, has yet to be extended beyond 1939. Nevertheless, there is no clear, evidential basis for Krozewski's view that the gentlemanly elite had lost its place by 1945, even though the state had become larger and had acquired a stronger technocratic element. The claim appears to rest on the assumption that the war and allied social change overturned or submerged the prewar order. But the upper ranks of the Labour Government, which Krozewski refers to, contained more gentlemen than proletarians: for every Bevin there were several Attlees and Gaitskells. As is well known, too, the Labour Government willingly shouldered the burdens of empire, and gentlemen such as Creech Jones and Andrew Cohen masterminded its progressive imperial policies.[58] The continuity of the 'Treasury view' within Whitehall has been well documented, as has its resistance to Keynesianism even after 1945.[59] The enduring vitality of the gentlemanly complement in the City has also been affirmed.[60] Moreover, Labour's Chamberlainite imperialist policies were partly subverted in the 1950s by a more traditional cosmopolitanism in which the City had an increasingly important role.[61] At the same time, the return to power of Conservative governments ensured the continuing prominence of the gentlemanly elite and created new opportunities for its patrician wing.[62] The striking visibility and evident resilience of the aristocratic and gentlemanly order were subjects of popular discussion among contemporaries. The familiar term, 'the Establishment', was coined in the 1950s in a critique of the continuing hold of Oxbridge and City elites over British policies and ideas.[63]

Accordingly, Krozewski's claim that our interpretation of the period after 1945 is little more than an inference from a historical legacy created in the nineteenth century seems to us to be an assertion that fails to do justice to the evidence, incomplete though it is.[64] We carried our argument forward because it became apparent in the course of our research that the gentlemanly order was sufficiently athletic to carry itself forward – in, through, and out of two world wars. Gentlemanly capitalism had an important part to play in government and the City throughout the 1950s. There is no compelling reason for separating it from policy-making or from what Krozewski calls 'the financial dimension'. For these reasons, its history is also part of the history of the state that Krozewski rightly wishes to see written. In mounting this defence, we also recognize that our description of the gentlemanly elite after 1945 needs to be filled out considerably and that relations between the elite and other influential groups, especially in allied branches of big business, need further investigation.[65]

Moreover, there is the important question, raised implicitly but not answered by Krozewski, of when and why the gentlemanly order withered away. The view sketched in *British Imperialism* still seems to us to point in the right direction.[66] Gentlemen were sufficiently recognizable in the 1960s and 70s by their dress, bearing, accent, and occupations to be objects of both emulation and satire. Thereafter, they steadily lost identity and visibility. Two events symbolize the change: the election in 1979 of Margaret Thatcher's 'new' Conservative government, which launched a sustained attack on the professions and public service, and the advent of 'Big Bang', which opened up the City in 1986. Standing behind these events were profound, underlying forces making for change: the creation of the welfare state, especially the widening of opportunities in higher education after 1945, the steady Americanization of the 'British way of life', structural shifts in the world economy, and of course the demise of empire itself. All continuities come to an end eventually. But the decline of the gentlemanly elite, like the fall of the empire, should not be proclaimed before its due time. The gentlemanly order survived, through successive transmutations, for as long as the conditions that nurtured it remained in place – and these were present through the twentieth century to the point where the long imperial story ended in decolonization.[67]

Krozewski opens his discussion of the international aspects of our argument by questioning our definition of imperialism, particularly our failure to give sufficient emphasis to the role of the state in the twentieth century and the difficulty of measuring infringements of sovereignty. Our response to the first point, as argued above, is to say that we believe we have contributed, however modestly, to an understanding of the nature of the twentieth-century state by drawing attention to the continued vitality of the gentlemanly order and its important role in policy-making. As for the difficulty of devising an index to record degrees of effective subordination, we would agree that this is indeed a formidable task. All solutions are constrained by the inherently intractable nature of the problem. However, the attempt is still worth making because it obliges historians to think analytically about a subject that has often been treated far too loosely. Some measures of dependence, such as trade and capital flows, can be identified quite precisely; others, such as cultural influences, cannot be recorded in quite the same way. But this does not mean that they cannot be recorded at all. The resulting assessment is then put forward for consideration in just the same way as that relating to any other large, complex historical issue. The difficulty of determining what is meant by imperialism is therefore no greater, at least in principle, than that of deciding the meaning of other weighty holistic terms, such as class, revolution or the state.

Krozewski goes on to make two points of substance regarding our treatment of the postwar colonial order. He qualifies what he calls our 'second continuity thesis' by denying that policy-makers aimed at revitalizing 'the old empire in an informal way' after 1960. This criticism appears to be aimed at the wrong target. In our view, the possibility of extending Britain's influence informally only surfaced late in the day because it was not until the mid-1950s that the formal decolonization of the empire, which had been repositioned and reinvigorated after the war and the loss of India, gained a prominent place on the agenda.[68] As it did so, however, a number of other developments were also claiming attention. From the late 1950s, Britain turned increasingly to the European Community and to the developed world generally; plans were made for establishing Britain as a financial centre within the emerging Pax Americana; decolonization was hurried on. After 1960 Britain still hoped to retain influence in her former empire, but these broader developments made any attempt to reconstruct a full-blown informal empire quixotic as well as increasingly unnecessary. Krozewski's second observation calls for a comparative approach to the study of the European empires in the postwar era, principally to determine the relationship between social structures, the state and international (financial) policy – though of course the agenda could be greatly extended. On this subject there is no difference between us: we were sufficiently aware of our own insularity in *British Imperialism* to make the same appeal,[69] and we have recently readvertised both the need and the opportunities.[70] The study of empires should span even more frontiers than it does at present; Krozewski is a historian who is especially well-equipped to respond to his own challenge.

V

The remaining five chapters of the book focus on the Far East and provide between them a fascinating insight into the workings of informal imperialism in the twentieth century. The essays on China deal with the British presence; those written from a Japanese perspective also show how Japan's informal influence in the region expanded in response to her own economic development, and how this, in turn, was related to the evolution of gentlemanly capitalism in Britain. In offering new evidence and new thinking, these essays point the way towards a comparative history of imperialism built on the merging of separate historiographical traditions – a wholly appropriate development, it might be thought, in an era of globalization.

Petersson's chapter on British policy towards China adds a new dimension to the study of a crucial period while also improving our understanding of the distinctive qualities of gentlemanly capitalism. As the most important foreign economic power in China, Britain had a vested interest in maintaining the political *status quo*. British China-watchers had been on the lookout for ways of opening China's economy to the wider world since at least the Macartney mission of 1792–94, but they were wary of any initiative that might undermine the stability of China because they recognized how disastrously counter-productive it would be.[71] At the turn of the century, they had good reason to fear that a combination of internal political weakness and foreign competition for access to China's resources, following the Sino-Japanese war of 1894–95, would end in partition. This outcome would have dealt a heavy blow to Britain's existing economic interests, which relied on the central government to service its foreign debt and on the free flow of trade through and between the widely scattered Treaty Ports. Partition, it was thought, would also retard the development, for at least a generation, of what most British observers regarded as being the greatest potential market in the world. The comparison with the Ottoman Empire, where a similar policy was adopted, is instructive; so, too, is the contrast with Africa, where political weakness manifested itself in a multiplicity of small polities that invited partition rather than preservation.[72]

In these circumstances, the gentlemanly capitalist strategy was to promote a form of financial 'inter-imperialism'[73] by locking the great powers into a policy that would both produce economic growth and uphold China's political unity. Petersson is quite correct in believing that this policy had distinctive gentlemanly-capitalist attributes. It relied on the hegemony of the City in world finance – a hegemony that was actively supportive of gentlemanly capitalism itself. It also depended on notions of financial cosmopolitanism and free trade that underwrote the City's international position and were deeply etched into the psyche of the gentlemanly capitalist politicians who orchestrated British policy in China.[74] Britain's plan for world development envisaged that benefits would flow to all participants.[75] China would be transformed into a modern state and all foreign powers would gain through increased opportunities for trade. It is undoubtedly the case that Britain's model of global economic development was more internationalist in its approach than that of any other major power. There was also a genuine streak of idealism in this plan for improving the world. Nevertheless, it should not be forgotten that the City's dominance and the survival of the whole gentlemanly enterprise in Britain were dependent on maximizing world trade and international financial flows and on keeping the peace.[76] It is in this context that Petersson's stress on the pacifist inclinations of gentlemanly capitalism has to be understood: it had less to do with an unreflective adherence to Cobdenite cosmopolitanism than with a shrewd assessment of where Britain's interests lay.

Petersson's stimulating assessment of these themes enables us to underline two of the distinctive qualities of gentlemanly capitalism. In the first place, as our foregoing remarks imply, gentlemen did not always stand aside for others. Gentility was the product of privilege. It imposed a code of conduct that emphasized the concepts of duty and service but also endorsed aristocratic and military values. Gentlemen were expected to show a degree of muscular prowess and were entitled to act forcefully to protect the weak or to defend the national interest. Restraint was called for in China; assertiveness manifested itself in Africa. The second feature that Petersson emphasizes is the relationship between co-operative imperialism and the national interest. This is a fascinating theme that needs more thought than it has received so far. On the principle that capital knows no frontiers, investment groups based in different countries established connections that cut across national interests in the late nineteenth century. Evidently, this development may not be captured by standard accounts of the history of modern imperialism that are based on the expansion of any one country. At the same time, as Petersson's subtle analysis reveals, the outlook of French and German financiers differed from that of the City, whether because governments that had different assumptions and priorities influenced them or because they adopted different lending policies. Above all, the French and German firms lacked the spacious world view of Britain's gentlemanly capitalists and the scale of operations that went with it.

In sharp contrast to Shunhong Zhang's judgement,[77] Petersson sees the Chinese case as being a prime example of gentlemanly capitalism at work. He refers to the period 1905–11 in particular as being the 'golden age' of gentlemanly capitalism in China. This was the time when relations between the great powers were such as to encourage them to fall in with Britain's own plans for China, and when British finance was able to revert to its preferred strategy of informal expansion. Petersson has performed an important service in identifying subdivisions in a period that we were obliged to treat as an entity, and his argument that British policy was at its least encumbered between 1905 and 1911 is a persuasive one. On the other hand, the detailed knowledge that led him to this conclusion may also have foreshortened his view of Britain's long-run position in China.

It seems to us that there is still a great deal to be said for treating 1895 as being the key date for the application of Britain's China policy. It was only then that China, in the wake of defeat at the hands of Japan, became dependent on foreign capital and thus faced the possibility of becoming, like the Ottoman Empire, subservient to foreign creditors. It was then that Britain took the lead in organizing an international loan that gave the Chinese government the opportunity to pay off its massive war indemnity. It was then, too, that other major powers acquired an interest in maintaining the existing imperial regime.[78] There is no doubt that China's instability in the late 1890s and early 1900s encouraged policies to become more predatory. British policy-makers were obliged to participate, whether they liked it or not, to delineate spheres of interest for themselves and to fight for concessions for their nationals. Nevertheless, the main aim of promoting the unity of China and of using joint-financing as a means of achieving it remained, and in the more benign atmosphere that accompanied the years from 1905 to 1911 it also flowered. Even so, Britain's success was not unqualified: international financial alliances were not easily forged, and the City's doubts about China's prospects sometimes slowed down progress markedly.[79]

British policy undoubtedly ran into much greater difficulties after 1911 as a result of the collapse of the imperial regime and changes in European politics. Yet the British stuck to their task: the 'one China' policy was resurrected through the Six-power Loan for the new regime in 1912. Petersson's account of this period can be amplified by noting that the policy ran into trouble in Britain itself, where it was assailed by a band of ungentlemanly capitalists, including some in the City who were excluded from the China loan market, which had fallen under the control of the Foreign Office, the Hongkong and Shanghai bank and a small coterie of merchant bankers and their foreign correspondents. Britain's cosmopolitan policy was also attacked by provincial industrial groups who resented the fact that it encouraged competition among European merchants in China in the interests of maintaining a united front in matters of finance.[80] However, these groups were unable to disturb the priorities of British policy, which remained essentially unaltered after 1911. Although modified to fit changing circumstances, the strategy continued to be applied throughout the 1920s, if with less success than in its heyday before the First World War. It made considerable progress in the 1930s, too, until it was destroyed, this time beyond repair, by Japan's invasion of China in 1937.[81]

VI

Shunhong Zhang's contribution is especially interesting not only for its substantive comments but also for the insights it offers into the thinking of a Chinese historian at a time when China appears finally to be 'opening up' to the outside world. At present, this process is more apparent in economic affairs than in political and intellectual spheres. As a national institution, the Chinese Academy of the Social Sciences, where Professor Shunhong is based, still has an important part to play in presenting the official view to the world. This may explain why Shunhong's starting point appears to be a rather basic and largely unreconstructed Marxism that is startling to scholars in the West (and probably in Japan too), where this approach, even in its refined versions, has lost considerable ground in recent years. His boldness in dealing with Western views of imperialism is to be admired, even though it does not always fit well with the detailed literature. Nevertheless, Shunhong may be ahead of the game rather than behind it: the developing debate on globalization, spurred on by the recent attack on the World Trade Centre in New York, is now giving renewed prominence to the history of material developments and is shifting attention from the cultural priorities elevated by postmodernism. Exactly how Marxist approaches can be related to the twenty-first century is a matter that has still to be addressed satisfactorily, but it seems certain that they will need to be applied imaginatively to new circumstances and not simply carried forward and clamped on a changed world.

Shunhong opens his essay by objecting to our definition of imperialism. Much of what he has to say is valid, at least in principle, as a way of extending our discussion. However, as a criticism of what we set out to do, it is misplaced. Our definition, as we made clear, was tailored to our purpose, which was concerned with *causes*, not with *consequences*. Shunhong believes that 'the crucial nature of imperialism is that one nation oppresses, exploits and enslaves another'. This may be so, but this conception is concerned with the results of imperialism, and cannot be used to refute an interpretation that treats only its causes. His conclusion that we have 'whitewashed' imperialism is wholly unfounded: we explicitly stated that we were not going to deal with the morality or the effects of empire-building;[82] accordingly, there is no basis for the inference that he has drawn. Moreover, Shunhong sets himself a series of unacknowledged difficulties in asserting that imperialism entailed fixed consequences. Aside from the well-known problems of defining exploitation, the record shows that the consequences of imperialism varied across space and through time. Marx himself held that capitalism was progressive as well as exploitative. It is unreasonable and unhistorical to suppose that the results of imperialism were identical or even broadly similar in cases as far from one another as New Zealand and Nigeria. In their chapter in this volume, for example, Akita and Kagotani draw attention to the developmental consequences of Japanese rule in Korea without supposing that this outcome absolves Japan from charges of oppression. The weight of evidence is against Shunhong in the case of China too: recent research has indicated that the late nineteenth century, when foreign powers began the process of opening China up, saw the beginning of economic development on a significant scale.[83]

Shunhong is on firmer ground in searching for weaknesses in our claims regarding the influence of gentlemanly capitalist interests. His main argument here is that we underestimated the importance of industry and the manufacturing lobby. However, as we have recently pointed out, it was never our purpose to deny the significance of the process of industrialization or to underplay the role of the manufacturing interest.[84] We ourselves drew attention, for example, to Palmerston's forceful policy in seeking to create markets for manufactured goods in the 1840s, though in our view this was a sign of the difficulties being experienced by British industry, not an indication of its effortless superiority.[85] What we claimed was that manufacturing interests failed to become the *dominant* force shaping British policy. Arguments to the contrary, though often asserted, have yet to be substantiated. Even Ward's careful restatement of the case for giving industrialization a more prominent role in the story of imperial expansion is based on the general proposition that wealth derived from industrialization underpinned Britain's expansion overseas, and not on detailed studies of the manufacturing lobby in action.[86] The issue is an important one but it also draws the discussion away from Shunhong's main concern with matters of agency and policy formulation.

On these subjects, Shunhong cites two principal examples in support of his position: Macartney's mission to China in 1792–94, and British loans to China at the close of the nineteenth century.[87] It is perfectly true, as Shunhong says, that Macartney was sent to China to promote British commercial interests.[88] However, this is not the same as saying that Macartney was acting as an agent for British manufacturing interests.[89] Macartney's twin aims were to extend the privileges of the struggling East India Company, which was searching for new sources of revenue, and to generate additional ways of paying for imports of China tea.[90] The chief means of attaining these goals was by expanding India's exports to China. Macartney's mission failed but the incentive remained. It helped to draw the British further into India to promote exports of cotton goods and indigo from Awadh (Oudh),[91] and it generated an important clandestine export trade in opium, which was shipped from western India to China.[92] If British manufactures could participate in the expansion of trade with China, then so much the better. But experience suggested that this was unlikely to happen on a significant scale, and experience proved to be a reliable guide: China was not opened up in the 1790s. When the East India Company's monopoly of trade with India was abolished in 1813, it was not because of pressure from British manufacturers;[93] indeed, British cotton textiles did not make sizeable inroads even into the Indian market, which was under British control, until the 1840s.

A century after Macartney's mission, when Britain again seemed on the brink of prising China open, the economic forces impelling overseas expansion had been transformed: foreign investment and invisible income had surged; the products of the industrial revolution had become established in many parts of the world. Shunhong makes the point that British industry, as well as British finance, gained from the limited opening of China at this time. Again, while this is true, it has also to be said that we did not attempt to argue a contrary case, though it is interesting to see that Britain, as a mature creditor, was also starting to lend money to finance sales of the products of other industrializing countries, including Germany, at this time. To this extent, there was the beginning of a conflict between the two interest groups. Nevertheless, our interpretation of the case of China did not depend on this point. Our argument was rather that finance was the more important of the two interests. China's economy was beginning to expand in the 1890s, but trade with Europe failed to take off.[94] Silk exports remained important, but exports of tea withered under competition from India, and imports of opium declined as cultivation of the opium poppy spread in China itself. Exports of 'muck and truck' items grew, but not on a scale that was capable of raising purchasing power to the point where significant imports of manufactured consumer goods could be sustained.

In these circumstances, the best prospects for business expansion lay elsewhere: in government loans, and investment in railways, mining concessions, shipping, and property in the Treaty Ports. This emphasis is endorsed by Petersson's contribution to this volume, which argues that the period 1905–11 was the 'golden age' of gentlemanly imperialism in China.[95] As he also suggests, British investment in Chinese government loans and in railway construction served both economic and political purposes. It gave the gentlemen of the Hongkong and Shanghai Bank, in particular, a position of influence in the formulation of British policy towards China during this period – one rarely aspired to and never achieved by British manufacturers.[96] As for the latter, we argued in *British Imperialism* that, after 1850, Britain's international economic policy evolved in such a way as to encourage foreign industrialization and to subject British manufacturing to severe competition at home. This argument is extended and amplified in the essays by Sugihara and by Akita and Kagatoni discussed below, and it provides an effective counter to Shunhong's claims about the importance of manufacturing interests in policy.

Shunhong's final criticism of substance concerns the process of decolonization after the Second World War. His basic argument is that our account is in error because it fails to give sufficient weight either to the liberating influence of the Soviet Union or to the rising force of nationalism. Shunhong takes this position because his perspective on the end of empire does not include the perception that the imperial powers might have been willing to concede independence for reasons other than external pressure.

We have already acknowledged that our interpretation of the period after 1945 was deliberately schematic:[97] what we did was attenuated; what we omitted was considerable. A full account of decolonization would certainly be obliged to allocate considerable space to the emergence of the Soviet Union as a superpower and to its influence on colonial nationalist movements. Our focus was the narrower one of showing that gentlemanly interests had a continuing part to play in the final stages of empire. To the extent that we brought other great powers into this story, we did so by concentrating on Anglo-American relations because these had a more direct bearing on Britain's policies towards the empire and on her international financial aspirations. All the same, Shunhong's claim that 'the Soviet Union was the greatest international force which contributed to the collapse of colonial empires' is surely an exaggeration. It ignores the fact that colonial nationalists drew heavily on the ideology of the Free World in staking their claims for independence, and it fails to recognize the extent to which the Soviet Union was itself perceived to be an expanding empire and not simply a benign, liberating force.

Shunhong complements his emphasis on the Soviet Union by suggesting that we also underestimated the strength of colonial nationalism. He seems puzzled by what he calls our 'inconsistency' in drawing attention to Britain's weakening grip on India and her changing economic interests there. However, the 'inconsistency' arises only because Shunhong's presuppositions do not allow him to accept that Britain's interests and British policy could respond to other influences. If this confining assumption is discarded, it becomes possible to see that both rising nationalism and changing interests were important in influencing the official mind. Moreover, Shunhong's interpretation ignores the fact that Britain had a well-established exit route from empire via the creation of dominion status, and that India herself was already moving towards self-government before the war. He fails to see, too, that the end of British rule in India was consistent with the repositioning of the empire elsewhere and that, during this 'second colonial occupation' resistance to British rule was dealt with firmly in places as far apart as Kenya and Malaya.

Shunhong concludes his discussion of the independence movements by dealing with the concept of neo-colonialism. His pre-formed view of imperialism obliges him to look for continuing subordination and oppression after the achievement of formal independence. Not surprisingly, he finds several examples. This outcome sits uneasily with his previous argument: the colonial power had just lost its empire because it was overwhelmed by the forces of nationalism, but was then able, so it seems, to exert neo-colonialist control once independence has been granted. Shunhong's assessment misses the important fact that the British were increasingly keen to decolonize from the mid-1950s onwards. The world economy was undergoing a fundamental transformation, and Britain's priorities were changing with it.[98] Moreover, empire had never been synonymous with the interests of gentlemanly capitalism, which had ranged far outside it before the 1930s, and by the mid-1950s were again seeking a wider, cosmopolitan field of enterprise. The British undoubtedly made an effort to work with and to influence colonial nationalists where they had interests to preserve. But they did not always succeed[99] and their commitment to the endeavour faded as they formed new attachments elsewhere in the era of post-colonial globalization that was just beginning.

VII

Kaoru Sugihara's essay adds a striking new dimension to the discussion of British imperialism and its impact on world economic development.

The argument he constructs builds on materials to be found in *British Imperialism* but takes the question of industrialization in 'late start' countries much further than we did. In doing so, he offers a perspective on the emergence of the world economy after 1870, and on Britain's part in creating it, that echoes Gilpin's characterization, published a generation ago, of Britain as a 'mature creditor'.[100] Our own interpretation of this theme was confined largely to Britain's relationship with the Dominions and India before 1939. Sugihara demonstrates that the same forces, transmitted by the City of London, were at work on a much wider scale and can provide important insights into the industrialization of East Asia in particular.

Sugihara's main contention is that the open regime promoted by Britain encouraged the spread of modern industry on a world-wide scale and thus eventually undermined Britain's imperial power. Whatever Britain's original intentions, her international economic policy indirectly allowed her own economy to be shaped by the industrialization of others. As this is a proposition of great importance, it is worth spelling out the basis of the argument in some detail. Until 1930, British policy was based primarily on the maintenance of the gold standard and free trade. Her role as the primary supplier of international services, 'lender of last resort', and foreign investor facilitated the growth of manufacturing industries elsewhere; her massive overseas investments created the need for recipients to repay their debts in sterling. These debts could be met, and sterling crises avoided, by exporting to the open British market. However, by allowing access to the British market in this way, free trade promoted manufacturing in debtor countries. It also limited Britain's bargaining power in international trade relations.[101] She had no way of negotiating reductions in the tariffs of countries that hindered exports of her own manufactures, despite the fact that, potentially, she had considerable market power. It has recently been argued, for example, that Britain's share of world trade was high enough, even in 1913, to produce a net gain in income had she chosen to impose tariffs on imported manufactures.[102] The free trade and foreign investment nexus also encouraged competitive industrialization in a more direct manner. Debtor nations could generate the sterling needed to meet their obligations not only by exporting commodities to Britain but also by excluding British goods from their markets by promoting import-substituting manufactures. Where Britain was able to impose 'free-trade imperialism', as in the Ottoman Empire down to the First World War and in China until the 1920s, this problem could be avoided. Where tariff autonomy remained or was recaptured, it could provide an important stimulus to industrialization, as in the case of Japan after she repudiated the 'unequal treaties' in 1899.

British policy changed in the 1930s, when the gold standard was abandoned and sterling became a floating currency, to which numerous other currencies were pegged. The system of preferences agreed at Ottawa also replaced the free-trade regime. Nevertheless, Britain's global relationships remained fundamentally unchanged. Trade preferences helped debtors to find a niche in the British market, while their serious balance of payments problems in the 1930s encouraged further efforts to promote import-substituting manufactures. We drew attention to this process in the Dominions, India and Argentina, where preferences and quotas in the British market were supplemented by pegging currencies to sterling at devalued exchange rates.[103] Sugihara shows that Japan did exactly the same with the yen after 1932, with the result that Japan effectively joined the sterling area. This connection helped to extend sterling's influence, but it also built up the industry that eventually fed Japan's militarization and made it possible for her to overwhelm the British empire in East Asia after 1941. China's short burst of industrialization in the late 1930s was promoted in much the same way.[104]

Sugihara recognizes how the open regime that exposed domestic industry to foreign competition also encouraged the growth of the service sector. As we emphasized in *British Imperialism*, this shift was fostered by the City of London and fuelled by its growing international business. The City became the most distinctive feature of Britain's economic development in the late nineteenth and early twentieth centuries, and its success underpinned the wealth and status of the gentlemanly elite.[105] Since the City depended on the growth of world trade and that growth depended on continuing industrialization in other parts of the world, Sugihara is right to say that the maintenance of gentlemanly capitalist structures in Britain into the twentieth century was a function of the evolving world economy.[106] Equally, he is correct to point out that the international economic system had room for only one finance-service complex to act as the midwife to world industrialization in this way. The reason for this, which perhaps he should have mentioned, is that income from international services was much smaller than that from goods at this time, and could only support one leading economy. It is worth observing in this connection that the dominance Britain had enjoyed in world exports of manufactures encouraged the openness and the global reach that made it easier for her to become the leading provider of international services.

Capitalizing on this opportunity, as Sugihara points out, required great experience and the generation of trust. The gentlemanly capitalist regime possessed these qualities in abundance, and it was this superiority that made it unique.[107] Since comparative advantage in finance and services is much more culture-specific than it is in manufacturing, Britain's supremacy in this sector – and the supremacy of the class that dominated it – lasted a great deal longer than its industrial leadership.

Much of Sugihara's argument reflects concerns expressed at the time by opponents of the economic priorities promoted by gentlemanly capitalism. Hobson, whom Sugihara refers to on more than one occasion, believed that the stream of British investment flowing abroad would eventually lead to the industrialization of Asia and to the corresponding deindustrialization of Britain unless there was a massive shift in purchasing power to divert capital to the home market.[108] Joseph Chamberlain, as we have just seen, also worried that the City-led foreign investment regime, in conjunction with free trade, would result in the destruction of British industry. Since he equated industry with power, and power with the strength of the empire, he concluded that the outcome would be disastrous for Britain's place in the world in the twentieth century. His ill-fated tariff reform campaign was designed precisely to counter this threat.[109] Britain's inability under the free-trade regime to negotiate with other industrializing nations infuriated the Tariff Reformers. In their view, unilateral free trade meant that, by manipulating their own tariffs, foreign countries could determine what Britain could and could not manufacture. Protection, therefore, was vital too if Britain was to shape her own economic destiny.[110] It was also argued that the adoption of free trade in the wake of successful industrialization had been a disaster – the ultimate cause of all the subsequent changes that Sugihara outlines and Chamberlain deplored. Free trade, it was alleged, had turned the terms of trade against Britain and encouraged overseas investment. Repayments of these investments in turn induced a horde of imports that undermined first agriculture and then industry. All the same, critics found it hard to deny that overseas investment had also flooded Britain with a 'golden rain' of invisible payments that was one of the most dynamic elements in the prosperity of the City and of the service economy generally.[111]

These commentators regarded the rise of the service sector as a sign of Britain's growing weakness. Sugihara, like Gilpin, seems to agree with their judgement. However, it is likely that the relatively small scale of Britain's resources and population would have made it impossible for her to retain her industrial dominance for long after 1850, whatever domestic or international economic policies she adopted. Moreover, Chamberlain's dream of overcoming Britain's inherent handicap of size by means of a united empire was unrealizable. In the circumstances, promoting a service economy in the context of global multilateralism was a reasonable option. The mix of finance, services, and industry was clearly strong enough to carry Britain through the First World War. Her contribution to the war effort was vital not only as a combatant but also as a financier of the anti-German coalition. When Britain's resources ran low, the United States stepped in to assist in 1917 as later on she did in 1941. One reason she did so, on both occasions, was that she favoured the open economy that Britain's system of free trade upheld.[112]

Sugihara occasionally comes close to the error of supposing that the City had both the political strength and the will to insist on free trade. In fact, free trade was entrenched because it attracted support from a very wide spectrum of interests, working class as well as propertied, and because the manufacturing sector was split over the issue before the late 1920s.[113] Moreover, the City's support for free trade was never fanatical. The key issue for the City was the maintenance of exchange stability: it could live with mild protection (which was much preferred to high taxation), as the functioning of sterling under the protectionist-preferential regime of the 1930s shows. It is this regime that attracts the attention of Akita and Kagotani, whose detailed case study further extends Sugihara's insights into British policy during the 1930s.

Sugihara concludes by relating his version of the causes of the Japanese 'miracle' to the ambitious and illuminating thesis advanced recently by Pomeranz.[114] Sugihara shows how the argument put forward in *British Imperialism* can inform the debate on the causes of Japan's industrialization; Pomeranz compares China and Europe in order to explain the first industrial revolution. Briefly put, Pomeranz suggests that Europe and China had reached comparable levels of development by the middle of the eighteenth century and that the 'great divergence' that followed can be attributed primarily to Europe's success in developing new sources of energy. This outcome was achieved partly by exploiting the region's own resources of coal and partly by colonizing land in the New World, thus adding to its stock of foodstuffs. Segments of the argument are familiar: Braudel, among others, made a similar claim about the relative levels of development of parts of Asia and parts of Europe, while the idea that wealth from the New World fuelled the industrial revolution is one that goes back a long way, and in its modern guise is associated principally with Eric Williams.[115] However, apart from the fact that Pomeranz has approached his task with impressive thoroughness and is also a sinologist who carries authority in that field, the novelty of his argument lies in the way he has attached it to the story of the rise of the Atlantic economy. Previous scholars argued either that profits derived from the new economy financed the industrial revolution, or that demand in the New World promoted Europe's manufactures. Pomeranz emphasizes instead the crucial contribution made by the Americas and the Caribbean to relieving the strain on Europe's scarce supplies of land.

Enlightening though it is, the European end of the argument is vulnerable on a number of counts. It is far from clear that the Malthusian aspect of the case will stand. As O'Brien has pointed out, Europe's self-sufficiency in foodstuffs extended into the nineteenth century, by which time the first industrial revolution was well under way.[116] Moreover, Pomeranz is inclined to refer to Europe as an entity, whereas, of course, the industrial revolution occurred in England before it spread elsewhere. Pomeranz's composite is therefore not well-tailored to fit the problem he seeks to explain. This difficulty probably accounts for the frequent insertion of parentheses referring to England and to the annotation 'especially Britain', when the author wishes to establish a more general point relating to the whole of Europe.[117] In effect, the European end of the argument rests largely on the English example, which Pomeranz has insufficient space to study in detail.

This is unfortunate because Pomeranz comes very near to recognizing the qualities of British 'exceptionalism', even if he ties them to a suspect argument about energy supplies. Throughout the book he emphasizes the distinctiveness of, and vital contribution made by, Europe's financial institutions, armed trading companies, and overseas colonization, and the way they were nurtured by a 'system of competing, debt-financed states', and he makes it clear that England was the prime example of these developments.[118] He then draws a contrast with China, where financial institutions were less advanced, and where the state had no incentive to promote overseas enterprise and consequently gave little backing to merchants engaged in foreign trade. However, having spread himself thinly over Europe, Pomeranz is unable to pursue the question of why England, standing as a virtual proxy for the continent, developed these attributes. At one point he is even driven to adopt the argument of last resort, namely that Europe's advantages were a 'fortunate freak'.[119]

All we would say at this point is that elements of the explanation that Pomeranz was reaching for are contained in *British Imperialism*, which unfortunately he did not cite. Had he referred to our argument (and bet-

ter still agreed with it), he would have built a case rooted not in freak-
ishness but in institutional developments since the Civil War and the
Glorious Revolution. He would also have been obliged to deal with the
fact that, as Sugihara points out, our interpretation was not directed to
explaining his problem, which was to find the causes of the industrial
revolution. At that point he would have had two options. He could
either have reformulated the problem so that the great divergence is
seen to be characterized by financial as well as by industrial developments, or he could have retained the original problem but traced the
links between the financial and the industrial revolutions in the eighteenth century. The forces represented by gentlemanly capitalism were
dominant in the first option and prominent, if indirectly, in the second
by financing the distribution of manufactures, by raising consumer purchasing power in the affluent Home Counties, and by promoting
imports and re-exports of colonial products. Either way, the argument
put forward in *British Imperialism* bears on the departure that Pomeranz
sought to explain, just as in the different circumstances of the twentieth century it helps to understand the rise of manufacturing in some
regions beyond Europe, as Sugihara demonstrates with reference to
Japan.

VIII

The contributions by Akita and Kagotani and by Kibata take the debate
about British imperialism in East Asia further by viewing the question
from a Japanese perspective, which necessarily received very limited
treatment in our work. Akita and Kagotani's essay is of particular interest as an attempt to extrapolate from our analysis of the Ottawa system
and the emergence of the sterling area in the 1930s.[120] It is consistent
with our interpretation, but it adds considerably both to what we said
and to our understanding of the international economy at that time,
and it has important implications for rethinking political relationships
between Japan, China and the British Empire in a period of mounting
international crisis.

We argued in *British Imperialism* that the imperial preference system
initiated at Ottawa in 1932, and the associated trade agreements made
with countries like Argentina, were concerned less with promoting the
sale of British manufactured goods than with ensuring that Britain's
debtors could continue to meet their sterling obligations and maintain
healthy sterling balances in London.[121] As the Ottawa system evolved,
it became primarily a set of devices for ensuring the stability of the

emerging sterling area and for keeping the sterling exchange rate steady against its main rival, the US dollar. We demonstrated that the chief outcome of the trade agreements was to enable the principal debtors to develop export surpluses, thus helping Britain to settle her own international obligations and to avoid successive sterling crises. We also drew attention to the fact that the need to economize on sterling in the 1930s gave some debtors, like Australia, new incentives to concentrate on import-substituting manufactures.[122] In other words, we claimed that the preferential system became a means of maintaining, in the difficult circumstances of the 1930s, the kind of financial and trade relationships that Britain had nurtured previously under the gold standard. Our discussion was centred on the direct relationships between Britain and other members of the sterling area. Akita and Kagotani expand this theme by showing that the ties between imperial members of the sterling area and foreign countries such as Japan were critical to the functioning of the system as a whole. We gave a hint of this in our brief discussion of the triangular relations between Britain, Australia and Japan in the late 1930s,[123] but without being able to establish the fact that this example was part of an even larger web of trade networks on which Britain's financial stability rested.

Akita and Kagotani clearly show that Japan's trading links with parts of the sterling area within the British empire became increasingly important in the 1930s. As they observe, historians have usually assumed that economic relations between Britain and Japan were focused upon the struggle for markets on behalf of their cotton textile manufacturers, whose mutual antagonisms were very strong.[124] Some scholars claim that these conflicts were important elements in the complex mix of forces that led to the final breakdown of relations between the two powers.[125] Others argue that Japanese policy was driven almost entirely by military pressures in the face of the perceived weakness of the British Empire in Asia, and that no amount of economic co-operation or appeasement would have prevented hostilities.[126] A third opinion emphasizes the tensions in Japanese policy between those who looked towards co-operation with Britain and the United States and those who saw aggression as the only solution to Japan's needs and aspirations.[127] The most detailed piece of new research on Anglo-Japanese trade negotiations in the 1930s is particularly interesting from our perspective because it shows that British governments did their best to rein in their militant manufacturers.[128] They made very few concessions to them, and their restraint was recognized and appreciated by their Japanese counterparts. Akita and Kagotani's analysis is wholly consistent with these recent findings. But it takes the debate further first by revealing more clearly than before the motives that lay behind each country's ability to be conciliatory on matters of trade, and secondly by shifting the focus of the discussion from trade to finance in ways that complement both our own work and that of Sugihara.[129]

Their interpretation, based in part on Sir George Sansom's contemporary record, holds that a complex complementarity developed between Japan and the sterling bloc in the 1930s, even though competition between Britain and Japan in visible trade, especially textiles, became more intense. Japan's purchases of raw materials from countries within the empire, such as India, Malaya and Australia, played a vital part in generating the export surpluses that enabled them to service their external debts and helped Britain to maintain her sterling balances during the world economic depression. In return, Japan received generous provision for her cotton exports in empire markets like India, despite the protests of Lancashire manufacturers. This process was assisted by the fact that the Japanese yen was undervalued after 1932; looked at another way, the British deliberately held the rupee at levels that gave investors confidence that India's external debts would continue to be met in full. The result, as Akita and Kagotani point out, was that Japan's exports of cotton goods to India were higher in the mid-1930s than they had been in the late 1920s, despite the world slump and the protectionist restrictions associated with Ottawa. In this way, Britain gave a significant boost to Japan's industrial growth while also nurturing the new sterling area.

It is important at this juncture to keep in mind the connections between economics and politics. India had been granted tariff autonomy in 1917 partly to ensure that revenue could be raised for payments that the Government of India had to make in London, and partly to persuade the Indian business class to co-operate with the Raj.[130] The Ottawa agreements and the trade negotiations with Japan were further extensions of a system that was intended not only to ease India's economic relations with Britain but also to pursue a collaborative policy with part of the middle class in India and thus weaken the radical nationalism of the Congress party. As Kagotani observes,[131] Britain wanted to maintain a supply of cheap consumer goods from Japan to prop up living standards in India and contain popular unrest. Indeed, Japan might have received even more open-handed treatment in India had not the Conservative government needed support from Lancashire's MPs at moments when political relations between Britain and India became so controversial that they threatened to split the Party.[132]

Looked at from the British perspective, it is clear that the original intention of the Ottawa agreements was to meet the world crisis by encouraging inter-imperial trade flows. Britain in particular wanted to see freer trade between empire countries, but the insistence of the Dominions and India on retaining protection meant that she had to make do with a system of mutual preferences. After that, the peculiar pressures exerted by Britain's position as a major international creditor, together with the traditional mind-set of British gentlemanly capitalists in the Treasury and other key areas of government, caused the agreements to evolve in a way that differed from the original intention. It was then that they became instruments facilitating the smooth operation of the sterling area. One fascinating aspect of Akita and Kagotani's work is to show how quickly the Japanese government grasped the essential elements of the British position. Policy-makers in Tokyo realized that to do business with the British empire effectively, and to maximize Japan's own interests, they needed to direct their efforts towards easing financial flows rather than towards promoting manufactured exports aggressively. They held to this policy, even though the interests of the manufacturing lobby in Japan sometimes stood in their way.

A further implication of Akita and Kagotani's work is to reveal how many segments of the multilateral trade network survived the crash of 1928–31 and were actively encouraged in the 1930s. Looking at the matter once more from a British perspective, we can say that the encouragement of multilateralism was a direct outcome of policy priorities favoured by gentlemanly capitalists.[133] Any system devoted to extending markets for Britain's manufactured exports would almost certainly have restricted international trade flows much more, as Sansom recognized. In practice, by expanding the sterling system and cultivating its relationships with other blocs, Britain tried to retain as much of the cosmopolitan world economy of the gold-standard era as was possible in the circumstances of the 1930s – and for the same reasons. In dealing with this theme, Akita and Kagotani also note the strong similarity between the way the Dutch, as well as the British, approached trade negotiations with Japan. The similarity suggests that financial concerns outweighed industrial ones in the Netherlands as they did in Britain. If this was indeed the case, it provides grounds for supposing that comparisons between international economic policies of Britain and the Netherlands would be well worth considering. The Dutch empire, based essentially on Indonesia, was far more important to the economic and political development of the Netherlands in the nineteenth century than has often been allowed; it has even been suggested that the Dutch produced a home-grown species of Britain's gentlemanly capitalist elite.[134] Whatever the outcome of this comparison, after it has been pursued into the twentieth century, it is clear from Akita and Kagotani's pioneering efforts that the idea that international economic relations in the 1930s were essentially about the creation of states of autarky is at best an oversimplification and at worst a misunderstanding. This much can be said with some confidence, even though the older stereotype still pervades much of the discussion of the subject, and even though additional work is needed to uncover just how intricate and interconnected the international economic system remained in the 1930s.

IX

Japan's invasion of China in 1937 is a key date in Akita and Kagotani's calendar of events; Kibata's elegant dissection of Anglo-Japanese relations in the 1930s confirms its importance. We agree with Kibata that until then it was possible that Japan would finally come to terms, politically and economically, with the British empire, despite her military build-up and aggressive stance towards China. After that date, military objectives overcame all others, and the war with China began a process of hostilities that led to the frontal attack on the British Empire in the Second World War.

If there was no inevitability about Japan's shift in policy from 1937, we can regard Britain's attempts to reach an accommodation with Japan as being more realistic than some historians are inclined to believe.[135] As Kibata notes, from the perspective of 1935–36 it was reasonable for Neville Chamberlain and his allies in the Treasury to suppose that there was an economic solution to the Japan–China problem and that the Japanese, as 'Orientals' themselves, could be valuable allies in Britain's drive to develop China. British business interests in China also began to favour the idea that Japan would galvanize China, thereby creating opportunities for Britain, too, while keeping the peace in the Far East.[136] In other words, the well known Leith-Ross mission, which Kibata sees as an example of gentlemanly capitalism, made some sense at the time. Admittedly, the mission was partly based on hubris. The chances of persuading the Chinese to join the sterling area formally were always remote: China managed to stabilize its currency without aligning it either to the dollar or to sterling.[137] Yet Leith-Ross's mission helped to stabilize the currency and to set up an effective central bank. Moreover, as Kibata notes, to the extent that Britain's economic initiatives stimulated

China's development, they moderated long-standing anti-British nationalism. Indeed, the prospects for sustained growth in China, and for continued British enjoyment of some of its fruits, seemed very promising immediately before the Japanese invasion.[138] However, there is no doubt that, despite Leith-Ross's attempt to placate the Japanese and even to involve them in the negotiations, his mission angered many observers in Tokyo who saw it as an attempt by Britain to dominate the Chinese market and to strengthen China against Japan.[139] Ambiguity was indeed present in Britain's policy towards China and Japan at this time, and it was not resolved until 1937, when a calculated decision was made, on the presumed balance of advantages, to support China.

Kibata's stress on the importance of industrial interests in backing British schemes for Chinese development is timely. We, too, drew attention to the role of the industrial lobby[140] principally in relation to the interest shown by Neville Chamberlain, the British Prime Minister of the day, in the Leith-Ross mission. Kibata extends our comments by referring to Ramsey MacDonald's ideas for developing the China market and to the Barnby Mission of 1934, which was supported by the Federation of British Industries and had official blessing.[141] Kibata's characterization of these initiatives as 'industrial imperialism' suggests a possible connection with Phimister's discussion of South Africa.[142] In the same way, Neville Chamberlain's policy of bringing industrialists into the discussions about China prompts interesting parallels with his father's approach to imperialism. As we have seen, Joseph Chamberlain wanted to assemble a new coalition of economic interests in support of his imperial policy. It is difficult to know whether to label it, and Neville's policy towards China, as 'industrial imperialism' or to see one or both as a modification of the more traditional gentlemanly capitalist approach. What is clear, however, is that Neville Chamberlain's initiatives, and the Leith-Ross mission itself, were both deplored by the Foreign Office, which feared that Britain's meddling in China's economic affairs would anger Japan and was likely to end in conflict.[143] A full assessment of this issue needs to bear in mind the fact that circumstances had changed greatly since the turn of the century. The industrialists of the 1890s were trying to sell textiles and railway equipment to China; those of the 1930s had formed transnational conglomerates and were beginning to invest in productive activities in China itself, often in association with indigenous entrepreneurs. The first group wanted to see China opened up and nationalists put down; the second were interested in developing the hinterlands of the great ports, which meant working with the nationalists rather than against them.

One of the merits of Kibata's paper is its reminder of how Britain's policy towards Japan and China was affected by perceptions of what was happening in other parts of the empire, most notably in India. However, though Britain had its share of Cassandras, Kibata may have underestimated the degree of optimism about the future of the empire expressed by British commentators in the 1930s. In the context of British policy towards Asia, it is interesting to see that the pessimists tended to come from the more traditional arms of the gentlemanly capitalist network – the Foreign Office and the upper ranks of the armed services – whereas the optimists were more likely to be found among the 'money men' and their allies – the City, emerging big business and the Treasury. Such contrasts should not be overdrawn: the Bank of England's records suggest that the Governor, Montagu Norman, was more sceptical about the outcome of Britain's financial initiatives in China than were either the Treasury or the City.[144] While both schools of thought were offering their different predictions of China's future, the British government tried to buy time, through appeasement, to enable Britain to rearm while still searching for a means of holding the international order, on which her economy was so dependent, in place. When Japan's invasion of China was followed by Hitler's strikes against first Czechoslovakia and then Poland, it became obvious that the future of the empire had come to depend upon the support of a republican, anti-colonial power: the United States.

X

Economic history and the history of political economy have lost favour in recent years. They have clearly failed to attract the same interest and enthusiasm as cultural history and the history of discourse in particular. However, the most obvious conclusion we draw from our reading of the contributions to this book is that the study of the economic dimension of the history of imperialism has great importance and vitality, and can still evoke research of the highest quality. The subject is far from being tired and dated, as its detractors have claimed.[145] It is also evident that, as in all good work, new questions are raised as old ones are answered: the essays in this volume suggest a host of research agendas yet to be tackled, and in doing so point to ways in which the scholarly frontier can be moved into new territory.

Bowen's essay amplifies our highly compressed view of the eighteenth century and prompts the question of whether 'peripheral gentlemanly capitalism' existed elsewhere, apart from America, before the nineteenth century. In parallel fashion, Krozewski's chapter expands our abbreviated treatment of the period after the Second World War and establishes the need to look more closely at the timing of the demise of gentlemanly capitalism in the metropolis itself in the second half of the twentieth century. Darwin's spacious contribution raises large issues relating to the interaction between economic events and political action and between domestic impulses towards imperialism and the international forces constraining them. Despite the immense amount of ink spilled over the partition of Africa, Phimister's concise assessment shows that many of the links between imperial expansion and the economic development of tropical and southern Africa remain either undiscovered or underresearched. The chapters dealing with Asia have research implications of equal importance. The broad survey by Shunhong opens up the possibility of further dialogue between Marxist and non-Marxist scholars on issues such as decolonization and neo-colonialism. Petersson's detailed analysis of the years between 1905 and 1911 is a model of its kind and should encourage studies of other regions that played host, reluctantly, to international diplomacy and cosmopolitan finance. By harnessing British imperialism to the study of industrialization in the Far East, Sugihara's chapter and the complementary contribution by Akita and Kagatoni point to the need for similar studies of Britain's relations with other parts of the globe. They suggest, too, that a closer investigation of the complex web of relations that held the international economy together after 1870 would be a rewarding exercise and might change our view of its evolution, especially during the crisis years of the 1930s. Kibata's essay adds to this new Asian perspective by showing how economics was linked to politics in the making and breaking of Anglo-Japanese relations, and not only in the 1930s, which is his own special interest.

Anyone familiar with the historiography of imperialism will be aware that there has been discussion recently of the emergence of a 'new' imperial history.[146] Like all such novelties, the term carries different meanings for different authors. They have in common the broad sense that imperial history, though ably studied by numerous scholars over many years, has lost the status it once enjoyed when empires were going concerns. From the 1960s it was gradually broken down, following the fate of the empire itself, and its various fragments were annexed by the rising power of Area Studies. Its appeal to younger scholars is limited, and in recent years has been confined largely to a restricted number of themes inspired by postmodernism. One reading of the term 'new' in relation to imperial history is that it consists of superimposing themes such as gender, race, science, art, architecture and the environment on older forms of the subject, perhaps to the point of liquidating them. This enterprise has already been launched, and has both departed from and added to the agenda inspired half a century ago by scholars such as Gallagher and Robinson. The issue is not whether these new topics are desirable additions to the repertoire, for it would be hard to deny their claims or their merits. The difficulty, which has yet to be addressed, is how to incorporate them in such a way as to produce an integrated programme for research and teaching.

A second meaning of the 'new' imperial history is one that seeks to rescue the central but neglected themes of economic and political history, to relate them not only to the role of the state but to forces that bypassed or permeated state agencies, and to place them in a long-term and comparative context.[147] The endeavour, though heroic enough in its ambitions, needs also to encompass cultural history and social history rather than be set against them. This design is a considerable departure from the postmodernist agenda, which not only relegates economic and political issues but is also hostile to the 'totalizing project' and the 'essentialism' inherent in studying structural change and continuity in the long run.[148] It will be apparent that it is this version of the new imperial history, or at least facets of it, that is set out in the present book. The approach adopted here connects in turn with other studies, such as Pomeranz's notable contribution discussed earlier, which promise to give new life and fresh appeal to large-scale, comparative histories of the material world.

The events of 11 September 2001 are certain to have a considerable impact on scholarship as well as on the wider world. When the twin towers of the World Trade Center were brought down, so too, surely, was the fashionable assertion that sophisticated thinkers speak only of perceptions and not of realities. On that day, reality made an instant come-back, tragically with a big bang. It was a reality, moreover, that could be understood only by placing it in a global perspective because it was a distant, different and poorly understood part of the world that suddenly 'struck back'. It then became apparent that to understand this world it was also necessary to grasp some of its past and, by a further step, to reach into the history of defunct empires in order to understand the economic, political and cultural impulses they transmitted and the reactions they provoked. In this circuitous way, globalization met history on 11 September. History, through the medium of historians, now has an opportunity to respond by re-energizing the study of those parts of the world that conventional histories of the nation state cannot reach.

Notes

1   Our title is adapted from a famous essay by E.P. Thompson, 'The Peculiarities of the English' in idem, *The Poverty of Theory and Other Essays* (1978), which discusses the unique features of the British form of capitalist civilization.

2   P.J. Cain and A.G. Hopkins, *British Imperialism, 1688–2000* (2001), pp. 1–19.

3   The first was R.E. Dumett (ed.), *Gentlemanly Capitalism and British Imperialism: the New Debate on Empire* (1999).

4   We make this point in response to the criticism that the concept of a gentleman, and by extension of gentlemanly capitalism, is too vague to be useful. See the valuable discussion in Penny Corfield, 'The Democratic History of the English Gentleman', *History Today*, 42 (1992), pp. 40–7; also our comments in *British Imperialism*, pp. 8–10.

5   On India see P.J. Marshall, 'British Society in India under the East India Company', *Modern Asian Studies*, 31 (1997), pp. 89–108.

6   David Armitage, *The Ideological Origins of the British Empire* (Cambridge, 2000).

7   H.V. Bowen, 'British Conceptions of Global Empire, 1763–83', *Jour. Imp. and Comm. Hist.*, 26 (1998), pp. 1–27. For a view 'from below', see Linda Colley, 'Going Native, Telling Tales: Captivity, Collaborations and Empire', *Past & Present*, 168 (2000), pp. 170–93.

8   Patrick K. O'Brien, 'Inseparable Connections: Trade, Economy, Fiscal State, and the Expansion of Empire, 1688–1815', in P.J. Marshall (ed.), *The Oxford History of the British Empire*, Vol. II (Oxford, 1998), pp. 53–77, and the further references given there.

9   Cain and Hopkins, *British Imperialism*, p. 77.

10 Bernard Semmel, *The Rise of Free Trade Imperialism: Classical Political Economy, the Empire of Free Trade and Imperialism, 1750–1850* (Cambridge, 1970), ch. 2.

11 For a concise restatement, see John Darwin, 'Imperialism and the Victorians: the Dynamics of Territorial Expansion', *English Historical Review*, CXII (1997), pp. 614–15.

12 Tony Ballantyne, 'Empire, Knowledge and Culture: from Proto-Globalization to Modern Globalization', in A.G. Hopkins (ed.), *Globalization in World History* (2002), pp. 115–40.

13 David Cannadine, *Aspects of Aristocracy* (1994), ch. 1.

14 P.J. Cain and A.G. Hopkins, 'The Political Economy of British Expansion Overseas, 1750–1914', *Economic History Review*, 2nd series, XXXIII (1980), pp. 474–81; idem, *British Imperialism*, pp. 82–7, and chs. 2–3; D.C.M. Platt, 'The National Economy and British Imperial Expansion before 1914', *Journal of Imperial and Commonwealth History*, 2 (1973–4), pp. 3–14.

15 *British Imperialism*, p. 658.

16 We argued against this view in *British Imperialism*. See, especially, ch. 11 and p. 311.

17 We are glad to acknowledge here, as in *British Imperialism*, the influence of Darwin's important article on this theme: 'Imperialism in Decline? Tendencies in British Imperial Policy between the Wars', *Historical Journal*, 23 (1980), pp. 657–79.

18 Though we are aligned with him on the broader, diplomatic considerations: see John Darwin, 'The Fall of the Empire State', *Diplomatic History*, 25 (2001), pp. 501–5.

19 *British Imperialism*, ch. 19 and chs. 22 and 25.
20 Ibid., ch. 20. Also P.J. Cain, 'Gentlemanly Imperialism at Work: the Bank of England, Canada, and the Sterling Area, 1932–1936', *Econ. Hist. Rev.*, 2nd. ser. XLIX (1996), pp. 336–57.
21 Pp. 335–6.
22 D.K. Fieldhouse, 'Gentleman, Capitalists and the British Empire', *Journal of Imperial and Commonwealth History* 22 (1994), pp. 531–41.
23 *British Imperialism*, pp. 312–17. We take this opportunity to advertise, again, the excellent unpublished PhD dissertations cited in notes 44 and 48, as they appear not to have been used, even by specialists on this subject.
24 See, for example, Juan R.I. Cole, *Colonialism and Revolution in the Middle East: Social and Cultural Origins of Egypt's Urabi movement* (Princeton, 1992), and Afal Lufti Al-Sayyid-Marsot, 'The British Occupation of Egypt from 1882', in Andrew Porter (ed.), *Oxford History of the British Empire* (Oxford, 1999), pp. 651–64.
25 *La France et l'Egypte de 1882 à 1914: intérêts économiques et implications poli- tiques* (Paris, 1997), pp. 535–70, 697–8. We are grateful to Professor Saul for helpful correspondence on this subject.
26 Phimister generously acknowledges this and provides the relevant citations.
27 P.J. Cain and A.G. Hopkins, 'The Political Economy of British Expansion Overseas, 1750–1914', *Econ. Hist. Rev.*, 2nd ser. XXXIII (1980), pp. 463–90.
28 Pp. 331–5.
29 A.G. Hopkins, 'The "New International Order" in the Nineteenth Century: Britain's First Development Plan for Africa' in Robin Law (ed.), *From Slave Trade to Legitimate Commerce: the Commercial Transition in Nineteenth-Century West Africa* (Cambridge, 1995), pp. 240–64, outlines a framework for treating this theme on a continent-wide basis. Jonathan Glassman, *Feasts and Riot: Revelry, Rebellion and Popular Consciousness on the Swahili Coast, 1856–1888* (1994), provides an illuminating case study.
30 Cloves accounted for about 25 per cent of the value of total exports from Zanzibar in the 1880s and ivory for about 40 per cent.
31 *British Imperialism*, pp. 331–5.
32 It need hardly be said that this is a far more complex matter than this sum- mary suggests. Specialists vary in their emphases on how strong the Sultanate was at the moment of partition. Compare, for example, Norman R. Bennett, *Arab versus European: Diplomacy and War in Nineteenth-Century East Africa* (1986) with Abdul Sheriff, *Slaves, Spices and Ivory in Zanzibar: Integration of an East African Empire into the World Economy, 1770–1873* (1987). This really is a case where 'more research is needed'.
33 The best statement of Kirk's policy, including his links with the 'unofficial mind' of imperialism, is now Roy Bridges, 'Towards the Prelude to the Partition of East Africa', in Roy Bridges, ed. *Imperialism, Decolonization and Africa* (2000), ch. 2.
34 *British Imperialism*, pp. 327–31.
35 Ibid., p. 331.
36 Ibid., p. 338.
37 See Trevor Lloyd, 'Africa and Hobson's Imperialism', *Past and Present*, 55 (1972), pp. 130–53. Lloyd makes this point in the broader context of arguing that, in general, flows of capital had little to do with imperialist expansion in Africa.

38 For example, David E. Torrance, *The Strange Death of Liberal Empire: Lord Selborne in South Africa* (Liverpool, 1996), p. 29. We are grateful to Professor Torrance for his advice on Selborne's views of the City and of imperial union, though he is not responsible for the stance we have taken here.

39 Kenneth E. Wilburn, 'Engines of Empire and Independence: Railways in South Africa, 1863–1916', in Clarence B. Davis and Kenneth E. Wilburn (eds), *Railway Imperialism* (1991), pp. 32–5. For Rothschild's views on informal empire in South Africa, see Niall Ferguson, *The World's Banker: the House of Rothschild* (1998), pp. 876–90.

40 Bill Nasson, *The South African War, 1899–1902* (1999), p. 29. This point, in turn, has to be placed in context: it was still the case that 75 per cent of the *Uitlanders* were British. Ibid., p. 27.

41 See Peter Henshaw, 'The "Key to South Africa" in the 1890s: Delagoa Bay and the Origins of the South African War', *Journal of Southern African Studies*, 24 (1998), pp. 527–43.

42 Nasson, *South African War*, p. 39.

43 Iain R. Smith, *The Origins of the South African War* (1996), pp. 268–9.

44 On Chamberlain's and Milner's philosophy, see P.J. Cain, 'The Economic Philosophy of Constructive Imperialism', in Cornelia Navari (ed.), *British Politics and the Spirit of the Age* (Keele, 1996), pp. 41–66.

45 Quoted in Iain R. Smith, 'Joseph Chamberlain and the Jameson Raid', in Greg Cuthbertson (ed.), *The Jameson Raid: a Centennial Retrospective* (Houghton, South Africa, 1996), p. 101.

46 We hope it will be clear that we are following a line of thought prompted by Phimister's interpretation of Selborne's memorandum, and not attempting a comprehensive explanation of the causes of the Anglo-South African war. A judicious recent assessment can be found in Nasson, *South African War*, which evaluates other important considerations – from Kruger's policy to the attitude of the mine-owners, as does Cuthbertson, *The Jameson Raid*.

47 Smith, *Origins*, pp. 157–60.

48 Phimister's earlier argument that the Transvaal's tariff independence was a barrier to union and to Britain's trade interests in South Africa takes on particular significance in this context. See I.R. Phimister, 'Unscrambling the Scramble for Southern Africa: the Jameson Raid and the South African War Revisited', *South African Historical Journal*, 28 (1993), pp. 218–19.

49 The detailed study is R.M. Kesner, *Economic Control and Colonial Development: Crown Colony Financial Management in the Age of Joseph Chamberlain* (Oxford, 1981). See also S.B. Saul, 'The Economic Policy of "Constructive Imperialism"', *Journal of Economic History*, 17 (1959), pp. 173–92.

50 On the Crown Agents, see David Sunderland, 'Principals and Agents: the Activities of the Crown Agents for the Colonies, 1880–1914', *Econ. Hist. Rev.* 2nd ser. LII (1999), pp. 284–306.

51 Cain and Hopkins, *British Imperialism*, pp. 195–6.

52 Torrance, *The Strange Death of Liberal Empire,* passim.

53 Ibid., p. 195, and pp. 181–95 generally.

54 Gerold Krozewski, *Money and the End of Empire: British International Economic Policy and the Colonies, 1947–58* (2001).

55 *British Imperialism*, p. 619, and our related comments on p. 9.

56 W.D. Rubinstein, 'Britain's Elites in the Inter-War Period, 1918–39', *Contemporary British History*, 12 (1998), pp. 1–18.

57 Ronald Robinson, 'The Moral Disarmament of African Empire', *Journal of Imperial and Commonwealth History*, 8 (1979), pp. 86–104.

58 Ronald Robinson, 'Andrew Cohen and the Transfer of Power in Africa', in W.M. Morris-Jones and G. Fischer (eds), *Decolonisation and After; the British and French Experience* (1979), pp. 50–72.

59 E.H.H. Green, 'The Influence of the City over British Economic Policy, c.1880–1960', in Youssef Cassis (ed.), *Finance and Financiers in European History, 1880–1960* (Cambridge, 1992), pp. 193–218.

60 Philip Augar, *The Death of Gentlemanly Capitalism* (2000).

61 Scott Newton and Dilwyn Porter, *Modernization Frustrated: the Politics of Industrial Decline in Britain since 1900* (1988).

62 See, for example, Philip Murphy, *Alan Lennox-Boyd: a Biography* (1999); and the patterns of recruitment revealed by A.H.M. Kirk-Greene, *Britain's Imperial Administrators, 1858–1996* (Basingstoke, 2000).

63 Hugh Thomas (ed.), *The Establishment: a Symposium* (1959). We note that Krozewski does not attempt to engage with our, admittedly limited, defence of the idea that gentlemanly capitalist elites continued to flourish after 1945, as presented in *British Imperialism*, pp. 620–2, or with the references contained therein. In this context, we would draw attention especially to W.D. Rubinstein, 'Education and the Social Origins of British Elites, 1800–1970', *Past and Present* 112 (1986), pp. 163–207.

64 We may refer here to the authority of Susan Strange, who felt that our argument had a great deal of contemporary relevance: See her review of *British Imperialism* in *Review of International Studies* 20 (1994), pp. 407–10.

65 Important recent contributions to this subject include: R.L. Tignor, *Capitalism and Nationalism at the End of Empire: State and Business in Decolonizing Egypt, Nigeria, and Kenya, 1945–1963* (Princeton, 1998); Philip Murphy, *Party Politics and Decolonization: the Conservative Party and British Colonial Policy in Tropical Africa, 1951–1964* (Oxford, 1995); Nicholas J. White, *Business, Government and the End of Empire: Malaya, 1942–1957* (Oxford, 1996).

66 Pp. 640–4.

67 Further assistance, if needed, can be found in Darwin's chapter, which also draws attention to the continuities between prewar and postwar Britain.

68 There were two prominent considerations: making friends rather than enemies out of nationalists by turning them into statesmen, and devising strategies for keeping colonies that might become independent 'sterling minded'. See, for example, A.G. Hopkins, 'Macmillan's Audit of Empire, 1957', in Peter Clarke and Clive Trebilcock (eds). *Understanding Decline: Perceptions and Realities. Essays in Honour of Barry Supple* (Cambridge, 1997), pp. 234–60.

69 *British Imperialism*, pp. 658–9.

70 Ibid., pp. 15–17.

71 Macartney, too, wanted influence, not annexation.

72 See *British Imperialism*, pp. 335–9, 379–80.

73 The phrase is from J.A. Hobson, *Imperialism: a Study* (1988 ed.), p. 332.

74 See Roberta Allbert Dayer, *Finance and Empire: Sir Charles Addis, 1861–1945* (1989).

75 The basic elements of the plan were put in place after the conclusion of the French Wars in 1815, when Britain turned her attention to 'winning the peace'. See Hopkins, 'The "New International Economic Order" in the Nineteenth Century'.

76 Paul Kennedy, *The Realities behind Diplomacy: Background Influences on British External Policy, 1865–1980* (1981), esp. Pt.I.

77 See below, p. xxx.

78 David McLean, 'The Foreign Office and the First Chinese Indemnity Loan', *Historical Journal* 16 (1973), pp. 303–21; F.H.H. King, *History of the Hongkong and Shanghai Banking Corporation*, II (Cambridge, 1988), pp. 264–75.

79 The most thorough account is E.W. Edwards, *British Diplomacy and Finance in China, 1895–1914* (Oxford, 1987).

80 David Kynaston, *The City of London: the Golden Years, 1890–1914* (1995), pp. 564–71.

81 *British Imperialism*, ch. 25.

82 Ibid., pp. 57–61.

83 See the summary in Hans van de Ven, 'The Onrush of Modern Globalization in China', in A.G. Hopkins (ed.), *Globalization in World History* (2002), pp. 167–93.

84 *British Imperialism*, pp. 6–7.

85 Ibid., pp. 63, 99–100, 102, 261.

86 For the reference and further comment, see *British Imperialism*, p. 7, n.18 and pp. 7–8, 50–3.

87 He also notes in passing the Opium Wars of 1840–42 and 1856–58, but the brevity of his comments on this subject precludes a short response, and there is insufficient space for a long one.

88 See P.J. Marshall, 'Britain and China in the Late Eighteenth Century', in Robert A. Bickers (ed.), *Ritual and Diplomacy: the Macartney Mission to China, 1792–1794* (1993), pp. 11–29. James L. Hevia's study, *Cherishing Men from Afar: Qing Guest Ritual and the Macartney Embassy of 1793* (1996), also cited by Shunhong, is an interesting postmodernist account but is of tangential relevance to the issue in hand.

89 Macartney's humanitarian, pacific and also prejudiced outlook is assessed by P.J. Marshall, 'Lord Macartney, India and China: the Two Faces of the Enlightenment', *South Asia*, 19 (1996), pp. 121–31.

90 The established means being shipments of silver. Macartney's involvement with India and the Company is dealt with by L.S. Sutherland, 'Lord Macartney's Appointment as Governor of Madras, 1780: the Treasury in East India Company Elections', *English Historical Review*, 90 (1975), pp. 523–35.

91 Rudrangshu Mukherjee, 'Trade and Empire in Awahd, 1765–1804', *Past and Present*, 94 (1982), pp. 85–106.

92 Amar Farooqui, 'Opium Enterprise and Colonial Intervention in Malwa and Western India, 1800–1824', *Indian Economic and Social History Review*, 32 (1995), pp. 447–73. This was also a key consideration in the subsequent annexation of Sind: J.Y. Wong, 'British Annexation of Sind in 1843: an Economic Perspective', *Modern Asian Studies*, 31 (1997), pp. 225–44. British shipping, and British merchants based in India and the Far East, gained significantly from the opium trade. See the important article by Freda Harcourt, 'Black Gold: P & O and the Opium Trade', 1847–1914', *International Journal of Maritime History*, 6 (1994), pp. 1–83.

93 Anthony Webster, 'The Political Economy of Trade Liberalization: the East India Company Charter Act of 1813', *Economic History Review*, 2nd ser. XLIII (1990), pp. 404–19.

94 Van de Ven, 'The Onrush of Modern Globalization in China', pp. 176–9.

95 Ch. 6 above.

96 See also *British Imperialism*, pp. 368–77, which notes Manchester's failure to prevent an increase in China's external tariff in 1902 (p. 371), and the inability of Paulings, the railway contractors, to tie British loans to the purchase of manufactured goods (pp. 376–7).

97 Both in *British Imperialism* (p. 619) and in our comments on Krozewski's essay in this volume.

98 *British Imperialism*, ch. 26.

99 Bill Warren, *Imperialism: Pioneer of Capitalism* (1980).

100 Robert Gilpin, *U.S. Power and the Multinational Corporation: the Political Economy of Foreign Direct Investment* (1975), especially chs. 1 and 2. Gilpin's study influenced our early thinking on this subject but has been rather neglected by historians, possibly because its title disguises its substantial historical content.

101 This is explored in P.T. Marsh, *Bargaining on Europe: Britain and the First Common Market, 1860–93* (New Haven, 1999).

102 A. Marrison, 'Insular Free Trade, Retaliation and the Most-Favoured-Nation Treaty, 1880–1914', in idem, *Free Trade and its Reception, 1815–1960* (Manchester, 1998).

103 *British Imperialism*, p. 241 notes the process before 1914. For the 1930s see ibid., pp. 471–2, 502–3, 508–9, 520, 527, 531, 539–40, 557–9, 594–6, 609, 615, 654–5.

104 Sugihara is mistaken in claiming that sterling was divorced from gold in the 1930s: it was exchangeable for gold but not at a fixed rate, as it had been before 1931. Moreover, the implication that, after devaluation in 1933, the US dollar was linked in some way to sterling is misleading. Sterling was managed with the aim of maintaining its stability against the dollar; from the Tripartite Agreement of 1936 onwards the dollar was tacitly recognized as being the *numéraire* of the system.

105 *British Imperialism*, ch. 3. See also C.H. Lee, 'The Service Sector, Regional Specialisation and Economic Growth in the Victorian Economy', *Journal of Historical Geography*, 10 (1984), pp. 139–55.

106 We made a similar point in a different context in *British Imperialism*, pp. 182–3.

107 Sugihara notes that Hong Kong played a key role as a British colony in servicing Asian industrialization after 1945. Since Hong Kong was run by a British gentlemanly elite, as Sugihara notes, this development might be seen as a modern manifestation of 'peripheral gentlemanly capitalism' of the kind discussed by Bowen with reference to the eighteenth century.

108 Hobson, *Imperialism*, pp. 304–19.

109 *British Imperialism*, pp. 190–1.

110 William Cunningham, *The Rise and Decline of the Free Trade Movement* (1904), pp. 115–17, and quoted in Cain, 'The Economic Philosophy of Constructive Imperialism', p. 51.

111 Ritortus, 'The Imperialism of British Trade', I & II, *Contemporary Review*, 76 (1899).

112 An extended version of this argument can be found in P.J. Cain, 'Was it Worth Having? The British Empire, 1850–1950', *Revista de Economica Historia*, 16 (1998), pp. 351–76, especially 362–72.

113 A.C. Howe, *Free Trade and Liberal England, 1846–1946* (Oxford, 1997); A. Marrison, *British Business and Protection, 1903–1932* (Oxford, 1996).

114 Kenneth Pomeranz, *The Great Divergence: China, Europe and the Making of the Modern World Economy* (Princeton, 2000).

115 Fernand Braudel, *Capitalism and Material Life, 1400–1800* (1973); Eric Williams, *Capitalism and Slavery* (1944).

116 Patrick O'Brien, 'Metahistories in Global Histories of Material Progress', *International History Review*, 23 (2001), pp. 365–7.

117 Pomeranz, *The Great Divergence*, for example, pp. 185, 282–5, 296.

118 Ibid., p. 19. See also pp. 178–9, where the generalisation about Europe is again qualified by being related to England.

119 Ibid., p. 207.

120 For a critical discussion of our position on the 1930s from a different angle of vision, see Angela Redish, 'British Financial Imperialism after the First World War', and our response in Dumett, *Gentlemanly Capitalism and British Imperialism*, pp. 127–40, 210–11.

121 *British Imperialism*, pp. 470–8.

122 Ibid., pp. 502–3.

123 Ibid., p. 504.

124 On the cotton-trade rivalries, see Ishii Osamu, 'Markets and Diplomacy: the Anglo-Japanese Rivalries over Cotton Goods Markets, 1930–36', in Ian Nish and Yoichi Kibata (eds), *The History of Anglo-Japanese Relations, 1600–2000, Vol. II: The Political-Diplomatic Dimension, 1931–2000* (Basingstoke, 2000), pp. 51–77. The three-cornered trade conflict between Britain, Australia and Japan in 1936–37 was clearly aggravated by British and Japanese cotton interests. Ibid., pp. 71–3.

125 Antony Best, 'The Road to Anglo-Japanese Confrontation, 1931–41', in Nish and Kibata, *The History of Anglo-Japanese Relations*, pp. 26–50.

126 See John Sharkey, 'Economic Diplomacy in Anglo-Japanese Relations, 1931–41', in Nish and Kibata, *The History of Anglo-Japanese Relations*, p. 103.

127 There is an excellent short presentation of the various choices open to Japan *vis à vis* Britain in the 1930s in Yoichi Kibata, 'Anglo-Japanese Relations from the Manchurian Incident to Pearl Harbour: Missed Opportunities?', in Nish and Kibata, *The History of Anglo-Japanese Relations*, pp. 1–25.

128 Sharkey, 'Economic Diplomacy', pp. 81–91, 102.

129 See ch. 10 and our comments above, pp. 235–6.

130 For a summary and further references see *British Imperialism*, pp. 549–50.

131 See ch. 8, pp. 157–9.

132 The trade negotiations between India, Britain and Japan in 1933–34 showed that the British were concerned more with the needs of Indian millowners than with Lancashire's demands. Sharkey, 'Economic Diplomacy', pp. 85–6.

133 *British Imperialism*, Ch. 20.

134 With a strong leaning towards finance and an accompanying cosmopolitan worldview. See Maarten Kuitenbrouwer, *The Netherlands and the Rise of Modern Capitalism: Colonies and Foreign Policy, 1870–1902* (Oxford, 1991); idem, 'Capitalism and Imperialism: Britain and the Netherlands', *Itinerario*,

18 (1994), pp. 105–16. Also the summary and references in A.G. Hopkins, 'Globalization with and without Empires: from Bali to Labrador', in Hopkins (ed.), *Globalization in World History*, pp. 223–4.

135 See notes 124, 125 above.

136 Peter Duus, Ramon Myers and Mark R. Peattie (eds), *The Japanese Informal Empire in China, 1895–1937* (Princeton, 1989), provides a comprehensive account of Japan's considerable economic and cultural presence in China.

137 *British Imperialism*, p. 608; Akita and Kagotani are in agreement here, but note too Sugihara's argument that both China and Japan were effectively linked, if not formally pegged, to sterling (see above, p. 235).

138 *British Imperialism*, p. 610; P.J. Cain, 'British Economic Imperialism in China in the 1930s: the Leith-Ross Mission', *Bulletin of Asia-Pacific Studies* 7 (1997), pp. 23–34: For a different view, see Shigeru Akita, 'British Informal Empire in East Asia: a Japanese Perspective', in Dummet, *Gentlemanly Capitalism*, pp. 147–52.

139 Best, 'The Road to Anglo-Japanese Confrontation', pp. 34–5.

140 *British Imperialism*, p. 609.

141 On the Barnby Mission, see also Kibata, 'Anglo-Japanese Relations', p. 9.

142 Above, p. 220.

143 On these tensions in British policy, see Gill Bennett, 'British Policy in the Far East, 1933–1936: Treasury and Foreign Office', *Modern Asian Studies*, 26 (1992), pp. 545–68.

144 For Norman's views on the Leith-Ross mission, see Bank of England archive G1/300/2525/2, file 13. It must be emphasized that this is a preliminary view: this is a subject that still awaits its researcher.

145 Dane Kennedy, 'Imperial History and Post-Colonial Theory', *Journal of Imperial and Commonwealth History* 24 (1996), pp. 345–63. We also expect that a cross-fertilization between our own approach and that represented by Kennedy would bear much fruit, as we tentatively suggest in *British Imperialism*, pp. 665–6.

146 See, for example, the 'Afterword' to *British Imperialism*; Hopkins, 'Back to the Future'; Dane Kennedy, 'The Boundaries of Oxford's Empire', *International History Review*, 23 (2001), pp. 604–22.

147 *British Imperialism*, 'Afterword'; Hopkins, 'Back to the Future; idem. *Globalisation in World History*.

148 We dissent here from Kennedy's categorization in 'The Boundaries of Oxford's Empire', which runs the postmodernist agenda and globalization together. Quite apart from the fact that the literature on globalization is heavily weighted towards economic and political issues, which are not given the same prominence by postmodernists, there are fundamental differences of approach to the writing of history, as this paragraph has pointed out.

Index